UTAH POLITICS AND GOVERNMENT

Politics and Governments
of the American States

Founding Editor

DANIEL J. ELAZAR

Published by the University of Nebraska Press
in association with the Center for the Study of
Federalism at the Robert B. and Helen S. Meyner
Center for the Study of State and Local
Government, Lafayette College

Utah Politics and Government

AMERICAN DEMOCRACY AMONG A UNIQUE ELECTORATE

ADAM R. BROWN

UNIVERSITY OF NEBRASKA PRESS

LINCOLN AND LONDON

Library of Congress Cataloging-in-Publication Data
Names: Brown, Adam R., author.
Title: Utah politics and government:
American democracy among a unique
electorate / Adam R. Brown.
Description: Lincoln: University of Nebraska Press,
2018. | Series: Politics and governments of the
American states | Includes bibliographical
references and index.
Identifiers: LCCN 2017053348
ISBN 9781496201805 (paperback: alk. paper)
ISBN 9781496207838 (epub)
ISBN 9781496207845 (mobi)
ISBN 9781496207852 (pdf)
Subjects: LCSH: Utah—Politics and government. |
Political culture—Utah. | BISAC: POLITICAL
SCIENCE / Government / State & Provincial.
Classification: LCC JK8416 .B76 2018 |
DDC 320.4792—dc23
LC record available at
https://lccn.loc.gov/2017053348

Set in Minion Pro by Mikala R Kolander.

CONTENTS

FIGURES

TABLES

Acknowledgments

Over the past decade, I have trained and mentored over two hundred undergraduates who have interned in the Utah Capitol. I thank them for sharing their experiences with me. Every year, they reignite the joy of discovery within me as I reenter the political arena vicariously through them. Their insights and ideas have inspired much of the analysis presented in this book, and their curiosity and enthusiasm energize me.

Many people have aided me in collecting and interpreting the data employed here. Luke Bell, Justin Chang, and Matt Beck labored as undergraduate research assistants and compiled much of the data on the Utah Supreme Court and the Utah Constitution. Thad Hall, Chris Karpowitz, and Quin Monson generously shared the raw data from their Utah Elected Officials Survey. I owe a special debt to Chris Karpowitz and Jeremy Pope for organizing a workshop at BYU's Center for the Study of Elections and Democracy and inviting a large group to read and comment on an earlier draft of this book. Feedback received at that workshop has improved this manuscript immensely, though faults obviously remain my own.

I offer special gratitude to my wife Janelle and our sons Hyrum, Alan, and Karl, for enriching my life and motivating me to keep pushing even when life pushes back harder than expected. To you I dedicate all my endeavors.

Introduction

Among Americans and foreigners alike, mentioning Utah conjures diverse reactions. World-class skiing. Mormons. The "Mighty 5" national parks. Exotic slot canyons. The Great Salt Lake. Schismatic polygamists. Majestic peaks. Charismatic wildlife. Bleak deserts. Cowboy films. The 2002 Winter Olympics. Green Jell-O. Sagebrush rebels. The Mormon Tabernacle Choir. Fry sauce. Noxious winter inversions. Butch Cassidy and the Sundance Kid. The Sundance Film Festival. Odd liquor laws. Pioneers. Utes. Ancient cliff dwellings and petroglyphs. Curious rock formations. Land speed records at the salt flats. The four corners. The Book of Mormon—both the scripture and the Broadway musical. The Salt Lake City Temple. Wilderness. If Utah were one of America's economic or cultural powerhouses—if Utah were a California, a Texas, a New York, or a Florida—these countless reactions would seem natural. Instead it seems that Utah—home to only 1 percent of the U.S. population and even less of its dry land—punches above its weight in American culture.

In politics, however, Utah punches below its weight, if it punches at all. Many reduce it to mere caricature: The reddest of red states, home to perhaps the nation's most homogeneous voters—religiously, culturally, and politically. Believing it foregone, presidential campaigns have ignored Utah for decades. Hillary Clinton's fleeting attention to Utah during her 2016 presidential campaign was the rare exception that proved the rule; when she dispatched her husband to headline a single fundraiser, then amplified that fundraiser with a single op-ed in a statewide paper, the national press marveled that any candidate would put Utah, of all places, in play.[1] Despite her efforts Clinton won only 28 percent of Utah's vote—right between Barack Obama's share in 2008 (34 percent) and 2012 (25 percent).

Utah votes Republican so reliably that one can hardly blame national campaigns for ignoring it. However, Utahns themselves infer too much from this neglect, acting as though their votes matter as little within Utah as outside it. In a poll I asked Utah voters to rate how much various political institutions "affect [their] personal life or financial situation."[2] They answered using a 5-point scale, ranging from 1 ("not at all") to 5 ("a great deal"). Respondents gave higher ratings to the U.S. Congress (4.2) than to the Utah Legislature (4.0); higher ratings to the U.S. president (3.9) than to the Utah governor (3.7); and higher ratings to U.S. courts (3.8) than to Utah courts (3.4). Overall 47 percent of respondents rated the federal government's influence on their lives higher than the state government's. Only 18 percent did the opposite.

These evaluations are misguided. Utah's legislature alone passes twice as many laws per year as the U.S. Congress, and Utah's courts alone hear twice as many cases per year as the nation's entire federal court system. Utah is hardly alone, of course: collectively, America's fifty state legislatures pass roughly one hundred times as many bills per year as Congress, and America's state court systems consider roughly one hundred times as many cases as the federal courts.[3] State governments are vastly busier than the federal government because they handle most of the policy realms that affect Americans' daily lives. State governments run public schools and universities, set punishments for crime, charter cities, regulate corporations, manage pollution, build freeways and reservoirs, maintain parks, generate electricity, fight fires, purify drinking water, certify marriages and adoptions, police the streets, inspect restaurants, issue professional licenses, and zone neighborhoods. State policy has more impact on Utah lives and wallets than federal policy.

Utahns nevertheless remain embarrassingly ignorant of their state government.[4] In the same poll mentioned above, I also asked Utah voters four simple factual questions about national politics, paired with four parallel questions about Utah politics. Respondents more easily identified the U.S. vice president (87 percent correct) than the Utah lieutenant governor (57 percent), the speaker of the U.S. House (65 percent) than the speaker of the Utah House (38 percent), and the U.S. Senate majority leader (67 percent) than the Utah Senate president (31 percent).[5] Respondents were also somewhat more likely to know that U.S. senators serve six-year terms (56 percent) than to know that Utah senators serve four-year terms (49 percent). Overall the average respondent answered 69 percent of the national questions correctly, compared to 44 percent of the Utah questions, a disappointing 25-point gap.

Most Utah voters fared barely better than guessing on these elementary questions, even though Utah government is so much more accessible to Utahns than the federal government. Utah's laws are made by citizen legislators who spend ten months of the year living in their districts and working nonlegislative jobs. When the legislature does convene, most Utahns live within an hour's drive of the capitol and can easily visit their legislator, testify in a committee hearing, and observe debates firsthand. Local officials—Utah's mayors, city councilors, county commissioners, school board members, and so on—are even more accessible. And in primary and general elections many Utahns cast votes in local races decided by only a few hundred ballots, a stark contrast to presidential races—yet 12 percent of Utahns who chose between Donald Trump and Hillary Clinton in November 2016 left without casting a vote in their Utah House of Representatives race.[6]

Maybe this neglect of Utah politics reflects the state's curricular priorities. Utah's core social studies curriculum for K–12 public schools includes three units on U.S. history and government but only one unit on "Utah studies"—and most of the "Utah studies" unit focuses on Utah's history, culture, geography, and economy, with minimal attention to Utah's state constitution and political system.[7] Likewise Utah's four-year universities require all undergraduates to complete a course in American national institutions as part of their general education requirements, but they require no instruction at all focused on state institutions. Perhaps voters pay little attention to Utah for the simple reason that the state of Utah has chosen not to teach about itself.

This book provides sufficient description of Utah's political processes to bridge these gaps, but it also has a broader purpose: to conduct a scholarly analysis of Utah politics within the broader American political setting. This book does not simply recount the governor's powers, sketch out the state's judicial system, or outline the state's legislative process; it contrasts each of Utah's political institutions against those found in the other forty-nine states and in Washington DC. Utah, it turns out, has much to teach us about governance, and careful analysis of Utah's political institutions can reveal what might happen if some of Utah's unique features were exported to other states or if features from other states were imported to Utah.

In the end this book's comparative analysis yields two major conclusions. First, Utah has more in common with the other forty-nine states than it gets credit for. Like all other states, Utah has a written constitution that it updates under predictable circumstances, as well as separate legislative, executive, and judicial branches that wrestle for power in predictable ways. More often than not, actors within these institutions behave in ways that affirm theories developed through observation of the other forty-nine states or of Washington DC. As elsewhere, for example, legislative leaders exploit their procedural authority to protect the majority party's interests (cf. Cox and McCubbins 2005; Cox et al. 2010). As elsewhere, governors have more influence over budgets than over policy (cf. Kousser and Phillips 2012). As elsewhere, the threat of a citizen initiative can spur legislative action (cf. Gerber 1996; Matsusaka 2010; Phillips 2008). As elsewhere, legislators prioritize their most sympathetic and politically active constituents (cf. Fenno 1978). As elsewhere, senior politicians make campaign contributions to their colleagues to advance their own political ambitions (cf. Cann 2008). As elsewhere, narrower interests organize more efficiently than broader public interests (cf. Olson 1965). True, Utah's institutions do differ in important ways from institutions elsewhere, and these institutions do occasionally have meaningful effects. For example, the Utah Legislature's unusually short General Session and unusually meager staff weaken rank-and-file legislators, thereby conferring unusual power on legislative leaders. Nevertheless these differences mostly arise at the margins. Excessive emphasis on Utah's uniqueness falsely implies that Utah politics are fundamentally different from politics elsewhere.

First, then, this book's analysis reveals that Utah has more in common with the other forty-nine states than many suppose and that theories of politics developed elsewhere apply in Utah far more often than not. But, second, this book also shows that Utahns themselves are unique. No territory struggled more than Utah to persuade Congress to grant it statehood and admit it to the union. Since the fall of southern segregation, no state has witnessed such virulent anti-federalism as Utah. Few states match Utah's devotion to the Republican Party. And, of course, Utah's most glaring difference, the one that drives all these others: no state exceeds Utah's religious homogeneity. More than half (56 percent) of Utahns self-identify to pollsters as Mormon, exceeding the homogeneity of Rhode Island (44 percent Catholic), Tennessee (43 percent white evangelical Protestant), West Virginia (40 percent white evangelical Protestant), and every other state.[8]

Compounding this religious difference, Utah's Mormon majority embraces not only a single religious tradition but a single church organization, one with a pronounced vertical hierarchy: the Church of Jesus Christ of Latter-day Saints (LDS). Sometimes top LDS leaders issue explicit calls to political action. When they do, Mormons comply so promptly that one study labeled them "dry kindling" waiting for a spark (Campbell and Monson 2007). More often, though, Mormon voters and politicians act without official prompting. In 1831 Tocqueville ([1831] 1969: 291) wrote the following about Protestant influence in the early American states: "One cannot . . . say that in the United States religion influences the laws or political opinions in detail, but it does direct mores, and by regulating domestic life it helps to regulate the state." Tocqueville could write the same words about Utah today (Magleby 2006). Mormonism shapes Utah politics more through its cultural influence than through explicit appeals from the pulpit. Several chapters review the LDS Church's direct and indirect political influence, especially chapters 1, 2, 3, and 5.

In his 1969 book, *Politics in the American West*, these religious differences led Frank Jonas to label Utah "the different state." Yet as later authors remind us, Utah is otherwise "an archetypical western state": "Sparsely populated, overwhelmingly urban, and rapidly growing" (Hrebenar et al. 1987, 113). More broadly Utah is an archetypal American state, with political institutions that, with only a few exceptions, operate like those in the other forty-nine states. As a result Utah politics (and this book) presents a study in contrasts: Its people are unique, but its institutions operate like institutions in other states.

On the whole, then, the most radical observation this book makes about Utah is that Utah is not particularly radical. Yes, Utah's Mormon heritage profoundly changes the citizenry's partisan and ideological leanings; at the same time, the institutions that translate these citizen pressures into public policies generally operate as theories developed elsewhere would predict. As much as LDS influence changes the players involved and the causes pursued, the underlying political processes broadly resemble those found in other states. Political scientists need not abandon all they know about politics when they cross the state line—a conclusion that suggests some optimism about the resilience of the general institutional model found in all U.S. states.

PLAN OF THE BOOK

This book begins with three chapters addressing Utah's uniqueness. Chapter 1 explores Utah's religious heritage and territorial history. From its initial pioneer settlements in 1847 until statehood in 1896, Utah Territory experienced repeated clashes between federal officials and Church leadership. Federal officials feared the Church's polygamy as much as its theocratic impulses; only when the Church showed credible progress toward abandoning both did Congress grant Utah statehood. Chapter 2 examines Utah's modern anti-federalism, tracing recurring clashes with the federal government back to the territorial period's political and religious legacy—a legacy amplified by modern disputes over public land management. Chapter 3 reviews Utah's complicated partisan history, from its decades-long stint as national bellwether to the eventual reemergence of a religious-partisan cleavage in the 1970s, producing today's Mormon Republican supermajority. Together these three chapters form a single narrative linking Utah's contentious territorial years and pioneer past to its modern sagebrush rebellions and Republican dominance. And together these chapters draw out Utah's most defining traits: a majority Mormon population, mistrust of federal authority, and a supermajority Republican electorate.

Subsequent chapters turn from Utah's people to its governing institutions, beginning with three chapters focused on Utah's lawmaking processes. Chapter 4 unfolds the Utah Legislature's internal operations, asking how part-time legislators craft policy when the state constitution allows them only seven weeks each year to pass new laws. Chapter 5 shows how constituents and organized interests compete to influence lawmakers and how Utah's rushed legislative session and understaffed legislature advantage organized interests; this chapter also examines the LDS Church's unique policy influence. Chapter 6 explains how Utahns have used their direct democracy powers to compel legislators to take actions they would otherwise avoid.

The next two chapters consider the other branches of government. Chapter 7 argues that Utah's governors enjoy more institutional authority than governors in any other state, though governors nevertheless have less influence over policy than does the legislature. Chapter 8 shows how Utah's merit-based selection of judges, coupled with its regularly updated yet brief state constitution, promotes consensus and reduces ideological sparring on Utah's appellate courts.

Chapter 9 takes the discussion local, laying out the role of Utah's cities, counties, and districts. These local governments exist only at the pleasure of Utah's state government, limiting their authority, yet local officials take their jobs seriously and long for greater constituent involvement. Chapter 10 applies the lessons from the foregoing chapters to show how legislators, the governor, and outside interests interact to produce the state's annual budget, the sum of all the state's policy endeavors. Chapter 11 concludes the book.

Some of this book's sources, such as the U.S. Census, official election results, and quotations from Utah's body of law (the Utah Code) require no explanation. For reference, this book also draws on the following data sources.

The Utah Legislative Voting Database

I have compiled a database of every bill considered and every vote held in the Utah Legislature during any of its annual General Sessions since 2007. The resulting database includes 9,084 bills, 218 legislators, 16,692 recorded voting events, and 812,423 individual ayes and nays. Unless otherwise noted, all discussions of legislative trends draw on this source. Detailed profiles of individual legislators' voting records—including their absentee rates, nay-voting rate, party support scores, ideology scores, and so on—are available via the author's website.[9]

The Utah Supreme Court Rulings Database

I have collected information on all 1,420 rulings issued by the Utah Supreme Court from 1997 through 2012, allowing for careful examinations of judicial ideology and decision making on Utah's five-member court. Discussion of voting patterns among Utah Supreme Court judges draws on this dataset.

The Utah Constitutional Amendments Archive

Utah amends its constitution by integrating new language directly into the text rather than tacking numbered amendments onto the end of the document. This differs, of course, from how the U.S. Constitution receives amendments. While this process makes the current version of the Utah Constitution much easier to read, it also makes it painfully difficult to reconstruct its historical development. I have used archival sources to locate every amendment ever proposed by the Utah Legislature or ratified by Utah voters since statehood. (By "proposed," I mean an amendment received the two-thirds legislative vote required to appear before voters for ratification.)

The Utah Legislator Survey

I administered a poll to all 104 elected members of the Utah Legislature during the Legislature's 2013 General Session between February 19 and 26. Legislative staff assisted in collecting the anonymous responses, some of which trickled in as late as March 5. Of 104 legislators, 46 responded, a respectable 44 percent rate. Still, the legislature's small size produces large margins of error: ±11.5 percentage points.[10]

Utah Voter Polls and Utah Colleges Exit Polls

Collaborating with researchers at Utah's other universities, Brigham Young University (BYU) researchers have fielded exit polls at least biennially since 1982. For several years BYU's Center for the Study of Elections and Democracy also fielded regular Utah Voter Polls, online surveys administered to a representative sample recruited during the exit poll.[11]

UTAH POLITICS AND GOVERNMENT

CHAPTER ONE

A Church and a State

Utah's unique 1847–96 territorial history, featuring clashes among Mormon pioneers, native tribes, mineral interests, and federal officials, still casts a long shadow. This chapter reviews this territorial history, but this is not history for history's sake. Abler historians have already risen to that task, and their work has deeply influenced this chapter.[1] Rather this chapter will emphasize only those actors and episodes that most shape Utah's modern politics. Above all else the territorial period witnessed stubborn conflict between federal authority and the LDS Church's theocratic ambitions. These clashes led Congress to repeatedly deny Utah's statehood petitions. Only when LDS leaders abandoned their most controversial practice— polygamy—and also their most obvious theocratic ambitions did Congress authorize Utah Territory to organize itself as the nation's forty-fifth state.

This chapter's review of the territorial era sets up arguments presented in the next two chapters. For the first decades after statehood, it appeared Mormons had reached an enduring accommodation with the federal government. By midcentury, however, seeds lying dormant since the territorial period began to sprout into two major features of Utah's modern politics: deep suspicion of federal authority (chapter 2) and a Mormon Republican supermajority (chapter 3).

INDIGENOUS PEOPLE AND EARLY EXPLORERS

Indigenous people dwelt in Utah long before the first white settlers arrived. The first hunter-gatherers arrived as early as 11,000 BC. Agriculture developed some two thousand years ago. Ancestral Puebloan people flourished in Utah's southeast, building and later abandoning cliff houses, granaries, and other stone structures.[2] Elsewhere the Fremont people built straw homes and settlements throughout northern and central Utah, leaving archaeological sites and petroglyphs scattered around the state, including around Utah Lake and Salt Lake.

These nations declined around 1,000 years ago as several Numic tribes arrived from the west: Paiutes settled Utah's southwest, Goshutes settled the west desert, the Shoshone settled around Salt Lake and Bear Lake, and the Utes settled much of the rest.[3] Spreading northward, the Navajo settled part of southeastern Utah. The four Numic tribes relied less on agriculture than did their Fremont and Ancestral Puebloan predecessors, perhaps because the climate had grown drier. They favored more nomadic lifestyles, traveling between various hunting and fishing grounds throughout the year.

Utah eventually fell under the Spanish claim. A minor expedition passed through what is now southern Utah in 1540. A later expedition, led by Atanasio Domínguez and Silvestre Vélez de Escalante, explored Utah more seriously in 1776 hoping to find a better route from Santa Fe, New Mexico, to the Spanish mission in Monterey, California. The Domínguez-Escalante expedition reached as far north as Utah Lake, where they met a large band of Numic-speaking people thriving on the lake's ample fishery. Their cousins elsewhere called this band the Timpanogos, in reference to the river mouth where they lived—today's Provo River, which empties into Utah Lake. The padres called them the Yuta Indians—later anglicized as Eutaw, then Ute—and called their home Yuta Lake and Yuta Valley. Impressed by the valley's farmland, fishery, timber, game, fresh water, and pastureland, they wrote that it could "support a city with as large a population as that of Mexico City" (quoted in Farmer 2008, 30). Indeed Utah Valley already supported the eastern Great Basin's densest population.[4] The padres continued their journey and never returned, but their journals and routes informed later traders and settlers, who soon introduced horses and firearms to the region.

Mexico inherited Spain's territorial claim upon winning independence in 1821. Like Spain, Mexico exercised no real influence in the region. Native tribes continued occupying the territory mostly undisturbed, despite their regular trading contacts with traveling merchants and slave traders.[5] They also began receiving visits from occasional American, French, and English trappers seeking furs for eastern markets. In the early 1840s the John C. Frémont expeditions passed through, producing additional maps and descriptions.

White settlement began in earnest with the arrival of the first Mormon pioneers on July 24, 1847. Joseph Smith had organized the Church of Jesus Christ of Latter-day Saints seventeen years earlier in western New York. His followers—calling themselves "Latter-day Saints" but nicknamed "Mormons" after their signature book of scripture, the Book of Mormon— began gathering in Kirtland, Ohio, and Jackson County, Missouri. Clashes between Mormons and their frontier neighbors often turned violent. In 1838, following the so-called Mormon War, Missouri governor Lilburn Boggs issued an "extermination order," evicting Mormons from the state: "The Mormons must be treated as enemies, and must be exterminated or driven from the state, if necessary, for the public good. Their outrages are beyond all description" (quoted in Greene 1839, 26). Smith personally led a delegation to Washington DC requesting federal assistance, but President Van Buren and other officials declined to intervene.

Eventually Mormons abandoned Missouri and Ohio in favor of frontier Illinois. Mormon missionary work collected converts from throughout the United States as well as from Europe, especially England, and missionaries directed their converts to gather in the church's rapidly growing Illinois settlement, Nauvoo. Owing to its size, Nauvoo received an unusually strong city charter from the Illinois Legislature that included authority to maintain a city militia, the Nauvoo Legion. While still serving as president of the Church, Smith was elected Nauvoo's mayor and appointed general of the Nauvoo Legion, uniting ecclesiastical, political, and military authority. Smith had organized the Quorum of Twelve Apostles years earlier to manage ecclesiastical affairs; while serving as mayor he organized an additional Council of Fifty to assist him with civic affairs. Eventually lingering hostilities from the Missouri period followed the Mormons to Nauvoo. Together with new conflicts stemming partly from Nauvoo's union of religious and civil authority, these tensions culminated in Smith's 1844 assassination. Nauvoo's population peaked around this time, rivaling Chicago's.[6]

Conflict continued between Mormons and their neighbors even after Smith's death. On January 29, 1845, the Illinois Legislature revoked Nauvoo's charter, dissolving its militia and municipal government (see Flanders 1965). Brigham Young eventually assumed leadership of the main body of Mormons, though smaller groups broke off behind other claimants. Concluding that long-term peace was impossible, Church leaders negotiated a temporary truce with their neighbors as they prepared for a cross-country exodus. Most Mormons left Nauvoo early in 1846, crossing the frozen Mississippi River to temporary settlements in Iowa and Nebraska.

Young resolved to lead the Mormons far from those he saw as persecutors into a land he thought nobody else would want, leaving the United States for what was then Mexican territory. Young and other Mormon leaders studied descriptions and maps of the area based on the Domínguez-Escalante journals, the Frémont expeditions, and other sources. Unable to decide between Cache Valley, Salt Lake Valley, or Utah Valley—all located in what is now northern Utah—Young led the expedition westward, concluding he would recognize the right place when he saw it.[7] As they journeyed they met the famous trapper and mountain man Jim Bridger, who warned Young that the Timpanogos people living along Utah Lake guarded their fishery jealously and, well-equipped with horses and firearms, would violently resist any settlement effort.[8] To avoid this conflict Young resolved to settle in the Salt Lake Valley, which served as a less populated buffer between Shoshone tribes to the north and their Ute rivals to the south. Young's wagon train entered Salt Lake Valley on July 24, 1847, commemorated in Utah today as Pioneer Day.

Young transitioned easily from organizing the migration to governing Utah's early settlements, assuming both religious and civic authority. The Nauvoo-era Council of Fifty had continued operating after Smith's death and helped organize the migration. For the first few years of Mormon settlement, Young and this Council governed their new desert home as a true theocracy, with religious and political power united under Young's supreme authority.

As Mormon pioneers poured into Salt Lake Valley, pressure built on Young to authorize southward expansion into Utah Valley. Fearing Bridger's warning, Young gave his blessing only reluctantly. In 1849 a group of settlers journeyed forty-five miles south from Salt Lake City to colonize what is now Provo. Bridger's prediction about the Timpanogos band proved accurate: several violent battles ensued within the year.[9] Soon enough, in a pattern familiar throughout American history, these clashes forced the Timpanogos band out of Utah Valley entirely and onto Uintah Basin reservations, as well as forcing most other Utah tribes off their traditional lands. Within a few generations Utah Valley's new white residents had collectively forgotten that the Timpanogos Utes had formerly occupied Utah Valley rather than the mountain reservations, and the name *Timpanogos* drifted from the river's mouth—now the Provo River—to a nearby mountain.[10] Over subsequent decades Young directed Mormon settlement far beyond Utah Valley, extending throughout modern Utah and into modern Idaho, Nevada, Arizona, California, and elsewhere.

THE UTAH WAR

Shortly after the first Mormons arrived in Salt Lake Valley, the United States won control of the region upon the conclusion of the 1846–48 Mexican-American War. Congress soon set about organizing its newly won lands into administrative territories. Young proposed vast boundaries for a new "State of Deseret" that would have included the entire watershed of the Colorado River north of Mexico, the entire Great Basin, and the southern coast of California from the Santa Monica Mountains to Mexico (including the existing settlements at Los Angeles and San Diego). In terms of modern boundaries, Young's Deseret included nearly all of today's Utah and Nevada, most of Arizona, about one-third each of California and Colorado, and pieces of Oregon, Idaho, Wyoming, and New Mexico—dwarfing modern Texas. The name *Deseret* came from a Book of Mormon word for honeybees; Young saw the honeybee's collective industry as a model for the Zion he hoped to build. Though the beehive and the word *Industry* remain prominent on the state seal and flag, Congress named the territory Utah to honor the Ute, or "Yuta," people. Congress also drew more modest boundaries that nevertheless included all of modern Utah, most of Nevada, and parts of Wyoming and Colorado. By 1868 Congress had reduced Utah Territory to the state's present boundaries.

Territories do not enjoy the same legal status as states. They are subordinate units of the federal government, just as today's cities are subordinate units of the state government. Although Utah residents had the opportunity to elect a territorial legislature from 1851 on, much political authority resided with the territorial governor, an unelected presidential appointee. With few ready alternatives, President Millard Fillmore appointed Brigham Young as the first territorial governor in 1851, further bolstering Young's theodemocratic union of civil and religious power.

In 1857, facing concerns about separation of church and state, President James Buchanan decided to replace Young with a non-Mormon governor, Alfred Cumming. Fearing that Mormon settlers would rebel at this news, Buchanan dispatched the U.S. Army to escort the new governor to Utah. Buchanan's decision to send the army to Utah without informing Young of his intentions triggered a series of events that nearly led to major military conflict between Utah and the federal government.[11] Young heard rumors of the army's march without knowing its mission. Fearing a renewal of the government-sanctioned hostilities familiar from Missouri and Illinois, he prepared to defend his people with force. Activating the territory's militia—called the Nauvoo Legion in homage to Smith's day—he sent advance teams to harass and hinder the army's progress by running off their horses, setting fire to grasslands in the army's path, and felling trees to block key passes.[12] These Mormon actions only served to further persuade the army's commander, Col. Albert Sidney Johnston, that he would indeed need to put down a Mormon rebellion before installing Cumming as governor.

The worst violence occurred in southwestern Utah's remote Mountain Meadows area, where war hysteria deepened suspicion of outsiders to the point that Mormon settlers joined with local Paiutes to slaughter some 120 noncombatants in a wagon train bound for southern California, plundering their goods; only the youngest children were spared.[13] Ultimately the so-called Utah War was resolved with minimal bloodshed except for Mountain Meadows. Negotiations between Young and the army led to the 1858 establishment of Camp Floyd a few miles west of today's city of Eagle Mountain, as well as Cumming's peaceful accession to the governorship. Thousands of federal soldiers remained at Camp Floyd in what became Utah's first major non-Mormon settlement. These soldiers soon returned east to fight each other in the Civil War. In July 1861 Camp Floyd—by then renamed Fort Crittenden—closed permanently.

SOLDIERS AND MINERS

The Union army returned a year later. Its new commander, Col. Patrick Connor, refused to rebuild the old Camp Floyd site, a two-day march from Salt Lake City. Instead he marched his men out of the old fort toward a new home. On October 29, 1862, with rifles loaded and bayonets fixed, Connor's men marched into Salt Lake City and planted the U.S. flag on the city's east bench, founding Camp Douglas. A contemporary non-Mormon writer adds this detail: "Connor could not possibly have selected a better situation for a military post, and certainly no place could have been more offensive to Brigham. The artillery have a perfect and unobstructed range of Brigham's residence, and with their muzzles turned in that direction, the Prophet felt awfully annoyed" (Stenhouse 1873, 603). On this and other occasions Connor showed his determination to remind Young of the federal government's superiority—even going so far as to keep artillery aimed at Young's house.

Colonel Connor soon sent his men to investigate rumored mineral deposits west of Salt Lake Valley.[14] The first metal mining claims were made in nearby Bingham Canyon in 1863. Though mining developed more slowly in Bingham Canyon than elsewhere in Utah, the Bingham Canyon mine eventually grew into the largest man-made excavation in the world. Where once stood a mountain, there now gapes a pit three-quarters of a mile deep and nearly three miles wide. This mining activity has visibly discolored a long stretch of the Oquirrh Mountains that mark the Salt Lake Valley's western edge. Known today as the Kennecott copper mine (for its former owners) or the Rio Tinto mine (for the current ones), the Bingham Canyon mine remains one of the world's most productive metal mines. Its cumulative output exceeds the combined value of the three most famous metal mining regions in the United States: the area of the California gold rush, of the Nevada Comstock Lode, and of the Alaskan Klondike rush. It has produced millions of tons of copper, thousands of tons of silver, thousands of tons of molybdenum, and hundreds of tons of gold.

Colonel Connor's efforts to develop Utah's mining industry, both at Bingham Canyon and elsewhere, earned him the moniker "the father of Utah mining." His mining operations and others exploded after the 1869 completion of the transcontinental railroad, which brought mining equipment and inexpensive labor into the territory. Thousands of non-Mormon immigrants flocked to Utah's mines over the next few decades, creating metal mining booms to the west of the territory's Salt Lake Valley and Utah Valley population centers and coal mining booms to their east.

Connor had already earned Young's ire by stationing federal troops in eastern Salt Lake City and aiming artillery at Young's house. Connor's energetic encouragement of the mining industry alienated Young further. The LDS leaders opposed development of Utah's mining industry, fearing that mining would interfere with their effort to build a collective, Zionistic economy—by promoting naked self-interest as well as by flooding the territory with non-Mormon labor. Young encouraged would-be prospectors to leave for California rather than corrupt Utah, but promised them they would regret it: "Go to California if you will; we will not curse you, we will not injure or destroy you, but we will pity you. People who stay will in ten years be able to buy out four who go" (quoted in Whitley 2006, 58). Another LDS leader, William Clayton, expressed similar views: "I do not enquire after gold, neither shall I trouble myself about it. . . . To me one thing is certain. If rich mines are opened in Utah, the Priesthood and honest saints will soon have to leave for some other region" (quoted in Whitley 2006, 60). Heedless of these warnings, major mining operations soon received investments from prominent Mormons, including Daniel H. Wells of the Church's First Presidency and LDS Apostles John Taylor, George Q. Cannon, and Moses Thatcher (Alexander 2007, 170–71). Young and other Church leaders soon ceased their public opposition to mining, which remains an important segment of Utah's modern economy.

TAMING THE THEOCRACY

Through all these years Mormon missionary work had continued in the eastern United States and abroad, and endless waves of Mormon immigrants journeyed to the new Zion. Most early pioneers came by covered wagon; some less fortunate migrants pulled their belongings in handcarts. By the 1860 census, only thirteen years after Young's 1847 arrival, Utah's population exceeded 40,000. After the transcontinental railroad's completion in 1869, the 1880 census counted 144,000 Utahns.

Meanwhile soldiers, miners, dissident Mormons, and other settlers grew into a burgeoning non-Mormon population, and Utah politics divided around a Mormon versus non-Mormon cleavage. In 1870 non-Mormon voters organized the Liberal Party to challenge Mormon political hegemony. Prior to that time Church-backed candidates ran without party labels and generally won without serious opposition; Mormons simply sustained on election day candidates previously selected by Church officials. Facing a newly organized opposition movement, pro-Church politicians organized the People's Party later that year. Newspapers split along the same lines. The Church-published *Deseret News*, founded in 1850, became an unofficial organ of the People's Party, regularly denouncing the Liberal Party. Dissident Mormons founded the *Mormon Tribune* in 1870, renamed it the *Salt Lake Daily Tribune and Utah Mining Gazette* a year later, and then sold it in 1873 to three Kansas businessmen, who turned the rechristened *Salt Lake Tribune* into an unofficial Liberal Party organ that regularly denounced Brigham Young.[15] The Liberal Party occasionally won upset victories, including in Ogden's 1889 municipal elections and Salt Lake City's 1890 municipal elections (Verdoia and Firmage 1996, 195–96).

Though Young had yielded the governorship after the 1857 Utah War, the emergence of the Liberal Party and People's Party reveals the Church's continuing effort to control both the Church and the government. Indeed Young had revived the Council of Fifty in 1862 to draft a constitution and (unsuccessful) statehood application, circumventing the federally appointed governor and the territorial legislature entirely. In 1870, while the territorial legislature was adjourned, Young convened the Council of Fifty again, this time as a shadow government that passed "laws," heard from Young, and prepared to assume power during Jesus Christ's imminent millennial reign (Alexander 2007, 141).

These naked theocratic ambitions fueled conflict between the Church and the federal government. Congress declined repeated statehood petitions in 1849, 1856, 1872, 1882, and 1887 (Verdoia and Firmage 1996, 189–97; Lyman 1986). Congress feared not only the Church's theocratic impulses but also the polygamy that LDS leaders sought to protect. Mormons had publicly embraced "plural marriage" soon after settling Utah, shocking Protestant consciences back east. At its first national convention, held in 1856, the newly established Republican Party vowed in its platform "to prohibit in the territories those twin relics of barbarism, polygamy and slavery" (quoted in Wills 1890, 41). Even before the Civil War eliminated the first relic, Congress acted on the second, enacting the Morrill Anti-Bigamy Act in 1862. Enforcement was delayed due to the Civil War, but eventually LDS leaders sought legal redress. In *Reynolds v. United States* (1879), the U.S. Supreme Court ruled unanimously that the First Amendment offered Mormon polygamists no protection from a monogamous marriage standard dating back centuries. Congress soon waged total war on polygamy, passing the Anti-Plural Marriage Act of 1887, more often known as the Edmunds-Tucker Act. This Act disincorporated the Church of Jesus Christ of Latter-day Saints, seized Church assets, barred polygamists from voting and from jury service, disenfranchised women, replaced sympathetic local (mostly Mormon) judges with federally appointed judges, and took other actions to compel an end to polygamy.[16] Church leaders sued on First Amendment grounds, but the Supreme Court again ruled against them (in 1890's *Late Corporation of the Church of Jesus Christ of Latter-day Saints v. United States*). Thousands were disenfranchised under this act, and top LDS leaders went into hiding to avoid arrest.

Brought to their knees, LDS leaders acted to end polygamy. Wilford Woodruff, Young's successor, renounced polygamy on behalf of the Church in October 1890.[17] Though it required several years and a few high-level excommunications, the mainstream Church of Jesus Christ of Latter-day Saints stamped out polygamy by the early twentieth century.[18] Traditionalists broke off to preserve polygamy and other early Mormon teachings; splinter groups remain scattered around Utah and the west even today, though in such small numbers that few Utahns know a living polygamist. Foremost among these are the Fundamentalist Church of Jesus Christ of Latter-day Saints (FLDS), known for living in oppressive enclaves and discouraging any contact with the outside world, and the Apostolic United Brethren (AUB), whose polygamous members denounce underage or coercive marriage and mingle with modern society, even appearing in the reality show *Sister Wives*.[19]

After ending polygamy LDS leaders also walked back their former theocratic ambitions. The Church-backed People's Party disbanded in 1891, encouraging its former (overwhelmingly Mormon) supporters to divide evenly into Republicans and Democrats.[20] The Liberal Party, equally eager for statehood, agreed on the value of integrating into the national parties and dissolved itself in 1893. Though prominent Mormons would remain active in politics for decades to come—most notably Reed Smoot served both as LDS apostle and U.S. senator from 1903 to 1933—LDS leaders would no longer offer a semi-official slate of candidates through the People's Party. Instead they hoped the religious-partisan cleavage that defined the territorial era would disappear forever; after all, if Mormons divided evenly into Republicans and Democrats, then neither party would have an incentive to demonize Mormons for electoral gain. However, religious-partisan cleavages die hard. The dissolution of the People's Party and Liberal Party set the stage for the partisan instability discussed in chapter 3. As that chapter will also show, the old religious-partisan cleavage eventually reemerged in the 1970s, when the Republican Party consolidated the Mormon vote. Ever since, Utah has remained solidly Republican.

THE FORTY-FIFTH STATE

The end of the territorial period could not have been more different from its start. In 1847 Utah was home to dispersed Native American populations, a small but fast-growing Mormon settlement, and vast untapped resources. By the 1890s white settlement had displaced native inhabitants onto shrinking reservations, a fierce religious cleavage divided Utah politically and socially, railroads crisscrossed the state, and industry—agriculture, mining, and manufacturing—had spread everywhere.

Most significantly, though, the LDS Church had renounced polygamy and shown clear signs of renouncing theocracy as well. Utah had finally "Americanized" (Magleby 2006, 180; Poll et al. 1989, 387–95). Congress reciprocated in 1894 by passing Utah's Enabling Act, authorizing the territory to hold a constitutional convention and send its proposed constitution to Washington for approval. Delegates convened on March 4, 1895, completed their work on May 6, and signed the final document on May 8. Utah voters approved their new constitution at the November 5 general election and selected new state officials at the same time. The federal government approved Utah's constitution, and on January 4, 1896, President Grover Cleveland proclaimed Utah the nation's forty-fifth state, admitted on an equal footing with the other states of the union.[21]

The 1894 Enabling Act dictated four mandatory ordinances that Utah's constitution would be required to include. To ensure that Utahns could not amend these ordinances out of their constitution after statehood, the

Enabling Act declared that these provisions would be "irrevocable without the consent of the United States"—that is, of Congress. At Utah's Constitutional Convention delegates copied these four mandatory ordinances verbatim from the Enabling Act into Article III of the Utah Constitution. Over one hundred years have passed since Utah's Constitutional Convention, and over one hundred amendments have been made to Utah's constitution in that time, yet these four mandatory ordinances still read today as they read in 1896.[22] Given that these ordinances cannot be changed without congressional consent, their longevity is hardly a surprise.

Two of these required ordinances reflect federal apprehension over the Church's theocratic ambitions: first, that "perfect toleration of religious sentiment shall be secured . . . provided, that polygamous or plural marriages are forever prohibited"; second, that the new state would maintain "a system of public schools, which shall be open to all the children of [Utah] and free from sectarian control." Mormons once fought hard to preserve polygamy, yet despite their continued political dominance of Utah's state government, they have made no attempt to rescind the state's constitutional ban on polygamy. Mormons view Joseph Smith, Brigham Young, Wilford Woodruff, and subsequent church presidents as prophets. Because the most recent prophetic statement on polygamy is Woodruff's 1890 renunciation of it, Mormons today view polygamy advocacy as heretical and pro-polygamy offshoots like the FLDS and AUB as apostates.[23] Proud though they may be of their pioneer heritage, more Mormons today call polygamy morally wrong (86 percent) than say the same about sex between unmarried adults (79 percent), abortion (74 percent), or drinking alcohol (54 percent), all of which violate LDS tenets (Campbell et al. 2014, 58). The federal government once ended polygamy over Mormon objections, yet modern Mormons evince no desire to reverse that ban today.

The Enabling Act's other two mandatory ordinances had less to do with religion than with an orderly transition from territory to state. First, the new state had to assume the territory's debts. Second, Utahns had to "agree and declare that they forever disclaim all right and title to the unappropriated public lands lying within the boundaries" of Utah "until the title thereto shall have been extinguished by the United States," with "all such lands . . . exempt from taxation by [Utah]." This latter requirement

reemerged as a major political issue a century later, when the Utah Legislature launched an effort to compel the federal government to transfer
all remaining public lands to the state, a battle discussed in chapter 2.

After these four required ordinances, the rest of Utah's 1895 constitution addressed matters typical to a state constitution: the structure and
operation of the legislative, judicial, and executive branches; the manner
of conducting state elections; a guarantee of certain civil rights; administration of public schools and universities; state revenue and taxation
procedures; amendment procedures; and so on. Essential provisions are
discussed in relevant chapters throughout this book.[24]

Like most states Utah amends its constitution heavily. Today it contains
almost eighteen thousand words, a 12 percent increase over its original
length. To amend the Utah Constitution, the Utah Legislature must first
propose an amendment by a two-thirds vote in each chamber; voters
must then ratify each proposed amendment at the ballot box. Using this
method, the legislature proposed 183 amendments between statehood
and 2015; voters ratified 118 of them. Put differently, the legislature has
proposed an average of 3.1 amendments per biennium; voters have ratified
an average of 2.0 of them.[25]

The U.S. Constitution contains around eight thousand words and has
received only twenty-seven amendments since 1789, most recently in 1992.
By contrast, Utahns needed only eighteen years—from 1998 to 2015—to
adopt as many amendments to their state constitution as the U.S. Constitution has received in 226 years. If anything, Utahns amend their constitution
even more now than in the past. Figure 1 plots Utah's amendment rate
over the 120 years since statehood, with amendments collapsed into four
thirty-year bins. The Utah Legislature proposed thirty-eight amendments
in the first thirty years after statehood (1896–1925), thirty-seven amendments in the second period (1926–55), fifty-three amendments in the third
period (1956–85), and fifty-five amendments in the most recent period
(1986–2015). Meanwhile voters show an increasing willingness to ratify
these amendments at the ballot box. Voters ratified fourteen amendments
in the first period, twenty-six in the second, thirty-one in the third, and
a whopping forty-seven in the fourth.

Comparing the Utah Constitution's high amendment rate to the U.S.

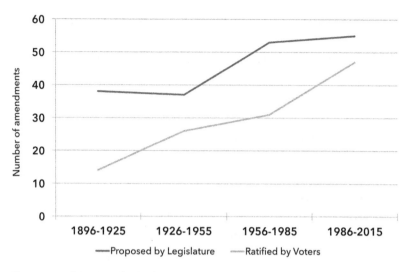

Fig. 1. Amendments to the Utah Constitution, 1896–2015. Compiled by the author.

Constitution's low rate may be unfair. Article V of the U.S. Constitution presents tremendous hurdles to would-be reformers, requiring two-thirds of each chamber in Congress to propose an amendment, which must then be ratified by three-fourths of the states. But even when comparing the Utah Constitution to its immediate peers—all the other state constitutions—it still has a high amendment rate. The median state constitution has twenty-seven thousand words—one-third longer than Utah's constitution—and receives as many amendments in twenty years (seventeen) as the U.S. Constitution has received since 1791.[26] Utah exceeds even this average; over the past twenty years, only one in seven states has amended its constitution more frequently than Utah.[27] In general, amendment rates are highest in states with longer and younger constitutions, as well as in states with laxer amendment procedures (Brown 2015). However, Utah is something of an outlier in this analysis. Though Utah has typical amendment procedures and an average-age constitution that is a little shorter than average—conditions that predict an amendment rate slightly below the average—its actual amendment rate exceeds the fifty-state average. It is not clear what makes Utah's amendment rate something of an outlier.

Utah's amendment activity does not reach all parts of the state constitution. The Utah Constitution contains 207 sections spread over twenty-four numbered articles. Since statehood, 147 of these sections have received at least one amendment. The remaining sections are mostly concentrated in Article I (with twenty untouched sections), which enumerates basic rights, and Article XXIV (with sixteen untouched sections), which deals with technical matters concerning the transition from territory to state and has long since lost its relevance. At the other extreme a number of articles have received so many amendments that essentially none of the original language remains, including Article VI ("Legislative Department"), Article VII ("Executive Department), Article VIII ("Judicial Department"), Article IX ("Congressional and Legislative Apportionment"), Article X ("Education"), Article XI ("Counties, Cities, and Towns"), Article XII ("Corporations"), and Article XIII ("Revenue and Taxation"). Lying in the middle are articles dealing with elections, labor, water rights, the state militia, forestry, public lands, and amendment processes.

Remarkably only 40 percent of Utahns even know their state has its own constitution—yet this constitution represents the very statehood that nineteenth-century Utahns fought so hard to achieve.[28] Creating a state is not a moment, of course, but a process. Like most state constitutions, Utah's is a detailed, regularly contested document that bears little resemblance to the original. And like all state constitutions, Utah's erects the arena where the state's political games are played, specifying the rules and procedures by which Utahns govern themselves. The Utah Constitution evolves because Utahns do.

LEGACIES OF THE TERRITORIAL DAYS

Utah's territorial period pitted the LDS Church's polygamy and theocratic impulses against federal authority. For ten years after his 1847 arrival, Brigham Young held unchallenged authority over civil and religious matters. He retained immense civil influence long after yielding the governorship in 1857. Only when the Church abandoned polygamy, disbanded the People's Party, and walked back its theocratic ambitions did Congress trust Utahns with erecting and administering their own state. Nevertheless statehood did not mark the end of Utah's clashes with federal authority any more than it marked the end of LDS political influence. Faulkner's words from *Requiem for a Nun* could have been written about Utah: "The past is never dead. It's not even past." As the next two chapters argue, most Utahns today retain their forebears' religion, mistrust of federal authority, and general political sensibilities. Chapter 2 examines Utah's ongoing clashes with federal authority, and chapter 3 traces Utah's partisan history, leading up to the 1970s reemergence of a religious-partisan cleavage.

CHAPTER TWO

A State and a Nation

Utah and Washington DC forced smiles after statehood, yet the marriage was rocky from the start. Utah voters elected LDS leader B. H. Roberts to the U.S. House in 1898. Fearing that the LDS Church would use Roberts to maintain political influence, the House refused to seat him, citing his polygamous past as a pretext. Five years later the Utah Legislature appointed Reed Smoot, an LDS apostle but never a polygamist, to the U.S. Senate in 1903. The Senate held contentious hearings for four years before finally seating him in 1907; senators even questioned Church president Joseph F. Smith.[1] After the Smoot hearings Utah increasingly "Americanized" culturally, socially, and economically, quieting these tensions for a time (Magleby 2006, 180; Peterson and Cannon 2015). Nevertheless power struggles between Utah and Washington DC have flared up regularly, especially in the 1940s, 1970s, and 2010s. In each case Utahns joined broader states' rights movements, though each of these movements reached its greatest intensity in Utah.

Utahns' unusually deep suspicion of the federal government stems from two sources. First, Utahns, especially Mormon Utahns, retain the old conflicts in their collective memory. Church curriculum teaches LDS youth a founding narrative that highlights the government's repeated failures to protect early Mormons: the 1838 Missouri extermination order, the 1844 assassination of Joseph and Hyrum Smith, the 1846 Nauvoo expulsion, the 1857 arrival of Johnston's Army, and the arrests of Church leaders and seizures of Church property resulting from the 1887 Edmunds-Tucker Act. Many LDS teens participate in summertime "treks," reenacting the pioneer journey. LDS leaders use these stories to build a global Mormon identity, even among those who lack pioneer ancestors. In a broadcast to Mormons worldwide, a German-born LDS apostle illustrated this strategy: "My own ancestors were living an ocean away at the time. None were among those who lived in Nauvoo or Winter Quarters, and none made the journey across the plains. But as a member of the Church, I claim with gratitude and pride this pioneer legacy as my own."[2] Just as the Civil War and Reconstruction left white southerners suspicious of federal authority for generations, the Church's celebration of pioneer perseverance against an indifferent or even hostile federal government leaves modern Mormons equally suspicious.

Second, Utah lacks control over most of its own territory. The federal government directly owns and manages 67 percent of Utah's land, mostly via the federal Bureau of Land Management (BLM), U.S. Forest Service (USFS), National Park Service (NPS), and Fish and Wildlife Service (FWS).[3] Most of these lands were too arid for pioneer settlement. As a result Utah ranks among the most urbanized states; most Utahns live in four of the state's twenty-nine counties, so that 75 percent of the state's population lives on 5 percent of its dry land.[4] Placing so much unpopulated Utah land under control of distant Washington bureaucracies creates a recipe for resentment.

Southern states share Utah's history of conflict with the federal government, and western states share Utah's public land management issues. Alone among the fifty states, Utah has both complaints, creating unusually fertile soil for antifederal movements to bloom. This chapter develops this argument, considering Utah's place in the federal system since statehood. To begin, I review American federalism broadly to highlight the many ways that modern states, including Utah, interact with the federal government; to be sure, Utah enjoys many positive, fruitful partnerships with Washington DC. Then I turn to the major areas of conflict, showing how Utah's territorial history and public lands issues led to explosive antifederal movements in the 1940s, 1970s, and 2010s.

AMERICAN FEDERALISM

Federalism requires more than the mere presence of central and regional governments. If a central government can overrule any decision made by regional governments, the system is unitary, not federal. For example,

Utah's state government has a unitary relationship with Utah's city and county governments; the legislature has unambiguous authority to over-rule any local governments' action. On the other hand, if the regional governments can ignore any decision made by the central government, the system is confederal, not federal; most international organizations are confederal, as were the Revolutionary-era Articles of Confederation and the Civil War–era southern confederacy. In a unitary or confederal system, one level governs only at the other level's pleasure.

Thus federalism by definition requires that neither level of govern-ment completely dominates the other and that neither level of government derives authority from the other. Instead both levels derive sovereignty directly from the people. Put differently, federalism implies that each level of government has at least one policy realm over which it makes final, binding decisions, even if one level has more responsibilities than the other.[5] America is federal because Utah—like all states—enjoys abso-lute control over some policy areas, while the federal government enjoys absolute control over others. States alone set sentences for most felonies, determine local speed limits, regulate land use and zoning, and set the local sales tax rate; the U.S. Congress alone raises an army, prints money, collects tariffs, and naturalizes immigrants.

The U.S. Constitution delegates certain powers to Congress and reserves others to the states. Of course many policy areas involve some degree of state and federal cooperation. Political science distinguishes between two broad flavors of federalism: dual and shared.[6] In dual federalism each level of government enjoys exclusive authority over a defined set of policy areas, with little if any overlap in their respective spheres. In shared federalism each level of government retains exclusive authority over a limited set of policy areas, but most policy areas involve shared authority and frequent cooperation.

Since ratification of the U.S. Constitution in 1787, broad expansions in federal power have shifted the relationship between Washington and the states from dual federalism toward increasingly shared federalism. In part these expansions reflect ever-broadening judicial interpretations of federal authority. For example, courts have read the U.S. Constitution's necessary and proper clause as conferring implied powers beyond those specifically enumerated in the constitutional text.[7] As a result federal courts today see most congressional acts as presumptively constitutional, even if they lack an obvious connection to an enumerated Article I power, as long as the congressional act does not infringe any specific rights guaranteed elsewhere in the Constitution. That is, federal actions are presumed to have a "rational basis within the knowledge and experience" of Congress, making them difficult to strike down.[8] Federal judges also read the U.S. Constitution's commerce clause broadly, upholding a variety of federal programs arguably affecting commerce within states more than between them.

The Tenth Amendment promises that "powers not delegated to the United States by the Constitution, nor prohibited by it to the States, are reserved to the States respectively, or to the people." These broad readings of the necessary and proper clause and commerce clause limit the Tenth Amendment's scope. After all, if these two clauses have the practical effect of authorizing Congress to reach beyond the Constitution's narrowly enumerated powers, then the Tenth Amendment's reference to "powers not delegated to the United States" retains little meaning.[9] Simply put, the Tenth Amendment offers states little protection against federal expansion.

For the most part, however, the American shift from dual to shared federalism has less to do with these judicial interpretations than with clever congressional strategies that pressure states to implement new policies they might not otherwise enact. By offering incentives to states that comply or threatening sanctions against states that do not, Congress can effect policy change indirectly, freeing it from finding constitutional justification for its actions.

On the incentive side, federal programs can encourage states to provide services they might not otherwise provide. Two major federal grant programs are Medicaid, which provides medical care for the poor, and Temporary Assistance for Needy Families (TANF), a cash assistance program for families with dependent children. Medicaid comes as a matching grant; for every dollar Utah spends on health care for the poor (subject to Medicaid guidelines), Congress adds $2.36.[10] By contrast, TANF comes as a block grant; even if Utah does not spend any of its own money on aid to the poor, the state receives federal money as long as it complies with congressional guidelines about how to spend it. Congress does not deliver these programs directly, so it does not need constitutional authority for them. Rather Congress simply makes money available to states willing to spend it according to congressional intent. Utah, like all states, accepts the money. For FY2017 Utah received nearly $80 million for TANF and over $1.5 billion for Medicaid; in total, federal transfers fund 25 to 30 percent of Utah's annual budget.[11]

Congress also has more forceful means at its disposal, of course: it routinely mandates that states will become ineligible for federal funding unless they adhere to the guidelines of some new program, an enforcement tool known as a crossover sanction or an unfunded mandate. For example, Congress voted in 1984 to cut federal highway construction grants in states with a drinking age lower than twenty-one; every state with a lower drinking age promptly raised it. Later the 2001 No Child Left Behind Act required states to administer standardized tests and make other costly reforms to public education or risk losing federal grants. Congress uses similar sanctioning schemes to compel state implementation of diverse environmental, civil rights, and public education mandates.

Federal growth has not rendered states irrelevant, of course. The Utah Legislature still enacts twice as many laws per year as Congress, and Utah courts issue twice as many rulings per year as federal courts. Moreover federal transfers fund only 25 to 30 percent of Utah's budget, leaving 70 to 75 percent entirely to the Utah Legislature. Most laws, most law enforcement, and most government programs still come from the states, not from Washington DC. All the same, the federal government's growth over the past two centuries remains an undisputed empirical fact.[12]

Whether or not this growth marks an improvement is the subject of intense dispute, especially in Utah.[13] After Barack Obama's 2008 electoral victory, he successfully worked with Congress to pass his signature health care reform, the Patient Protection and Affordable Care Act ("Obamacare"), in March 2010. The federal government's steady growth over preceding decades had already fueled antifederal sentiment among certain elements, though it mostly remained on the back burner. But this new federal program caused these simmering sentiments to boil over, spilling into the forefront of the national discourse. In 2010 a new Tea Party movement rallied not only against Obama's health care reforms but against the federal government's long-growing role.

Utah legislators embraced this Tea Party groundswell by forming the Patrick Henry Caucus, proclaiming in their video manifesto that "states

[were] fighting back."[14] They recruited like-minded state legislators nation-wide to join their cause, but with less success than they found at home. Members of the Patrick Henry Caucus successfully enacted a series of aggressive anti-federal bills during the movement's 2010–11 zenith. In the 2010 General Session these bills included HB67, prohibiting any Utah agency from implementing any part of the federal Affordable Care Act without receiving specific advance approval from the Utah Legislature;[15] SB11, declaring any firearm manufactured and sold within Utah exempt from all federal firearms regulations since those federal laws were generally justified under the U.S. Constitution's interstate commerce clause; HB234S1, denouncing the federal REAL ID Act, passed in 2005 by a Republican Congress and signed by a Republican president, as "inimical to the security and well-being" of Utahns and "adopted in violation of the principles of federalism contained in the Tenth Amendment of the United States Constitution";[16] and SB250, which sought to roll back the Seventeenth Amendment to the U.S. Constitution (providing for direct election of U.S. senators) by encouraging Utah's political parties to consult with the legislature when nominating candidates for the U.S. Senate.

The next year additional anti-federal bills included HB220, requiring Utah's public schoolteachers to refer to the United States as a "compound [federal] Constitutional republic" to emphasize states' role;[17] HB76, creating a new Federalism Subcommittee within Utah's Constitutional Defense Council to mull legal challenges to federal actions; and SJR25, a non-binding resolution "declar[ing] the need for a restoration of American federalism and a decentralization of government power." After this brief heyday the national Tea Party movement waned and the Patrick Henry Caucus's founders moved on from politics.[18]

Though the Tea Party movement was national, it found its greatest support in Utah. At its height in 2010, 34.9 percent of the average state's residents had a positive view of the movement. Support was higher in southern and western states. Among the eleven former Confederate states, the average rose to 37.5 percent; in the intermountain West (excluding Utah) it rose to 39.0 percent. In Utah, which combines the South's memory of nineteenth-century federal antagonism with the West's public lands disputes, a whopping 45.0 percent of respondents had a positive view of the Tea Party.[19] No wonder, then, that only Utah witnessed the Patrick

Henry Caucus's organized legislative assault on the federal government. And no wonder that even as the Tea Party movement waned nationally, it birthed in Utah a multiyear fight over federal management of public lands.

ORIGINS OF UTAH'S FEDERAL LANDS

Historically the loudest arguments for states' rights came from slaveholders during the Civil War and from their segregationist descendants a century later. This tainted heritage has sometimes made it politically unsavory to raise states' rights arguments today. Since the 1970s, however, states' rights arguments have come not from southern white supremacists but from western ranchers, grazers, miners, and off-road enthusiasts—with Utah in the thick of everything.

Vast swathes of western land are managed by the Bureau of Land Management, National Parks Service, U.S. Forest Service, Fish and Wildlife Service, and other federal agencies. Together these four agencies control 63 percent of Utah's land, with the BLM alone controlling 43 percent.[20] These four control 81 percent of Nevada, 62 percent of Idaho, 61 percent of Alaska, 53 percent of Oregon, 48 percent of Wyoming, 44 percent of California, 38 percent of Arizona, and so on throughout the West, with minimal federal ownership east of the Rockies.[21] Like some of its western neighbors, Utah's state government craves more control over how those lands are managed, apparently because it hopes to increase tax receipts by privatizing land or promoting extractive industries like grazing, mining, and oil exploration, even at the expense of preservation.[22]

The federal government has owned vast tracts of land since the founding, and assembling this public domain played a significant role in uniting the first thirteen states as they warred against Britain.[23] The colonies' joint 1776 Declaration of Independence proclaimed thirteen sovereign states—independent from Britain as much as from one another. Fearing the violent and bloody expansionist wars that might follow a successful campaign against Britain, the thirteen states drafted terms for a permanent alliance, the Articles of Confederation, yet state-to-state rivalries still gave small states lacking expansive western claims nightmares. Maryland in particular refused to sign the Articles until New York and Virginia ceded their massive (and overlapping) western claims to the new Congress of the Confederation. As war with Britain stretched from one year into another,

Maryland's would-be allies grew increasingly frustrated with Maryland's intransigence. Eventually they yielded; New York agreed to cede its western claims in 1780, five years after the war's first shots at Lexington and Concord, with Virginia following suit soon after. With the largest two claims extinguished, Maryland ratified the Articles early in 1781. By the time the war ended, Congress owned land between the Appalachians and the Mississippi nearly as large as the thirteen states combined, so that "the forging of the national public domain coincided with the creation of the United States itself" (Wilson 2014, 14). During the Revolutionary era this joint ownership of unsettled lands united the colonies and helped guarantee postwar peace.

Acting under authority of the Articles, the postwar Congress enacted the 1784 and 1787 Northwest Ordinances, authorizing the new confederation to own, manage, and sell these lands. These ordinances declared that the new territories would eventually be organized into states, yet they also declared that Congress would retain exclusive authority over unsold lands within these future states. The 1787 Constitutional Convention strengthened these ordinances by including the "federal territory and property clause" in Article IV of the new Constitution: "The Congress shall have power to dispose of and make all needful rules and regulations respecting the territory or other property belonging to the United States."

When Congress passed an 1894 Enabling Act authorizing Utah to draft a constitution and form a state government, it required Utah's new constitution to affirm the federal government's exclusive authority over unsold public lands within the new state, with those lands exempt from state taxation and with proceeds from any future sales accruing solely to the national treasury. Similar provisions appeared in enabling acts for Alaska (1958), Arizona (1910), New Mexico (1910), Nevada (1864), North Dakota (1889), South Dakota (1889), Montana (1889), Washington (1889), and other states.[24] These provisions merely echoed what had been true since the Northwest Ordinance. Like other states admitted to the union, Utah agreed to these terms, stating in Article III of the Utah Constitution that Utahns "do affirm and declare that they forever disclaim all right and title to the unappropriated public lands lying within the boundaries hereof . . . until the title thereto shall have been extinguished by the United States."

Through most of the nineteenth century congressional policy favored selling western lands, both to promote western settlement and to repay war debts. Early on, countless settlers claimed the most favorable lands. As migration later slowed, Congress began sweetening the terms of sale to encourage settlers to claim more marginal lands. For example, the Graduation Act of 1854 reduced the price by 87.5 percent on land that remained unsold thirty years after being listed for sale; the Homestead Act of 1862 allowed settlers to purchase a 160-acre lot at a steep discount as long as they remained on the land for five years and made certain improvements; and the Morrill Act of 1862 sought to make western settlement more attractive by providing land grants to each state to create colleges.[25]

Eventually only the most arid lands remained unsold—those least suited to settlement or agriculture. Dry, rocky lands may be unsuitable for farms and cities, but they suit extractive industries just fine. Soon squatters were running unregulated mining, logging, quarrying, and ranching operations on those unsold public lands. Most of these extractive users remained for only a short time and then moved on, giving them little incentive to purchase title outright. As a result congressional land policy began to shift from selling to managing unsold lands. Congress began with a series of mostly ineffective laws targeting these transient uses of the public domain: the 1872 General Mining Act, the Timber Culture Act of 1873, the Timber and Stone Act of 1878, and the Free Timber Act of 1878, for example.[26] Congress also began giving unusually scenic or resource-rich lands special management designations—national parks, national forests, and national wildlife refuges—and later created specialized agencies to manage them: the NPS, the USFS, and the FWS.[27] The leftover lands eventually wound up in the Bureau of Land Management's portfolio. Though federal land sales all but ceased by the end of the nineteenth century, it was not until 1976 when the Federal Land Policy and Management Act officially declared what had long been true in practice: remaining public lands would no longer be sold but rather held indefinitely and managed by the BLM, NPS, USFS, and FWS.

Extractive industries can no longer buy BLM land for their operations, but they seldom wanted to even when those lands were available for sale a century ago, preferring to work one area for a time and then move on. Recognizing the transient nature of these industries, the modern BLM, acting under the mandate of the Federal Land Policy and Management

Act, issues temporary leases and permits for these activities. In doing so the BLM operates under a "multiple use" mission intended to balance extractive, recreational, and conservationist goals. The USFS has a similar multiple-use mission. Multiple use has the impossible goal of pleasing everybody, which feeds the conflict between western interests and federal managers.

UTAH'S SAGEBRUSH REBELS

Ranchers, miners, loggers, and oil speculators have always been the BLM's loudest critics. Whiffs of rebellion began as early as 1946, the year the old General Land Office became the Bureau of Land Management. A decade earlier Congress had passed the Taylor Grazing Act, requiring ranchers to pay grazing fees to run cattle on federal lands. In 1946 angry ranchers and western politicians convened in Salt Lake City to plan a response. A sympathetic member of Congress from Wyoming followed up by introducing federal legislation transferring grazing land to the ranchers who had squatted on it for generations, though the bill went nowhere.[28] Critics elsewhere lambasted this Utah-led land transfer effort. Reminding readers that ranchers chose for decades to run their cattle freely on public lands rather than purchase title outright, one critic minced no words: "The Cattle Kingdom never did own more than a minute fraction of one percent of the range it grazed: it was national domain, it belonged to the people of the United States. Cattlemen do not own the public range now: it belongs to you and me. . . . But they always acted as if they owned the public range and act so now; they convinced themselves that it belonged to them and now believe it does; and they are trying to take title to it."[29]

Attacks like these ended the 1940s land transfer movement, but grumbling continued. Lingering discontent erupted again thirty years later in the so-called Sagebrush Rebellion when Congress passed the Federal Land Policy and Management Act, which officially ended land sales and introduced processes enabling conservationists to challenge ranching, grazing, and mining leases. Utah's newly elected senator Orrin Hatch responded with federal legislation authorizing a transfer of most federal lands (except national parks and national monuments) to the states. During an August 1980 presidential campaign stop in Salt Lake City, Ronald Reagan pledged his support, declaring himself a sagebrush rebel.[30] Tempers cooled once

Reagan won the White House, though Hatch's transfer bill nevertheless failed in 1981.

By the 1990s the Sagebrush Rebellion was once again relegated to the back burner, where it might well have stayed—save for Bill Clinton and the Antiquities Act. Congress had enacted the Antiquities Act in 1906. Over the preceding thirty-four years, Congress had created the nation's first eight national parks, starting with Yellowstone. Creating each park required an act of Congress, and congressional study could take months or longer. In 1889 some cowboys stumbled upon spectacular cliff ruins in southwestern Colorado, not far from the Utah line. Within a short time looters had broken down ancient walls and used centuries-old roof beams as firewood in their search for relics they could sell. By the time Congress created Mesa Verde National Park in 1906, what little protection their designation could offer came too late for most of the area's antiquities.

Hoping to prevent a repeat of this sad scenario, Congress passed the 1906 Antiquities Act to grant the president unilateral authority to quickly protect irreplaceable sites on public lands. The Act allows presidents to designate a national monument on any federal land to protect sites of "historic or scientific interest," with boundaries limited to "the smallest area compatible with proper care and management." Theodore Roosevelt promptly tested the law's limits, declaring eighteen new national monuments during his presidency, five of which Congress later upgraded to national parks: Grand Canyon, Olympic, Lassen, Pinnacles, and Petrified Forest.[31] Four of Utah's "mighty five" national parks began as presidential designations under this Act: Zion (by President Taft), Bryce Canyon (by President Harding), Arches (by President Hoover), and Capitol Reef (by President Roosevelt). Utah also contains many smaller national monuments created under this authority, including Timpanogos Cave, Cedar Breaks, Dinosaur, Hovenweep, Natural Bridges, and Rainbow Bridge.

With this context President Clinton might be forgiven for underestimating local reaction to his 1996 proclamation creating the 1.8-million-acre Grand Staircase-Escalante National Monument in southern Utah. Then again perhaps Clinton did foresee the firestorm that would result. After all, he sought no consultation from Utah's congressional delegation or state government as he prepared his monument designation, choosing instead to provide them only twenty-four hours' notice before acting. He did not even visit Utah to make the announcement. Instead, in September 1996, at the height of his campaign against Bob Dole for reelection, Clinton held a ceremony across the border in Arizona at Grand Canyon National Park declaring the news. Utahns reacted furiously. Even Utah's lone Democratic member of Congress, Bill Orton, introduced legislation seeking to limit the Antiquities Act, saying, "We cannot continue to allow people from inside the beltway, who have never set foot in Utah, to make decisions affecting us without any kind of congressional oversight."[32]

Once again tempers cooled with time, and once again the western battle over public lands waned—until the 2010–11 Tea Party and Patrick Henry movements revived anti-federal sentiment both nationally and in Utah. Extractive industries seized the moment to press back on federal land management policies. In some cases these clashes threatened violence. In spring 2014, for example, Cliven Bundy brought dozens of armed militiamen to his Nevada ranch to resist BLM efforts to remove his cattle from lands closed to grazing; the BLM stood down, though Bundy and his accomplices were arrested and charged two years later.[33] Later that year Phil Lyman, an elected commissioner in Utah's San Juan County, led an ATV ride through Recapture Canyon, which the BLM had closed to protect Ancestral Puebloan artifacts. After Lyman's arrest, Utah governor Gary Herbert and other prominent officeholders publicly contributed to Lyman's legal defense fund, and the Utah Association of Counties declared Lyman "Commissioner of the Year" for his activism; all the same, Lyman was sentenced in December 2015 to ten days in jail.[34] A few weeks later two of Bundy's sons and several accomplices staged a month-long armed occupation of a federal wildlife refuge in Oregon before authorities captured them.[35]

Only Lyman's protest ride occurred within Utah, yet all these events had unavoidable Utah links. Though Bundy and his sons confronted the federal government in Nevada and Oregon, they are Mormons who explicitly linked their anti-federal struggle to Mormon scripture and to Utah's territorial struggles. A Bundy ally in the Oregon occupation identified himself to media only as "Captain Moroni," a heroic Book of Mormon figure. The Bundys pressed this narrative so relentlessly that the LDS Church felt compelled to respond with a statement "condemn[ing] the armed seizure of the [Oregon refuge]" and urging "conflicts with government [to] . . . be settled using peaceful means."[36]

Utah's state government has pursued a less physical but equally audacious approach. In 2012 the Utah Legislature passed Representative Ken Ivory's HB148, demanding that the federal government transfer most federal lands within Utah to the state by December 31, 2014.[37] Utahns may have agreed in their constitution to "forever disclaim all right and title to the unappropriated public lands," but the bill's proponents maintain Utah did so with the tacit understanding that the federal government would continue offering those lands for sale rather than managing them directly. With two-thirds of the state's territory under federal management, a potential land transfer has enormous economic stakes.[38]

The federal government allowed HB148's deadline to pass with minimal comment, despite Utah's threat of litigation.[39] Utah's Commission for the Stewardship of Public Lands, a study committee created indirectly by HB148,[40] contracted an outside legal analysis for $500,000. Ultimately this legal analysis concluded there was "credible support" for legal theories that "have value as the basis for claims in litigation"—lukewarm language at best—with full legal costs estimated at $13,819,000.[41] Later a separate legal analysis released by the Conference of Western Attorneys General—representing state attorneys general from Alaska, Arizona, Colorado, Idaho, Montana, Nevada, New Mexico, Oregon, Utah, Washington, and Wyoming—cast doubt on these findings, concluding that federal land management authority under the U.S. Constitution "has no limitations."[42]

As of this writing, long after HB148's 2014 transfer deadline, Utah has yet to bring suit. Meanwhile presidential use of the Antiquities Act has kept disputes over federal management of Utah lands alive. Shortly before leaving office, President Barack Obama proclaimed a vast new Bears Ears National Monument in southeastern Utah, protecting its scenic, archaeological, and other natural values.[43] A year later President Donald Trump reduced the Bears Ears National Monument from 1.3 to 0.2 million acres and the Grand Staircase-Escalante National Monument from 1.9 to 1.0 million acres, dividing the two large national monuments into five small ones.[44] In doing so Trump asserted that the Antiquities Act authorizes presidents not only to create national monuments but also to rescind them, a claim that, at this writing, is being challenged in court.[45]

THE ANTI-FEDERAL STATE

Time will tell whether the Utah Legislature's land transfer effort will succeed. Proponents expect local control to result in streamlined management policies that promote resource development and expand Utah's tax base; opponents prefer the federal government's more conservationist approach and worry that the state will do too little to protect antiquities, sensitive species, dispersed recreation, and scenic vistas.[46] The specific merits or drawbacks of state ownership are not the point of this chapter, however. Rather this chapter demonstrates the depth and resilience of pro-state, anti-federal sentiment within Utah. The 1946 Salt Lake City conference promoting ranchers' land rights, the late 1970s Sagebrush Rebellion, the Patrick Henry Caucus's anti-federal assault in 2010 and 2011, the Tea Party movement's unusually strong support in Utah, the Bundys' Mormonism-infused armed protests, and the Utah Legislature's land transfer gambit—all these are mere manifestations of Utah's persistent suspicion of federal authority.

To be sure, Utah has enjoyed many fruitful collaborations with the federal government. In particular it has received tremendous federal assistance in delivering fresh water to the densely populated Wasatch Front. A vast network of canals and aqueducts collects snowmelt that would otherwise flow toward the Colorado River and instead diverts it into the Provo River and other Great Basin tributaries by way of several large reservoirs, including those at Deer Creek, Jordanelle, Strawberry, Starvation, and Upper Stillwater. Erecting this vital water infrastructure took more than half a century, and the federal Bureau of Reclamation provided much of the financing. Utah has also collaborated on defense policy, playing host to Hill Air Force Base, the Dugway Proving Ground, the Utah Test and Training Range, a National Security Agency data center, the Tooele Chemical Agent Disposal Facility, the Kearns Army Air Base, Camp Williams, the now-defunct Green River Launch Complex, and other major installations. And when the Great Recession struck in 2009, federal stimulus funds kept Utah's state budget afloat. It would be a mistake to see Utah's relationship with the federal government as entirely antagonistic.

Still, since the end of the southern civil rights battles, no state has witnessed such powerful and consistent resistance to federal authority as Utah. This chapter has argued for two major causes of this antifederal sentiment. First, Mormon Utahns actively preserve a culturally unifying narrative celebrating early believers' perseverance against an indifferent and occasionally hostile federal government. Intentionally or not, these stories have the incidental effect of nurturing suspicion of federal officials. Second, federal control of two-thirds of Utah's territory makes it inevitable that some Utahns will find fault with federal land managers; multiple use cannot please everyone.

Utah's 1940s and 1970s land transfer efforts eventually waned, producing no real change. Its 2010s land transfer quest may end the same way. However, Utah will continue to share with the South an inherited memory of past federal conflict, and Utah will continue to share with its western neighbors frustrations over federal land management. These two considerations will keep Utah fertile ground for future anti-federal outbursts. Utah's next Sagebrush Rebellion may lie only a few years out.

CHAPTER THREE

A Peculiarly Republican People

In the 2012 presidential election Utahns delivered 73 percent of their votes to former Massachusetts governor Mitt Romney, rejecting Democratic incumbent Barack Obama by a three-to-one margin. Perhaps Romney's smashing victory reflected Mormon voters' excitement to support the first Mormon running as a major party's nominee, a breakthrough dubbed "the Mormon Moment."[1] In truth, though, Romney's success reflected no more than Utah's continued love affair with the Republican Party. After all, George W. Bush won essentially the same vote share (72 percent) eight years earlier. And in 2014 Utah voters elected the second most Republican state legislature since 1926, adding two more Republicans than they had elected two years earlier during the supposed Romney surge.[2] Though it clearly did not hurt, Romney did not sweep Utah because he was Mormon; he swept it because he was Republican.

It has not always been so. In Utah's first election as the nation's forty-fifth state, held in 1896, voters placed seventeen Democrats, one independent, and no Republicans in the new Utah State Senate, along with forty Democrats, one independent, and two Republicans in the new Utah House of Representatives. Everything flipped twelve years later: in 1908 voters placed eighteen Republicans and no Democrats in the Utah Senate, along with forty-three Republicans and two Democrats in the Utah House. Everything flipped once again eight years later: Democrats won every seat in the Utah Senate and all but one seat in the Utah House. Figure 2 plots these wild swings in each chamber of the Utah Legislature, with the U.S. House shown for comparison.[3] The Depression brought partisan

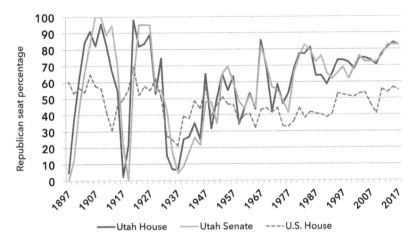

Fig. 2. Partisan control of the Utah Legislature since statehood. Compiled by the author.

stability, and Utah soon emerged as a swing state. Only in the 1970s did the Republican Party become dominant.

This chapter reviews this partisan history, arguing that the reemergence of a religious-partisan cleavage—suppressed since the 1890s dissolution of the People's Party and Liberal Party—defines Utah's modern politics. In the 1970s Utah voters began sorting along religious lines; Mormons became Republican and others became Democrats. These circumstances make Utah today an overwhelmingly Republican state. I then argue that single-party dominance has had three major effects on Utah politics: less turnover among officeholders, less turnout among voters, and more factional bickering within the Republican majority. I conclude by considering what Utah's socioeconomic trends portend for its partisan future.

BECOMING A REPUBLICAN STATE

Chapter 1 reviewed the religious cleavages that defined nineteenth-century politics in Utah Territory. In those days the Mormon majority supported the Church-backed People's Party against the secular Liberal Party. In pursuit of statehood civic and religious leaders acted to disband the People's Party in 1891. In doing so they explicitly hoped that the state's old religious-partisan cleavage would fade as Mormons and non-Mormons divided evenly into the national Republican and Democratic parties.[4] More to the point, they also hoped that neither national party would have any incentive to attack Mormonism if both parties had Mormon supporters. After all, the Republican Party's founding 1856 platform denounced "those twin relics of barbarism, polygamy and slavery," and Republican politicians led the territorial era's anti-Mormon crusades.

With the People's Party gone, however, these grand visions failed to materialize. Rather than divide evenly into the national parties, Mormons flocked to the Democratic Party, eschewing the anti-Mormon Republicans: "The Mormon people detested the GOP as much as they loathed Satan's legions" (Alexander 2007, 202). Alarmed, the Church's First Presidency, its highest governing council, asked Democratic-leaning Church officials to remain quiet as it sent out prominent Mormon Republicans recruiting for the GOP. Though it remains difficult to separate fact from folklore, one possibly apocryphal story relates a Church leader's failure to persuade any members of a particular congregation to sign up as Republicans. Frustrated, he resumed his appeal: "Brothers and sisters, you have misunderstood. God needs Republicans" (quoted in Fox 2006, 4).

Stories like these may exaggerate the recruitment method. Still, Mormon voters sensed the Church's endorsement and moved right, swinging from overwhelmingly Democratic to overwhelmingly Republican. Reeling from their losses, jilted Mormon Democrats ended their silence and responded with their own recruitment appeals. This battle for Mormons' partisan loyalties contributed to the tremendous partisan swings narrated earlier.[5]

Mormons aspire to follow their prophet.[6] In the territorial days the LDS-aligned People's Party showed them how to do so. After statehood, with the People's Party disbanded, Mormon voters struggled to discern where their prophet wanted them to go. Perhaps, after so many years of following the Church's lead on politics, lay-level adherents simply failed to grasp that LDS leadership favored an even partisan split. As a result Mormon voters' allegiances shifted with shifting partisan cues.

Things finally stabilized in the Depression. Mormons and non-Mormons alike embraced Franklin Delano Roosevelt's Democratic platform and his New Deal, finally muting Utah's religious cleavage. Ironically this partisan stability came even as Church president Heber J. Grant, formerly a Democrat himself, began actively urging his flock to resist the New Deal and "the dole," encouraging them to give the emerging Church welfare program a chance to succeed rather than support federal recovery efforts. Despite Grant's vocal opposition, Utah voted for Roosevelt all four times he ran, a development Grant called "one of the most serious conditions that has confronted me since I became President of the Church" (quoted in Winder 2007, 251). (In later years LDS leaders would adopt a strict political neutrality policy.)

Utah soon emerged as a true swing state. For four decades it voted for every winning presidential candidate but one.[7] This competitive era ended in 1976, when Utahns voted decisively for Republican Gerald Ford over the ultimate winner, Democrat Jimmy Carter. Republicans have dominated Utah ever since, controlling the Utah House of Representatives since 1975 and the Utah Senate since 1977. Republicans also control all four elected executive positions, including state auditor (since 1969), treasurer (since 1981), governor (since 1985), and attorney general (since 2001). All five state supreme court justices were appointed by Republican governors; all were confirmed by Republican state Senates. Only five of the twenty Utahns to represent Utah in the U.S. House and U.S. Senate between 1981 and 2017 have been Democrats; since 2015 all seven have been Republicans. Without question Utah has become an overwhelmingly Republican state.

Utah became Republican because Mormons became Republican. As late as the 1960s Mormons "tended to be about equally divided between Democrats and Republicans" (Mauss 1994, 49). As the 1970s dawned, however, new issues—civil rights, anticommunism, abortion, and homosexuality—began to break up Roosevelt's New Deal coalition, pulling social conservatives nationally toward a newly resurgent Republican Party.[8] Certain outspoken LDS leaders signaled their flock to follow. Asked in 1974 by a reporter whether a good Mormon could be a "liberal Democrat," for example, LDS apostle (and future LDS president) Ezra Taft Benson replied, "I think it would be very hard if he was living the gospel and understood it" (quoted in Turner 2016, 66). Later in the 1970s official LDS opposition to the proposed Equal Rights Amendment reinforced these signals. And in the 1990s–2000s official Church involvement in a series of same-sex marriage contests that increasingly pitted Republicans against Democrats, especially California's 2008 battle of Proposition 8, implied a new partisan signal.

There have always been and continue to be prominent Mormon Democrats. James E. Faust, a Democrat who once served in the Utah Legislature, was called as an apostle in 1978, later serving in the LDS First Presidency from 1995 through 2007. And the highest political office ever held by an American Mormon was occupied by Harry Reid, a Democrat who led the U.S. Senate from 2007 through 2015. Moreover outspoken Democrats like Marlin K. Jensen and Larry Echo Hawk have held prominent positions as LDS general authorities.

Nevertheless Church cues gave new social issues like abortion, women's rights, and homosexuality extra weight in the Mormon-dominated mountain West. Marchant-Shapiro and Patterson (1995) demonstrate that Mormons became increasingly Republican not because of generational change or newly mobilized voters but because of partisan conversion. Mormons' partisan realignment did not happen overnight of course; the process took many years, culminating around 1980 (Beck 1974; Monson et al. 2013). Since that time Mormons have been among the most reliably Republican blocs, making modern Utah a reliably Republican state.[9] Mormons have long considered themselves a "peculiar people";[10] they might also call themselves a peculiarly Republican people. One recent book even makes the extraordinary claim that twenty-first-century Mormons are more politically distinctive than Mormons were at statehood (Campbell et al. 2014).

Much has been written about Mormons' move to the right. Less has been written about Utah's other voters. As it turns out, Utah's non-Mormon voters changed too: as Mormons moved right, other Utahns moved left.[11] By the 1970s and 1980s the old religious-partisan cleavage that defined the territorial days—a cleavage once embodied in the People's Party and Liberal Party—reemerged under Republican and Democratic banners. Polling data reveal this religious-partisan cleavage. In 2016 over sixty thousand American adults participated in the Cooperative Congressional Election Survey (CCES). Using this rich data set, I estimated a model of voters' partisan identification using the demographic variables age, education, sex, and race.[12] Consistent with well-known patterns, this statistical model finds that survey participants are more likely to identify as Democrats if they are young, college-educated, female, or nonwhite. There is nothing new here—yet.

The results get more interesting, however, when we add three additional variables: whether the respondent lives in Utah, identifies as Mormon, and—the kicker—is *both* Utahn and Mormon. That last variable produces novel insights since it allows a comparison of Mormon Utahns to non-Mormon Utahns. When all other variables are set to their median values, a typical American respondent has a 42 percent predicted probability of identifying as a Democrat and a 39 percent probability of identifying as a Republican. These are baseline predictions, and they feel intuitively about right. For a Mormon (from any state), the Republican probability jumps to 65 percent; for a Utah Mormon, this probability rises further, to 78 percent—39 percentage points higher than the typical American. For a Utah non-Mormon, however, the Republican probability plummets to 34 percent—5 percentage points lower than the typical American.[13] True, the +39-point gap for Utah Mormons is far larger than the −5-point gap for Utah non-Mormons; nevertheless both groups are statistically different from the American population as a whole. Mormon Utahns are (very) unusually Republican, and non-Mormon Utahns are (somewhat) unusually Democratic.

Religion defines Utah's partisan boundaries even more today than in the past. When the first Utah Colleges Exit Poll was conducted back in 1982, 68 percent of Mormon respondents identified as Republican, while 60 percent of non-Mormons identified as Democrats. Thirty-two years later the 2014 Utah Colleges Exit Poll found an even starker divide: 80 percent of Mormons were Republican, while 64 percent of non-Mormons were Democrats.[14] Mormon identification correlated with partisanship at 0.32 in the 1982 poll, but at 0.54 in the 2014 poll.[15] Correlation coefficients range from 0 (no relationship) to 1 (perfect relationship), so this rise from 0.32 to 0.54 marks a tremendous increase. And as figure 3 shows, the correlation between Mormon identification and partisanship has risen steadily with time. The religious-partisan cleavage may have emerged in the 1970s, but it has since grown steadily.

Ideology also matters, of course. Nationally Democrats have become more liberal and Republicans have become more conservative over recent decades.[16] This national trend toward ideological polarization has reached Utah as much as anywhere else. As shown in figure 3, biennial exit poll data reveal a rising correlation between partisanship and ideology—and this correlation has always exceeded the correlation between religion and partisanship.[17] All the same, it is striking that Mormonism correlated more

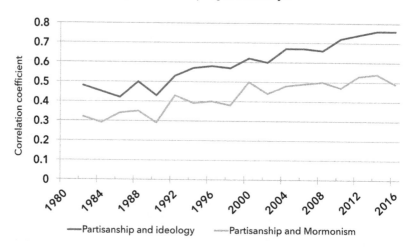

Fig. 3. Correlates of partisanship in Utah. Calculated by the author from data in the 2014 Utah Colleges Exit Poll.

strongly with partisanship in 2012 and 2014 than ideology did from 1982 through 1992.

In Utah, then, the partisan story runs deeper than the facile claim that Mormons nationally tend to vote Republican. In Utah social and cultural differences between Mormons and other Utahns bleed into partisan differences. In the territorial era the People's Party and Liberal Party explicitly defined themselves around this religious-partisan cleavage. After the decades-long volatility that followed the dissolution of these two parties the religious-partisan cleavage faded and Utah emerged as a swing state. By the late 1970s, however, the old religious-partisan cleavage had reappeared with a vengeance.

Mormons constitute only a slim majority of Utah residents, and their share continues to decline. Nevertheless Mormons vote at high rates, giving them disproportionate political influence. In the 2016 Utah Colleges Exit Poll, 59 percent of voters self-identified as Mormon—a steep drop from the 77 percent mark in the 1982 and 1986 polls, and even from the 67 to 69 percent recorded in 2004, 2006, and 2010, but still a comfortable majority. Utah is Republican because Mormons are—and because Mormons vote at high rates.

EFFECTS OF SINGLE-PARTY DOMINANCE

Though Republicans dominate Utah, Utah is not the most politically imbalanced state. That honor goes to Massachusetts (Democratic), followed by Idaho (Republican), West Virginia (Democratic), and then Utah (Republican). Rounding out the top ten are North Dakota (Republican), South Dakota (Republican), Alaska (Republican), Arkansas (Democratic), New Mexico (Democratic), and Rhode Island (Democratic).[18] Extreme, enduring partisan imbalance is simply a fact of life in many states—a fact of life with three predictable effects.

First, partisan imbalance reduces turnover among officeholders. For example, consider the percentage of legislators in Utah's House of Representatives who are freshmen.[19] During the four turbulent decades that followed statehood, at least 50 percent of Utah's representatives were freshmen at any given time. Several elections during this period—in 1900, 1902, 1916, 1922, and 1932—produced a House with 80 percent or more freshmen, an incredible and possibly risky turnover rate.[20] Eventually, however, turnover waned. In 1943, for the first time ever, the Utah House convened with fewer than 50 percent freshmen. As Utah transitioned from a swing state to a reliably Republican state, turnover declined further. During the 1990s average turnover fell to 24 percent; during the 2000s it dropped to 20 percent. Figure 4 shows the declining percentage of freshmen in the Utah House since 1901. The dark line plots the percentage of freshmen following each biennial election; the other line averages these percentages by decade to highlight the downward trend. In today's one-party Utah most legislative turnover results from voluntary departures and intraparty nomination battles; general election losses are almost unheard of.

Second, Utah's partisan imbalance has also decreased voter turnout.[21] Voters anywhere are less likely to participate in elections that appear foregone.[22] From 1960 through 1980, the tail end of Utah's swing state period, voter turnout rates in Utah were always at least 10 percentage points higher than the national average, without a single exception. Turnout rates began declining during the 1980s and early 1990s as Utah voters realized their elections had grown uncompetitive. In 1996, for the first time on record, Utah's turnout rate fell below the national average, where it has remained ever since. Figure 5 shows the difference between Utah's voter turnout rate

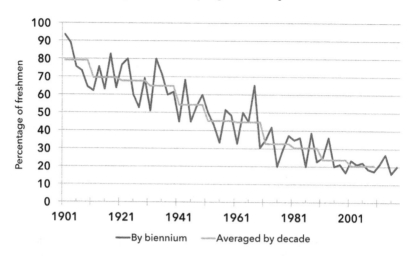

Fig. 4. Turnover in the Utah House of Representatives. Calculated by the author.

and the national average for each presidential election since 1960. The two lines represent different ways of calculating turnout. The dark line uses a less accurate turnout formula (turnout as a percentage of voting-age population, or VAP) that is available over a longer timespan; the lighter line uses a more accurate formula (turnout as a percentage of voting-eligible population, or VEP) that extends only to 1980. Both formulas show the same result: turnout declined in Utah relative to the national average as the state's elections became less competitive.[23] Not even Romney's 2012 "Mormon Moment" could reverse the tide.

Third, Utah's partisan imbalance elevates intraparty battles among various Republican factions over traditional Republican-Democratic conflicts. When the two major parties are closely balanced and competing for power, partisans on both sides have strong incentives to ignore intraparty squabbles and focus on the larger interparty clash.[24] But when one party enjoys decisive, indefinite dominance, internal divisions within the majority party can emerge unchecked.[25]

In Utah's capitol the running joke is that the state has a three-party system: the Democratic Party, the Republican Party, and the other Republican Party. The first Republican Party unites the more ideological "true believers," who embrace a deep skepticism of government's ability to do

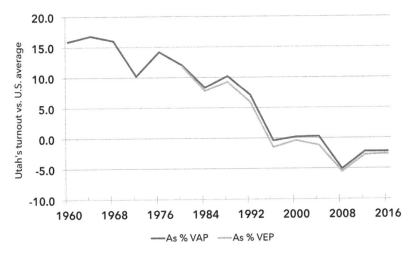

Fig. 5. Presidential election turnout in Utah. Source given in text.

anything right. This group reacts cynically to new federal policy proposals and usually favors a market approach even for such long-established
state functions as public education. The second Republican Party prefers
a more pragmatic rather than ideological approach, searching for policy
solutions that will yield the best results even if those solutions require
some ideological compromise. Relative to voters and politicians nationally,
both Republican factions are unambiguously conservative. However, one
could reasonably label the first faction very conservative and the second
merely conservative or even center-right.

This intra-Republican split arises not only in the capitol but also among
voters. In the 2016 Utah Colleges Exit Poll 40 percent of self-identified
Republicans described their ideology as "strongly conservative," compared
to 44 percent "moderately conservative"—roughly the same proportions
that arise year after year in these polls.[26] Perhaps the most heated and
enduring clash between these two factions has concerned whether to take a
market or managed approach to K–12 public education. After a major clash
over publicly funded private school vouchers in 2007, the 2008 exit poll
found that 25 percent of Utah Republicans "strongly" favored vouchers, 29
percent "somewhat" favored them, 24 percent "somewhat" opposed them,
and 22 percent "strongly" opposed them—about as even a distribution

as ever arises in polling. Though vouchers have faded as a political issue, this intra-Republican clash over public education flares up in arguments over charter schools, teacher retention, school performance evaluations, curriculum design, and school funding generally.

Because Republican voters are divided, Republican officeholders divide also.[27] Utah legislators have organized a variety of caucuses—that is, legislative clubs—to facilitate strategic coordination among those Republicans who share particular goals. Recent years have witnessed the rise (and sometimes fall) of the pro-business Conservative Caucus, the anti-federal Patrick Henry Caucus, the pragmatic Mainstream Caucus, the rural Cowboy Caucus, and the family values Common Sense Caucus—all founded by Republican legislators wishing to promote a particular Republican agenda.

These intraparty squabbles have led to litigious disputes over how the party chooses its candidates. After all, throughout most of Utah whichever candidate wins the Republican nomination is all but guaranteed to win the November general election. Traditionally Utah's Republican Party chose nominees through a caucus-convention system. Republican voters would gather on caucus night for local precinct-level caucus meetings, sometimes attracting only a few dozen voters per precinct, and in a three- to four-hour meeting would select delegates to represent the precinct at the party's state and county conventions. A few weeks later these Republican delegates would convene at the state and county Republican conventions to select the party's nominees.[28] Delegates to the statewide Republican convention would select nominees for statewide office—that is, for governor, attorney general, U.S. Senate, and so on—while delegates would break out by district to select nominees for the Utah Legislature and other district-based offices. In practice this meant that several hundred delegates participated in choosing nominees for statewide office, but only a few dozen participated in choosing nominees for each Utah House district and for other local races. If the delegates deadlocked—meaning the second-place candidate won at least 40 percent of the delegate vote—then the top two Republican candidates for a particular office would appear before Republican voters in a state-funded primary election.

In most states political parties have long since abandoned caucus-convention systems in favor of direct primaries for all races.[29] In a direct primary would-be Republican candidates gather signatures to qualify for a state-run primary race, and Republican voters simply show up on primary election day and mark a secret ballot to indicate which Republicans they would like to see represent the party in November.

Defenders of Utah's caucus-convention system claim it empowers the most politically informed and engaged citizens, though research does not support this claim.[30] Rather what sets apart caucus-convention participants is their ideology. Because caucus-convention systems are not only time-consuming but can involve public rather than private voting, they tend to attract more ideologically extreme participants than primaries. As such, Utah Republicans who serve as convention delegates are more ideologically extreme than typical Utah Republicans who attend caucus night, who in turn are more ideologically extreme than typical Utah Republicans who participate in primary elections.[31] In part these differences reflect simple math: the Utah Republican Party allocated only 3,806 state delegate slots in 2016, yet 246,529 votes were cast in that year's Republican primary.[32] A primary electorate sixty-five times larger than the delegate base will unavoidably include more ideological diversity.

On the occasion that convention delegates deadlock and send the contest to a primary, stark differences can emerge between delegates and voters. In 2016 at the Republican state convention Governor Gary Herbert lost to insurgent challenger Jonathan Johnson by 45 to 55 percent. If Johnson had cleared 60 percent of the delegate vote, he would have claimed the nomination outright; because Herbert stayed above 40 percent, however, party rules mandated a primary election. Herbert later smothered Johnson in the Republican primary, 72 to 28 percent. No scandals or shocking news shook up the race; rather the 246,529 Republican voters who participated in the June primary had very different views from those of the 3,806 Republican delegates at the state convention.

A similar situation had a different outcome six years earlier. In 2010 several candidates challenged the incumbent U.S. senator Bob Bennett for the Republican nomination. An April poll found that Bennett had nearly three times as much support as his strongest challenger, Mike Lee, among Republican voters generally.[33] Before Bennett and Lee could face off in a primary, though, state delegates weighed in at the Republican convention—and removed Bennett from consideration, sending Mike Lee and Tim Bridgewater to the Republican primary instead, where Lee emerged victorious.

Few Utah races involve serious intraparty battles like these. When they do arise, however, they often pit the far-right ideologues against the center-right pragmatists. Because the caucus-convention system favors the ideologues while primaries favor the pragmatists, the nomination method itself has become politicized. After Bennett's defeat, well-known center-right Republicans formed Count My Vote to agitate for a direct primary in all races, doing away with the caucus-convention system entirely. As the next caucuses neared, in 2012, with Bennett's defeat still looming large, the LDS Church declared its "[concern] with the decreasing attendance at these caucus meetings," saying that caucuses "are best served by a broad representation of Utah citizens." The statement concluded by urging LDS adherents to attend party caucuses.[34] Count My Vote supporters welcomed the Church's implicit critique of the caucus system, using it to promote their proposal further.

The legislature responded by passing SB54, creating a dual path to the ballot: would-be Republican candidates could appear on a primary election ballot either by winning the traditional caucus-convention delegate vote or simply by gathering enough signatures. Though this bill was passed by a Republican legislature and signed by a Republican governor, the Utah Republican Party unleashed a series of lawsuits challenging the state's authority to regulate party nominations. Though the party won a few minor legal victories (with a few legal actions still unresolved as of this writing), SB54 remained mostly intact for the 2016 elections and appears on track to remain the law going forward. SB54 did not eliminate the caucus-convention system, but it did ensure that candidates with enough popular support can still appear on a primary election ballot regardless of what happens at the convention.

These battles over Utah's nomination system illustrate the broader intra-Republican disputes that permeate modern Utah politics. Policy battles in Utah pit Republicans against Republicans more than against Democrats. Republicans nationally also have their own internal conflicts of course; as one book recently observed of the national GOP, "The fault lines of internal debate and conflict tend to separate conservative purists who reject compromise and value constant symbolic confrontation from more pragmatic colleagues who prefer to pick their battles and demonstrate achievements in governing" (Grossman and Hopkins 2016, 12). Nevertheless these intraparty rifts are usually overlooked at the national level as Republicans target their common opponent, the Democrats. In Utah, however, long-term supermajority Republican dominance reduces competition with Democrats, leaving intraparty disputes unchecked.

Utah's erratic partisan swings stabilized during the Depression. After several subsequent decades as a swing state, Utah became a reliably Republican state by the 1980s. Since that time single-party dominance has had three predictable effects: low turnover among officeholders, low turnout among voters, and low unity among Republicans. Unless changing demographics or newly emerging issues trigger a realignment that reduces Mormon partisan homogeneity, these three effects will endure.

READING THE TEA LEAVES

Like much of the West, twenty-first-century Utah has experienced rapid growth and diversification. Utah's population grew by 38 percent in the 1970s, 18 percent in the 1980s, 30 percent in the 1990s, and 24 percent in the 2000s (see figure 6). The 2010 census counted 530,716 new residents since 2000, resulting in a total statewide population of 2,763,885. Only two states (Nevada and Arizona) surpassed Utah's 24 percent growth rate during this period. This rapid growth earned Utah a third congressional seat in 1980 and a fourth in 2010. Continued growth could earn the state a fifth seat in 2030, if not sooner (Brown 2013b).

Utah's population has always been concentrated along the Wasatch Front, that is, Weber, Davis, Salt Lake, and Utah counties, only four of Utah's twenty-nine counties. At the center of it all lies Salt Lake County, home to 37 percent of the state's population—over one million residents. Combined, the four Wasatch Front counties house 75 percent of the state's population despite having only 5 percent of its dry land.[35] Meanwhile the ten least populous counties contain 35 percent of the state's land but only 2 percent of its population. The only meaningful population growth outside the Wasatch Front is in the neighboring spillover counties—Tooele, Cache, Wasatch, and Summit—and in distant Washington County, home to St. George in the state's southwestern corner. These settlement patterns reflect the scarcity of water and arable land throughout much of the state.

Even within the Wasatch Front counties the population has grown increasingly urbanized. Consider Salt Lake and Utah counties, home to 56

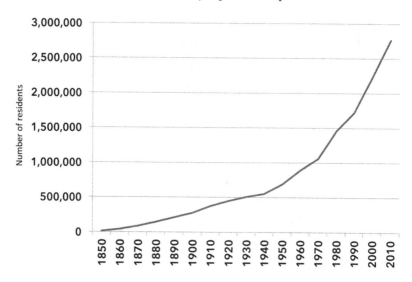

Fig. 6. Decennial census estimates of Utah's population.

percent of the state's population. Within living memory most residents in these two counties were clustered around two urban cores, Salt Lake City and Provo-Orem, with vast rural tracts separating them. Those two urban centers have long since reached their capacity, though; the 2010 census reported only 2.6 percent growth for Salt Lake City and 7.0 percent for Provo. Instead growth has shifted to the historically rural and suburban areas between these two population centers. The 2010 census reported 51 percent growth for West Jordan and 149 percent growth for Lehi, both of which lie between Provo and Salt Lake City. The few green spaces that remain along the Wasatch Front are rapidly filling in.

Utah's growth and urbanization bring both religious and ethnic diversity. On the religious front the Latter-day Saint share of Utah's population has declined since peaking in the late 1980s. In 1987, 78 percent of Utahns appeared on official LDS membership rolls; by 2015 only 68 percent did. Though LDS rolls grew by 60 percent during this period, from 1,277,000 to 2,040,171 members, the state's overall population grew even faster (by 82 percent), from 1,644,306 to 2,995,919.[36] Of course official LDS statistics may overstate the Mormon share of the population, since former members who have ceased attending church meetings remain on LDS membership lists unless they formally request removal. Using survey research methods rather than LDS reports, the Pew Research Center found that 55 percent of Utahns self-identified as Mormon in 2014, a decline from 58 percent in 2007.[37] Mormons, then, remain a clear but shrinking majority within Utah. Nevertheless they turn out to vote at higher rates than non-Mormons, giving them outsized political influence. In 2016, 59 percent of exit poll respondents in Utah self-identified as Mormon, including 46 percent identifying as "active" in their religious practice.[38]

Growth has also brought ethnic diversity, with the state's white superma-jority slowly giving way to a growing Hispanic presence. Of Utah's 530,716 new residents in the 2010 census, 156,781 (30 percent) were Hispanic. Statewide the Hispanic population grew by 78 percent (from 201,559 to 358,340) between 2000 and 2010, bringing it to 13 percent of Utah's total. By contrast, Hispanics represented only 9 percent of the population in 2000 and 5 percent in 1990. Almost every county saw its Hispanic pop-ulation grow during the 2000s, but the most dramatic growth occurred in Utah's older cities. Salt Lake City and its immediate neighbors (West Valley City, Taylorsville, and Murray) now have large Hispanic minorities, ranging from 19 to 33 percent of their total populations. In fact some of these cities would have lost population between 2000 and 2010 if not for Hispanic growth. Taylorsville's 3,909 new Hispanics offset a decrease of 3,250 whites; Salt Lake City's 7,383 new Hispanics offset a decrease of 3,853 whites. Meanwhile growth in the state's newer suburban communities has been driven largely by white movement away from these urban cores. South Jordan, for example, gained 18,030 whites in the 2010 census but only 2,046 Hispanics. As a result Utah's older urban areas are becoming more Hispanic while its newer suburban communities remain mostly white, a classic example of so-called white flight.

Utah's dynamic population growth has been matched by steady eco-nomic growth, with the state's real gross domestic product (GDP) more than doubling in the past twenty years. Figure 7 presents Utah's real GDP (in chained 2005 dollars) since 1977. Other than the 2009 recession, Utah has enjoyed robust growth, though it is nevertheless not a particularly wealthy state. Nationwide America's income per capita was $47,669 in 2015; Utah's was only $39,045, ranking forty-third among the states. Utah's relatively low income per capita reflects the state's high fertility rate. The

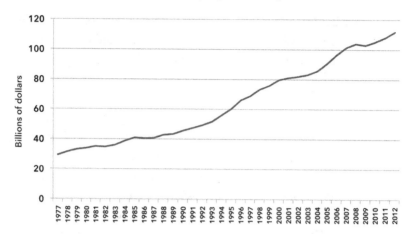

Fig. 7. Annual estimates of Utah's gross domestic product in chained 2005 dollars, from the U.S. Bureau of Economic Analysis.

average American woman bears 1.93 children over the course of her life. Utah's rate, at 2.50, is the highest in the nation, followed by Alaska (2.35), South Dakota (2.27), and Idaho (2.24).[39] Another way to measure fertility is to count the number of live births each year per 1,000 women ages fifteen to forty-four; from 2004 through 2014 Utah's average birthrate (88.6) was 35 percent higher than the national average of 65.5. Utah's high fertility rate depresses income per capita in two ways. First, it means more children share in the wages of each household. Second, it means Utah has more stay-at-home parents out of the paid workforce.

Overall Utah has a diverse economy that defies simple characterizations. As is common throughout the country, state and local governments are a major sector, employing 14 percent of Utah's workforce according to 2010 estimates from the U.S. Bureau of Economic Analysis. In addition to public schools and universities, this sector includes police, public utilities, firefighters, public libraries, public parks, and the like. No particular sector dominates in Utah's diversified economy; after state and local governments, the next largest sectors were retail (11 percent), health care (10 percent), and manufacturing (9 percent). Tourism makes a major contribution (8 percent), especially where there are ski resorts or southern national parks. Increasingly a growing technology sector—the so-called Silicon Slopes— has developed around the Salt Lake–Utah County line.

Taken as a whole these demographic and economic indicators reveal a state where rapid population growth has fueled and been fueled by economic growth. Eventually this growth and diversification may threaten the Republican Party's decades-long dominance. The 2016 Utah Colleges Exit Poll found that 81 percent of self-identified "active" Mormons identify as Republicans, compared to only 28 percent among non-LDS respondents. Moreover 60 percent of white respondents identify as Republicans, compared to only 26 percent among Hispanic respondents, Utah's largest and fastest-growing minority group. If these left-leaning demographic groups—that is, non-Mormons and Hispanics—continue increasing their share of Utah's population, they may someday change Utah's partisan balance even if white Mormons remain solidly Republican.

This chapter has explored the awkward attempt to eliminate religious-partisan cleavages and integrate Utah's voters, regardless of religion, into the national parties. In the early twentieth century this effort produced mixed messages that caused Utah to vacillate wildly between Republican and Democratic control. Only when the Depression hit did Utah finally integrate into the national system, to the consternation of LDS president Grant, later emerging as a competitive swing state. In the 1970s and 1980s the religious-partisan cleavage reemerged, shaping Utah into a reliably Republican state as Mormons became Republicans and other Utahns became Democrats. Single-party dominance brought with it low turnover among officeholders, low turnout among voters uninterested in uncompetitive elections, and regular clashes among various Republican factions.

Thus far I have emphasized Utah's uniqueness—its uniquely heated territorial period (in chapter 1), its uniquely strong anti-federal sentiment (in chapter 2), and its unique Mormon Republican supermajority (in chapter 3). The next several chapters will shift to Utah's governing institutions: its state legislature, its governor, its courts, and its local governments. Unique though Utah's people may be, its governing institutions operate in far less atypical ways.

CHAPTER FOUR

Legislating in the People's Branch

America's founders expected Congress to dominate the federal government. Presidents would play a modest role, staffing the executive branch and ensuring its smooth operation while leaving the actual policy decisions to Congress.[1] Apart from a few notable exceptions, eighteenth- and nineteenth-century presidents largely accepted this limited role. By the twentieth century, however, American presidents began consistently claiming broader authority. Theodore Roosevelt (1913, 479) argued that the president should "act upon the theory that he is the steward of the people, and that . . . he is bound to assume that he has the legal right to do whatever the needs of the people demand," a perspective subsequent presidents have apparently embraced (see James 2005).

Congress has more than obliged this expanded vision of the presidency, delegating much of its legislative authority to the executive branch and empowering executive agencies to enact legally binding regulations. In today's administrative America, Congress does not decide which endangered species to protect; the Fish and Wildlife Service does, under authority of the Endangered Species Act. Congress does not decide which new medicines to approve; the Food and Drug Administration does, under authority of the Food, Drug, and Cosmetic Act. Congress does not set pollution limits; the Environmental Protection Agency does, under authority of the Clean Air Act, Clean Water Act, and other laws. In countless areas Congress has declared only broad policy goals, then empowered an executive agency to fill in the details. More often than not Congress serves as America's policymaking supervisor rather than its actual policymaker.[2]

The situation in Utah could hardly be more different. Utah's legislature jealously guards its legislative authority. In the relatively few cases where the legislature has delegated rule-making authority to executive agencies, such as the Alcoholic Beverage Control Commission and the Air Quality Board, the legislature imposes strict limits on each commission's authority and places equally strict limits on the governor's ability to appoint his or her supporters as commissioners. In Utah it is the legislature, not the executive branch, that sets state policy.

Occasional exceptions prove the rule. In June 2008 Governor Jon Huntsman announced his "Working 4 Utah" plan, shifting many state employees from working five eight-hour days to four ten-hour days. He defended this program on several grounds: Closing state buildings each Friday would save electricity, reduce traffic congestion and vehicle emissions, and allow citizens to access state services outside their own 9 a.m. to 5 p.m. working hours. U.S. presidents regularly take far more consequential unilateral actions; George W. Bush unilaterally announced that intelligence agencies would employ waterboarding and other aggressive interrogation techniques on suspected terrorists, for example, and Barack Obama unilaterally announced a series of executive orders protecting millions of unauthorized immigrants from deportation. By comparison Huntsman's "Working 4 Utah" order seems trivial.

Nevertheless legislators felt the governor inappropriately challenged their policymaking supremacy. They responded in 2011 with HB328, requiring most state employees to work a traditional five-day workweek. (By then Gary Herbert had succeeded Huntsman as governor.) While debating the bill legislators repeatedly emphasized that it was the legislature's prerogative to set state policy, not the governor's. That is, they emphasized that they were less concerned about the substantive merits of Huntsman's order than by the fact he had made an order at all. Citing the Utah Constitution, one legislator marveled on the House floor "how this ever happened without any Legislative challenge."[3] The bill sailed through both chambers. When it arrived on Governor Herbert's desk, he vetoed it—not because he preferred the four-day workweek but because he wished to assert the governor's authority to manage executive branch personnel. Herbert denounced HB328 as "an unwarranted intrusion on the power granted to the Governor in . . . the Utah Constitution to faithfully execute the law."[4] Legislators promptly overrode his veto. A Republican governor had created the "Working 4 Utah" program; a Republican leg-islature reversed it; a Republican governor vetoed that reversal; and a Republican legislature overrode that veto.

The "Working 4 Utah" episode illustrates just how vigorously the legisla-ture guards its authority to set state policy. Utah governors seldom attempt the sort of unilateral policy change Huntsman ordered in 2008. Though Huntsman's order seemed directly tied to his gubernatorial authority to manage executive branch employees, the legislature nevertheless bris-tled at being sidelined. In any issue domain those seeking policy change within Utah quickly find that there is really only one place to go: the Utah Legislature.

After first describing the general structure and processes of the Utah Legislature, I evaluate its operations in light of theories of legislative behav-ior developed through the study of the U.S. Congress and of other states. Unlike the preceding three chapters, which emphasized Utah's unique-ness, this chapter concludes that the Utah Legislature operates much as American legislatures elsewhere do. In particular I argue that in the Utah Legislature, as elsewhere, procedures create power; that is, Utah's legislative leaders can exploit their procedural authority to prevent certain bills from ever reaching the floor. However, I further argue that Utah's unusually short legislative session and dearth of professional staff exacerbate these effects, since rank-and-file legislators have less time and fewer resources than legislators elsewhere to independently evaluate legislation.

ORGANIZING A CITIZEN LEGISLATURE

The Utah Legislature consists of two chambers, the seventy-five-member Utah House of Representatives and the twenty-nine-member Utah Senate, a total of 104 legislators.[5] Compared to other state legislatures, Utah's is on the small side; only eleven states have a smaller house, and only five have a smaller senate.[6] Of course Utah also has a small population. As such, each Utah house district includes around 40,000 residents, while each Utah senate district includes 100,000.[7] Nineteen states have fewer constituents in their house districts while twenty-nine have more, placing Utah near the middle.[8] Utah representatives stand for reelection every two years; Utah senators stand for reelection every four years, with half

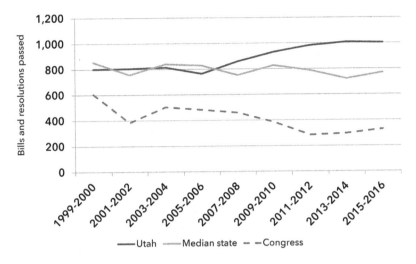

Fig. 8. Bills and resolutions passed per biennium in the Utah Legislature, the U.S. Congress, and in the median state legislature. Utah data were compiled by the author. Congressional data are from Congress.gov. Median legislature data were calculated by the author from various annual editions of the *Book of the States*, published by the Council of State Governments, which uses even-odd rather than odd-even biennia. Median legislature data include all session types; Utah data include only General Sessions.

standing for reelection at a time. Legislators may run for reelection as many times as they like; there are no term limits.

Unlike the U.S. Congress and some state legislatures, the Utah Legislature is limited by the Utah Constitution to one forty-five-day General Session each year, beginning on the fourth Monday of January and ending in early March. Legislators may introduce as many bills as they like, on any topic they like, during this brief session—and they do, as shown in figure 8. Since 2011 the Utah Legislature has passed three to four times more bills per year than the U.S. Congress—partly because the legislature has become more active and partly because Congress has slowed down.

Utah's high bill passage rate may reflect the state's single subject rule. As found in Article VI, Section 22 of the Utah Constitution, this rule requires that "no bill shall be passed containing more than one subject, which shall be clearly expressed in its title." The U.S. Congress might not pass many bills, but some of those it does pass are massive omnibus bills addressing diverse subjects. Though Utah's single-subject rule may help explain why it passes more bills than Congress, however, the rule does not explain why Utah has also passed more bills than the median state, since all but nine state legislatures have a similar rule.[9] Compared to Congress and most state legislatures, Utah legislators have less time to write laws and a smaller, more homogeneous population to serve, yet they nevertheless pass more bills and resolutions.

Outside the frenetic forty-five-day General Session, legislators gather for periodic "interim day" discussions, but they cannot take any binding actions—that is, they cannot hold floor votes—except under limited circumstances detailed in Article VI of the Utah Constitution. For example, legislators can gather during the interim for a veto override vote, but they cannot consider new or revised legislation at the same time. The Utah Senate can call itself into a confirmation session to consider gubernatorial nominees, but, once again, it cannot consider any legislation or other business unrelated to the nominee in question. Likewise the Utah House can call itself into an impeachment session to consider proceedings against any state officer, but it cannot consider any legislation.

If some urgent policy matter does arise during the interim, legislators may enact new legislation only if the governor formally calls them into special session. However, the governor declares the special session's purpose, and legislators cannot consider any legislation unrelated to this declared purpose. For example, Governor Huntsman called the legislature into special session to cut the state budget when the economy entered recession in late 2008, and Governor Herbert called a special session in late 2011 to draw new electoral districts after the U.S. Census released its 2010 population estimates.

Utah's 104 legislators organize themselves with leaders, committees, and caucuses.[10] The four most important caucuses are the House Republican Caucus, the House Democratic Caucus, the Senate Republican Caucus, and the Senate Democratic Caucus. These four party caucuses meet regularly to discuss legislative strategies, establish a united policy front, and work out compromises. Legislators may also form private caucuses if they wish to organize around common policy goals; internal divisions among Republicans have prompted the formation of the Conservative Caucus,

Patrick Henry Caucus, Mainstream Caucus, Common Sense Caucus, Public Lands Caucus, Cowboy Caucus, and other legislative alliances.

In each chamber the majority party caucus nominates the chamber's presiding officer—the speaker of the house or the senate president—who is formally seated after a vote of the entire chamber. Within each chamber these presiding officers appoint a Rules Committee chair to manage the chamber's flow of legislation and an Executive Appropriations co-chair to coordinate the annual budget effort. Officially the presiding officers and these appointed leaders serve their entire chamber; in practice, of course, retaining their posts requires only retaining majority party legislators' support.

After nominating a presiding officer, each chamber's majority party caucus rounds out its leadership team by electing a majority leader, majority whip, and majority assistant whip. Each chamber's minority party caucus appoints a shadow leadership team consisting of a minority leader, minority whip, minority assistant whip, and minority caucus manager. Broadly speaking, majority and minority leaders coordinate their caucus's legislative agenda and develop strategies to enact that agenda; whips and assistant whips, by contrast, feel out where legislators stand prior to important votes and promote party unity, serving as a link between leadership and rank-and-file legislators.

Separate from the party caucus system, legislators are also organized into committees. Each chamber's presiding officer has complete authority to decide which legislators will serve on which committees and to appoint each committee's chair. By legislative rule each committee must have a partisan balance reflecting the chamber's overall balance, and each committee chair must come from the majority party, but the presiding officer faces no other restrictions in forming these committees. The committee system consists primarily of standing committees, appropriations subcommittees, and interim committees.

Standing committees hold hearings on all routine bills, which must generally pass a standing committee vote before coming to the house or senate floor. Each chamber has its own set of standing committees separate from the other chamber's, although they are organized along similar jurisdictional lines. For example, the House Education Committee hears bills dealing with k–12 public schools, as does the Senate Education Committee.

Appropriations subcommittees specialize in budget bills. To expedite house-senate cooperation on the budget, all legislators from both chambers belong to the universal Joint Appropriations Committee. This 104-member committee exists only on paper and never convenes; instead it is divided into several appropriations subcommittees along jurisdictional lines. These joint house-senate subcommittees have two co-chairs, one from each chamber, who take turns presiding at subcommittee meetings. The Executive Appropriations Committee, consisting of legislators from both chambers' majority and minority leadership teams, coordinates the work of these various subcommittees and has ultimate responsibility for assembling the annual budget (discussed in greater detail in chapter 10).

Standing committees and appropriations subcommittees meet only during the General Session. Outside of session legislators serve on interim committees, which are structured along similar jurisdictional lines as the standing committees. Like appropriations subcommittees, interim committees are joint committees, with a co-chair from each chamber. Interim committees conduct studies and other preparatory work for issues likely to emerge in the next General Session.

The legislature maintains a modest staff, but nothing compared to the U.S. Congress's massive staff. Of 21,362 total U.S. congressional staffers, 10,791 work as personal staff for a specific member of Congress, while the remaining 10,571 work on behalf of a congressional committee, a support office (such as the Congressional Research Service), or in some other capacity (Ornstein et al. 2012, table 5-1). The 10,791 personal staffers work at the pleasure of whichever member of Congress hired them; they assist with constituent communications, media relations, policy research, scheduling, and speechwriting. The average U.S. senator employs thirty-nine personal staffers, and the average U.S. representative employs sixteen.

By contrast, rank-and-file Utah legislators have no personal staff at all except for a single undergraduate intern during the General Session. Otherwise they receive no personal assistance unless they pay for it themselves. However, legislators do benefit from a few shared staff resources. The Office of Legislative Research and General Counsel (LRGC) provides legal advice to the legislature, drafts legislators' bills in legal language, and staffs standing and interim committees. The Office of the Legislative Fiscal Analyst (LFA) advises appropriations subcommittees and the Executive

Appropriations Committee as they assemble the annual budget; LFA also estimates the financial impact of all bills. The Office of the Legislative Auditor General conducts performance and compliance audits on state agencies to ensure state funds and programs are implemented consistent with the legislature's intent. Combined, these three staff offices employ around a hundred people, including secretaries and receptionists—a far cry from the twenty-one thousand working for the U.S. Congress.[11]

State legislatures with long sessions, large staffs, and high legislator salaries are known as "professional" legislatures, while legislatures with short sessions, small staffs, and low legislator salaries are "citizen" legislatures (see Squire 1992, 2007). California legislators, the nation's most professionalized (other than those in the U.S. Congress), earn over $100,000 per year; they receive personal staff in addition to committee staff and other shared staff; and they handle legislative business year-round. In California legislative service is a full-time profession. In contrast, Utah legislators earn so little (roughly $16,500) and spend so little time legislating that they typically keep a full-time job unless they are retired or independently wealthy. Most have flexible jobs that can bend around the legislative schedule; many work as realtors, developers, attorneys, or bankers. Indeed low legislator salaries and difficult hours deter many potential candidates from running.[12] Legislative service in Utah is a part-time activity, hence a "citizen legislature." In fact the Utah Legislature is among the least professionalized in the nation, ranking forty-ninth for session length, forty-fourth for salary, and forty-fourth for staff support (Hamm and Moncrief 2008, table 6-1). When these three factors are combined into a standard index of overall professionalism, the Utah Legislature ranks forty-sixth, placing it between Maine, Montana, South Dakota, and Wyoming.[13]

Because Utah has a citizen legislature, political life fluctuates in a boom-to-bust cycle, with legislators spending inordinate amounts of time on politics during the General Session but far less during the interim. In the Utah Legislator Survey I asked legislators how many hours they devote each week to their work as a state legislator, including "any activities you would not engage in if not for your elected position." On average, legislators report spending sixty-five hours per week during the session but only thirteen during the interim. The nature of the work also varies, as shown in table 1.[14] During the interim legislators report spending one-quarter

Table 1. How legislators spend their time

	SESSION	INTERIM
Meeting with activists, lobbyists, stakeholders	9.4 hours	3.3 hours
Interacting with constituents	9.4	4.7
Researching and crafting legislation	11.4	3.3
Attending committee hearings or floor time	31.6	4.8
Attending other meetings with legislators	9.1	2.8

Source: From the author's Utah Legislator Survey.

of their legislative time interacting with constituents; during session they spend more total hours with constituents—9.4 hours rather than 4.7—but this represents only one-seventh of their total time commitment, as time spent crafting legislation and attending legislative meetings skyrockets.

No matter where their time goes, legislators clearly work harder than their $16,500 salary suggests.[15] Overall legislators report working more than a thousand hours per year, producing an effective wage of only $16.42 per hour.[16] At that wage a full-time employee with two weeks off would earn $29,240 per year, which is just over half of Utah's 2014 median household income of $53,481. For a family of four, $29,240 is only slightly above the federal poverty line ($24,600). It is not much of a stretch to claim that Utah legislators earn poverty wages.

LEGISLATIVE PROCESS

The Utah Constitution says almost nothing about how the legislature should make laws, imposing only a few general requirements: legislative meetings must be public; decisions must be published in a journal; nonbudgetary bills must deal with only a single subject; each bill must have its title and number read three separate times in each chamber; and a majority of each chamber's legislators must support a bill before it can become a law. The Utah Constitution does not mention legislative committees, legislative leaders, procedural motions, or limits on debate.

Instead it broadly empowers each chamber to "determine the rules of its proceedings and choose its own officers."

Following this provision each chamber has adopted its own rules, aptly known as the house rules and the senate rules. (There are also joint rules and interim rules governing joint committees and other matters concerning both chambers.) It is these procedural rules—not the Utah Constitution—that govern most of the legislative process. Because each chamber writes its own rules, each chamber is also free to amend its rules, which requires passing a special resolution through the chamber; each chamber can also choose to ignore its rules, which requires only a motion to "suspend" the rules for a specific instance. This section reviews the procedural steps a bill must follow to become a law—assuming, of course, that no rules are suspended.

First, no idea, no matter how clever, receives legislative consideration unless some legislator chooses to sponsor it. To pass through both chambers a bill needs both a sponsor (who introduces the bill in his or her own chamber) and a floor sponsor (who introduces the bill into the other chamber after it has passed through the primary sponsor's). A senator cannot sponsor a bill through the house, nor can a representative sponsor a bill through the senate, hence the need for a floor sponsor. A bill can originate in either chamber; if it starts in the senate, it will move to the house after the senate passes it.

Legislators do not write bills themselves. Instead they describe their idea to a full-time drafting attorney in LRGC, a process referred to as "opening a bill file." The LRGC drafting attorney researches the body of existing law—known as the Utah Code—to identify all sections potentially affected.[17] The drafting attorney then produces a bill that inserts (with underlines) or removes (with ~~strikethroughs~~) language from the Code to achieve the legislator's goals.[18] Drafting attorneys refrain from stating their opinion on the bill; they simply draft whatever bills legislators request. If, however, legislative attorneys spot a potential violation of the state or federal Constitution, they can attach a written "legislative review note" spelling out the bill's legal risks.

Legislative rules require drafting attorneys to process bill requests in the order received, provided that legislators may mark up to three requests as "priority bills," which jump the regular queue. To preserve flexibility down the road, legislators sometimes open "boxcar" bill files far in advance of the legislative session without giving the drafting attorney details about what the bill should include. These boxcar bills appear in the public bill list as "Numbered by title without any substance." Opening a boxcar allows a legislator to hold her place in line without wasting one of her three priority designations. Just as a boxcar on a train is an empty trailer waiting to be filled, a boxcar bill is an empty bill file waiting for substance. The catch, though, is that legislative rules require bill files to include a bill title, and the Utah Constitution states that bill titles must be germane to the bill's actual substance. As a result many boxcars have broad titles like "Revenue and Tax Amendments," "Education Amendments," or "General Government Amendments."

LRGC assigns each bill a number such as HB073, SB051, HJR002, SR001, or SCR018. Bills originating in the house start with H, while bills originating in the senate start with S. After that a B indicates a standard bill—that is, a law that changes the Utah Code. R, JR, and CR indicate resolutions, which do not change Utah Code: an R indicates a resolution involving only one chamber, such as a resolution modifying a single chamber's rules; JR indicates a joint resolution involving both chambers but not requiring the governor's signature, such as a joint resolution proposing an amendment to the Utah Constitution or modifying the legislature's joint rules; and CR indicates a concurrent resolution requiring the governor's signature. Most concurrent resolutions, along with many joint resolutions and single-chamber resolutions, have no legal effect but merely honor some Utahn for a recent accomplishment or declare some other nonbinding message. After this prefix bills receive a number indicating their drafting order. Numbers are reused each year.

Once the sponsoring legislator has approved the drafting attorney's work, the bill goes to the Office of the Legislative Fiscal Analyst to estimate the bill's fiscal impact. LFA shares the bill with any state agencies potentially affected by it to request their feedback. LFA then attaches a fiscal note to the bill summarizing its expected revenues and expenses. Pursuant to Utah law, fiscal notes must separately estimate a bill's impact on the state budget, on local governments' budgets, and on Utah individuals and businesses (see Utah Code §36-12-13, 2016). Bills projected to require an appropriation of $10,000 or more from the state budget are subject to special procedural rules, addressed below. Although every bill must have a fiscal note attached, legislators will sometimes say a bill costing less than $10,000 "doesn't have a fiscal note."

If the bill's sponsor serves in the Utah House, the bill's formal legislative journey begins when it is introduced on the house floor. The house clerk announces the bill's number and title, a step called the "first reading." (The Utah Constitution requires three readings in each chamber.) After introduction the speaker sends the bill to the House Rules Committee, which reviews the bill and recommends to the speaker which house standing committee should hear the bill. The bill then returns to the house floor, where the clerk announces the House Rules Committee's recommendation. The speaker then formally refers the bill to committee—usually, but not always, following the Rules Committee's recommendation.

After giving at least twenty-four hours' notice, the assigned standing committee can hold a public hearing on the bill if the committee's chair chooses to hear the bill at all. The committee invites the bill's sponsor to present the bill and then hears public comment. Eventually the standing committee takes one of five actions: amend, substitute, hold, table, or recommend.[19] The committee can amend the bill by making minor changes to its language; it can substitute the bill with an entirely rewritten bill dealing with the same subject; it can hold the bill until a future meeting, giving the sponsor time to respond to committee members' concerns; it can table the bill, in which case the bill remains temporarily under the committee's jurisdiction but will not be considered again unless two-thirds of the committee votes to untable it;[20] or it can have a final up-or-down vote on whether to recommend the bill for further consideration.

If the committee recommends the bill, it returns to the house floor.[21] The house clerk announces the committee's endorsement on the floor, a step called the "second reading." After a minimum twenty-four-hour waiting period, the entire seventy-five-member house holds a floor debate and then votes on the bill, a step known as the "third reading." During floor debate representatives recognized by the speaker may amend, substitute, "circle" (hold), or table the bill. For major bills, legislators will have already discussed the bill in a party caucus meeting, and they may have already agreed on amendments or substitutions to propose during floor debate. Unlike committee hearings, the public may not testify in floor debates. If floor debate runs long, any representative can make a "previous question" motion to cut off debate and hold an immediate vote. Every bill requires thirty-eight votes to pass, even if some of the representatives are absent.

If the bill passes the house, its house sponsor will recruit a senator as floor sponsor to shepherd the bill through the senate, since representatives cannot participate in senate procedures. Legislators choose their floor sponsors carefully, preferring to work with somebody known for getting bills passed. This dynamic appears distinctly in figure 9, which plots the relationship between each legislator's primary sponsorship and floor sponsorship. In the figure each circle denotes an individual legislator (with representatives in the left panel and senators to the right), while the solid line depicts the linear trendline. Legislators who sponsor more bills (horizontal axis) receive more cross-chamber requests to serve as floor sponsor (vertical axis). The relationship is especially strong for senators, since the seventy-five representatives have only twenty-nine senators to choose from when recruiting a floor sponsor.

Senate procedures resemble house procedures, but with a few key differences. As in the house, each bill is introduced with a first reading when the senate secretary announces its number and title on the senate floor. The Senate Rules Committee then examines the bill and recommends a specific standing committee to consider it further. Back on the senate floor the senate president formally refers the bill to a standing committee—usually, but not always, the committee recommended by Rules. After at least twenty-four hours' notice, the senate standing committee can hold a public hearing on the bill. Senate committees have the same five options as house committees: amend, substitute, hold, table, or recommend favorably. If the committee votes to recommend the bill, it returns to the senate floor, where the senate secretary announces the committee's recommendation.

At this point the senate differs from the house. The house debates each bill on the floor only once, but the senate debates each bill twice. After a twenty-four-hour waiting period the bill has its first senate floor debate and vote, known as the "second reading." If at least fifteen senators vote in favor of the bill, it advances to a final floor debate and vote (after another twenty-four-hour waiting period), known as the "third reading." Because the senate holds two floor votes on each bill, senators who wish to see changes made to a bill often announce "aye on two" rather than "aye" to

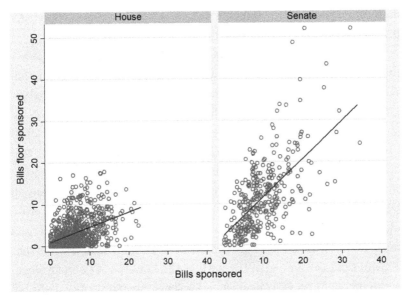

Fig. 9. Floor sponsorship plotted against primary sponsorship, 2007–16 General Sessions, with linear trendline and modest jitter added to separate overlapping points. Each mark represents a legislator-year; a legislator who served in multiple years will have a separate mark for each year. Compiled by the author.

informally signal to the bill's sponsor that their "aye" on the second reading will become a "nay" on the third if the bill is not improved.

Senators pride themselves on being the more august, deliberative chamber, and the senate's decision to debate every bill twice reflects its desire to be seen as more thoughtful and careful. All the same, senators do not seem to value their two-vote process in practice. For one thing, they are more likely to miss a bill's second reading vote than its third reading vote; on average 13.4 percent of senators are absent during a second reading vote, but only 10.8 percent are absent for a third reading vote.[22] Moreover senators waive the two-vote requirement for nearly one in three bills (29 percent), sometimes using the consent calendar process (detailed below), but more often simply by suspending the requirement to vote twice. One can hardly blame them, since senators surely know that they seldom change their vote between the second and third reading anyway: 74 percent of bills that have two floor votes receive the same vote margin both times, while 90 percent gain or lose two or fewer "aye" votes.[23] All the same, the senate clings to its two-vote requirement.

As they approach their final floor vote, bills with a large fiscal impact— that is, bills expected to require an appropriation of $10,000 or more from the state budget—encounter special procedural rules. Costly house bills are automatically tabled prior to the final senate floor vote; costly senate bills are automatically referred to the House Rules Committee prior to their final house floor vote. These bills are released for a final floor vote only if the end-of-session budget bills appropriate funding for them.

Regardless of whether a bill originates in the house or the senate, all bills except single-chamber resolutions require both chambers to approve identical language, even down to the punctuation marks. If a bill gets through the house but then receives amendments in the senate, the senate will send the amended bill back to the house for a "concurrence" vote. Only if the house concurs with the senate amendments will the bill proceed to the governor for a signature. If the house refuses to concur, it sends the bill back to the senate requesting that the senate recede from its amendments. If the senate refuses to recede, the house speaker chooses three representatives to confer with three senators chosen by the senate president in a special conference committee. If the conference committee agrees on a compromise, the compromise bill returns to the originating chamber's third reading calendar for a new vote, then proceeds again to the second chamber (see JR3-2-603).

The Utah Constitution requires that every bill be "read by title three separate times in each house" unless a two-thirds supermajority within a particular chamber suspends this requirement, hence the odd-sounding "first reading," "second reading," and "third reading" language used above. The legislature tracks bills by organizing them into separate calendars based on this terminology.[24] The House Third Reading Calendar, for example, lists (in order) bills waiting for their third reading in the house—that is, for their floor debate and vote. The Senate Second Reading Calendar lists bills waiting for their first senate floor vote, and the Senate Third Reading Calendar lists bills waiting for their final senate floor vote. The Senate Concurrence Calendar lists bills awaiting a concurrence vote—that is, requests to concur with house amendments or to recede from senate amendments. Of course "calendar" may be a misnomer; these calendars contain no dates, only an ordered list of bills waiting their turn, with special markings to indicate bills with large fiscal notes and bills that have been circled (held). Only the House Time Certain Calendar and Senate Time Certain Calendar list specific times; these calendars list bills that are ready for their third reading but which have been scheduled for a specific time so that some dignitary can be present for the vote. (Bills under a committee's jurisdiction do not appear on either chamber's floor calendar.) Each chamber has internal rules governing when to consider bills from each calendar. For example, each chamber sets aside separate days to hear bills originating in the house rather than the senate.[25] This latter provision prevents either chamber from prioritizing its own member's bills over the other chamber's.

Each chamber also has a Consent Calendar—not to be confused with the Concurrence Calendar—for simple, noncontroversial bills. If some standing committee votes unanimously to recommend a bill to the floor, the committee can further recommend that the bill be placed on the chamber's Consent Calendar. After three days bills on Consent proceed to a final vote without any floor debate. The three-day delay gives legislators time to object to a bill's placement on Consent. If a handful of legislators (six in the house or three in the senate) petition to remove the bill from their chamber's Consent Calendar, it will revert to the chamber's standard reading calendar.

Legislative rules officially relax a few of these procedures during each General Session's final week. First, the twenty-four-hour waiting periods disappear during the session's final three days, meaning a bill can move immediately from one step to the next (see HR4-3-101 and SR4-3-102). Second, bills no longer receive floor consideration in the order received; a few days before the session ends, both chambers remove all pending bills from their floor calendars and refer them to their respective chamber's Rules Committee, which reorders the bills based on legislative leaders' priorities. (Legislators call this "sifting.") Bills can also be reprioritized by motion from the floor, usually by the chamber's majority leader.[26]

PROCEDURES CREATE POWER

Opportunities to kill or water down a bill arise at every step in the legislative process, but majority party leaders and committee chairs have especially outsized influence. Three procedural steps deserve special emphasis here. First, both chambers require all newly introduced bills to be sent to the chamber's respective Rules Committee for initial review—but neither chamber's Rules Committee has any obligation to actually release bills it receives.[27] Each chamber's presiding officer selects the chamber's Rules Committee chair and members carefully to ensure that undesirable bills—bills that will make the majority party look bad, that will cause fights within the majority party, or that legislative leaders simply dislike—never get out of Rules. These bills can get stuck in a chamber's Rules Committee for the entire session.

Second, each chamber's presiding officer, with advice from the chamber's Rules Committee, decides which committee will hear each bill. Standing committee chairs have tremendous influence over bills under their committee's jurisdiction. For example, standing committee chairs decide whether to place bills on the committee agenda at all; committee chairs also manage debate during committee hearings and can choose to give disproportionate speaking time to one side or the other.[28] Recognizing all this, bill sponsors work to get their bills assigned to friendly committees. In 2014 SB54 (controversially) appeased the Count My Vote movement by creating a dual path to the ballot. Usually the Senate Government Operations and Political Subdivisions Committee would hear bills dealing with election law. Because the senate president supported this bill, though, he referred it to the friendlier Senate Business and Labor Committee, chaired by SB54's sponsor, Curt Bramble.

Third, bills remaining on either chamber's floor calendars in the session's final days are sent to the respective chamber's Rules Committee for reprioritization. Very few bills pass before the session's final days—in 2017, 56 percent of bills that passed received their final vote in the General Session's seventh and final week—so most bills must survive this sifting process. Reprioritization presents a final opportunity for majority party leadership to advance or bury a bill.

Though all these procedures serve the innocuous purpose of managing the immense flow of legislation during the General Session, they also create opportunities for majority party leadership in each chamber to help or hinder individual bills. In other words, procedures create power.[29] Each chamber's presiding officer—the speaker of the house or the senate president—has firm control over these critical procedural steps, either directly or through his or her appointed allies on that chamber's Rules Committee.

These presiding officers must retain majority party legislators' support if they wish to remain in leadership, possibly giving them an incentive to privilege Republican-sponsored bills while burying Democratic-sponsored bills. After all, it is far harder for legislative leaders to compel rank-and-file legislators to vote a certain way than to simply privilege or impede bills using their procedural powers.[30] As such, one might naïvely expect that minority party legislators would receive worse and worse treatment as the majority party's seat share grows. If so, then Utah's Republican supermajority would kill every Democratic bill with impunity. Broadly speaking, though, studies of American legislatures generally find that majority party leaders feel more threatened by a large minority party than a vanishingly small one. Put differently, when a supermajority party controls an overwhelming seat share, as in Utah, majority party leaders have little reason to fear the minority party's voice.[31]

Patterns in the Utah Legislature confirm this general logic. Figure 10 plots the percentage of Democratic- and Republican-sponsored bills that receive a floor vote in either chamber (dashed and dotted lines) and that actually pass (solid lines). In Utah Democratic-sponsored bills start at a severe disadvantage since they generally seek to push policy in a liberal direction despite the state's sharply conservative tilt; thus we should expect fewer Democratic- than Republican-sponsored bills to pass, even if every bill received an equal chance. Nevertheless Democratic-sponsored bills pass at nearly the same rate as Republican-sponsored bills. More to the point, Democratic-sponsored bills are also nearly as likely to receive at least one floor vote as Republican-sponsored bills. Though legislative leaders could hinder or kill Democratic bills by holding them in Rules, sending them to hostile committees, deprioritizing them in the session's final days, or exploiting other procedural controls, they rarely do so, choosing instead to give minority party bills a fair chance. A former speaker of the Utah House, Rebecca Lockhart, regularly proclaimed her preference to let the legislative process play out rather than favoring some bills over others with her powers: "This House . . . is a place where process, beautiful and messy, continues to ensure great policy becomes great law."[32]

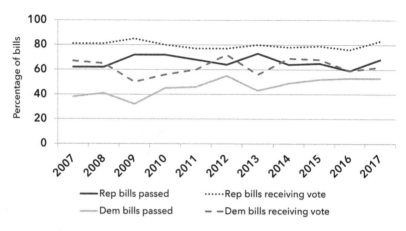

Fig. 10. Partisan batting averages in the Utah Legislature. Compiled by the author.

All the same, legislative leaders do exploit their procedural powers often enough that legislators remain wary. Responses to the Utah Legislator Survey affirm the importance of these critical steps—especially the standing committee's outsized role. The survey asked legislators, "How important is each of the following in shaping the bills that the Utah Legislature passes (or does not pass)?" Legislators rated several procedural steps on a 5-point scale from "not at all influential" to "highly influential," with 3 being the neutral midpoint. Figure 11 charts legislators' responses.[33] On average, legislators rated all steps above 3, but committee hearings received an exceptionally high score of 4.4. Floor debate (in both chambers) ranked second, followed by party caucus meetings and Rules Committee actions.

VETTING BILLS IN A SHORT SESSION

In the seventy-five-member house, the average representative introduced 6.7 bills in 2017, passing 4.0; in the twenty-nine-member senate, the average senator introduced 10.6 bills, passing 8.2. Some legislators far exceed these averages, of course, running twenty or more bills each year. These introductions add up to a tremendous workload. Over the past decade legislators have introduced 700 to 830 bills per year, with 540 to 650 coming to at least one floor vote and 430 to 540 actually passing.[34] Figure 12 depicts these trends.

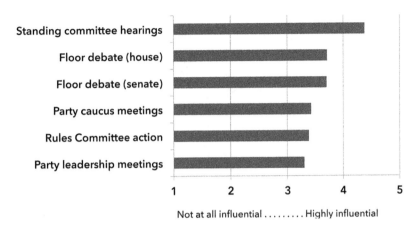

Fig. 11. Legislators' opinions of the most important procedural steps, from the author's Utah Legislator Survey.

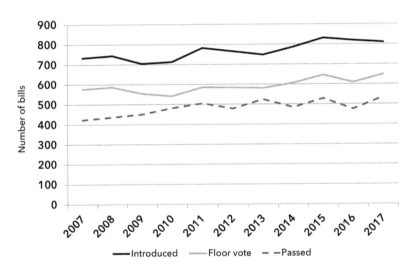

Fig. 12. Bills introduced, heard on the floor, and passed during General Sessions. Compiled by the author.

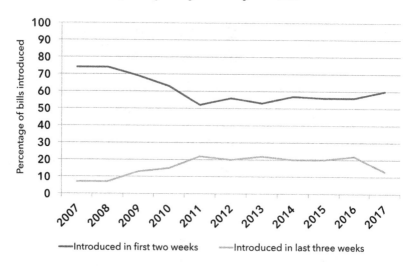

Fig. 13. Timing of bill introductions during General Sessions. Compiled by the author.

The forty-five-day General Session translates to only thirty-three working days once weekends and holidays are removed. If all a session's bills were heard at a constant rate over the session's workdays, legislators would introduce twenty-one to twenty-five bills per day and pass thirteen to sixteen of them, a dizzying pace. Of course legislators spend much of their time in committee hearings, caucus meetings, and other obligations. As such, the legislature schedules a maximum of only 120 hours for floor time over the entire General Session.[35] Even if all of those 120 floor hours were spent debating legislation, passing five hundred bills would mean spending only fourteen minutes per bill.

In practice most bills receive far less floor consideration, partly because so much floor time goes to daily opening ceremonies, speeches from visiting dignitaries, unscheduled recesses, committee reports, and other activities, and partly because legislators seldom have their bills ready for consideration by the General Session's first day. In recent years legislators have introduced as many as 177 bills during the final three weeks of each year's seven-week General Session, forcing the legislature to process these late-appearing bills at breakneck pace. As shown in figure 13, legislators began procrastinating bill introductions around 2009 and 2010, eventually

Table 2. Time spent vetting bills in
General Sessions of the Utah Legislature

YEAR	AVERAGE AGE OF BILL AT TIME OF FIRST VOTE, IN DAYS
2007	17.9
2008	15.9
2009	15.6
2010	14.4
2011	13.1
2012	13.6
2013	13.6
2014	16.8
2015	16.0
2016	15.9
2017	17.2

Source: Calculated by the author.

settling into their current pattern, in which barely over half the session's bills are introduced within the General Session's first two weeks, and nearly a quarter are introduced in the final three weeks.[36] With so few bills ready when the General Session opens, standing committee hearings and floor time routinely adjourn early in the General Session's first days due to a lack of bills. All this means that legislators spend far less than 120 hours on the floor during a typical session.

The result, of course, is that legislators and the public alike have scant time to digest most bills. As shown in table 2, enacted bills typically age only thirteen to sixteen calendar days between introduction and final passage, providing very little time for thorough legislative vetting. Vetting time bottomed out in 2011, when the average bill aged only thirteen days before passing. Late introductions caused much of this decline in vetting time.

As a result the legislature grows especially frantic in its final week. In 2017 the legislature passed 301 bills—56 percent of the total passed that year—in the session's seventh and final week. Rushing bills to passage has consequences. U.S. congressional leaders sometimes intentionally create situations wherein representatives must vote on major legislation without giving them enough time to read and study the bill in advance; research shows that doing so causes rank-and-file members to rely more on recommendations from party leaders rather than exercising their independent judgment (Curry 2015). In Utah, legislative leaders need not intentionally create a voting rush; the Utah Constitution's forty-five-day session limit does that already. This research from the U.S. Congress suggests that the Utah Legislature's frantic pace gives legislators less opportunity to read and evaluate bills, increasing their reliance on legislative leaders and trusted colleagues.

Because the average bill receives only a few minutes' consideration on the Utah house or senate floor, most vetting must happen earlier in the process, during standing committee hearings. Even there, though, legislative schedules allot an average of only thirty standing committee minutes per introduced bill.[37] Even in committee, then, legislators dispatch many bills too quickly to fully digest them. One hardly wonders that so many legislators explain their bills on the floor by saying, "This is a simple bill that makes some adjustments to legislation we passed last year." In fact variants on this floor speech became so common in the legislature that Speaker Lockhart addressed it in her 2013 opening day remarks: "If you hear anyone say, 'This is really a very simple bill,' that should be your first warning. A little restraint today, means a lot less trouble down the road."[38]

HOW LEGISLATORS DECIDE

One word summarizes most floor votes in the Utah Legislature: consensus. Since 2007 only 2 to 4 percent of house votes and 1 to 2 percent of senate votes have failed, as shown in figure 14 (note the restricted 0 to 20 percent vertical axis shared by the next several figures). In part this high success rate reflects the important work that committees perform before bills arrive on the house or senate floor. Standing committees are expected to either kill bad bills or amend them into something more palatable. On the occasion a committee does advance a divisive bill, it is likely to be amended

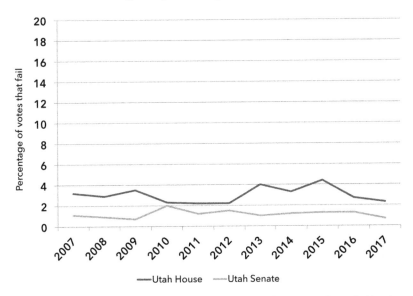

Fig. 14. Percentage of floor votes that fail during General Sessions. Compiled by the author.

on the chamber floor prior to its final vote. As a result controversial bills seldom reach the floor without significant amending, freeing legislators from many difficult choices. Indeed this is the primary reason that rank-and-file majority legislators delegate so much procedural power to their chamber leaders: so the leaders can prevent difficult bills from coming to the floor, saving members from politically awkward votes (Cox and McCubbins 2005).

Not only do most floor votes succeed, but they typically do so with overwhelmingly large margins, with Republicans and Democrats voting on the same side. The average house floor vote since 2007 has passed with support of 92 to 94 percent of legislators; the average in the senate is even higher, at 95 to 97 percent.[39] Party-line votes, in which the majority of Republicans vote against the majority of Democrats, seldom occur. Since 2007 only 9 to 16 percent of each year's house floor votes and 5 to 8 percent of senate floor votes have been decided along partisan lines, as shown in figure 15. Clearly Utah's legislative Democrats have learned to choose their battles carefully. Because they hold such a small share of legislative seats, they cannot accomplish much by voting against every Republican

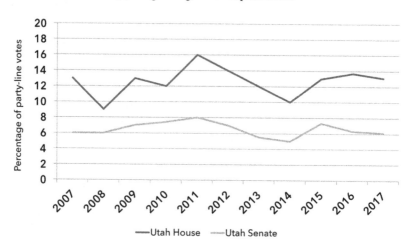

Fig. 15. Frequency of party-line votes during General Sessions. Compiled by the author.

proposal. Instead their strategy involves compromising with Republicans whenever possible and voting against Republican bills only in the most objectionable cases. This strategy has helped legislative Democrats build enough goodwill with their Republican colleagues that Democrats have been able to pass a surprising percentage of their bills, as discussed earlier.

With so many pressures on their time during the hectic forty-five-day session, legislators often must leave the voting floor briefly to tend to other matters. In the house 5 to 8 percent of representatives miss a typical floor vote; in the senate the rate rises to 9 to 14 percent, as shown in figure 16. Because most votes pass by overwhelmingly large majorities, one might expect that legislators would be more likely to skip votes on the simplest bills. As it happens, a large-scale study of absenteeism in thirty-five state legislatures (including Utah) finds that legislators are more likely to miss close votes than lopsided ones, as well as votes on important bills such as budget bills—presumably because reelection-minded legislators sometimes wish to avoid taking a clear stance on troublesome issues (see Brown and Goodliffe 2017). The same study found that absenteeism rises in states with short sessions—like Utah—especially among legislators sponsoring a large number of bills.

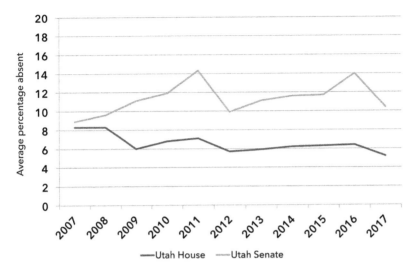

Fig. 16. Absentee rates in the Utah Legislature. Compiled by the author.

Though most bills pass overwhelmingly, enough difficult bills make it to the floor to expose cross-party as well as intraparty ideological differences. Applying a technique developed by U.S. congressional researchers, I calculated an overall ideology score for each legislator based on his or her floor voting records.[40] The scores are placed on an arbitrary scale from −100 (most liberal) to +100 (most conservative). The scores have only relative meaning, not absolute meaning; that is, there is no score that means "liberal" or "conservative," but a higher score indicates a legislator who is relatively more conservative than other legislators. The gaps between scores are therefore meaningful; legislators scoring 10 points apart exhibit more similarity in their voting behavior than legislators scoring 50 points apart.

Figure 17 presents the distribution of scores from the 2016 Utah House. Democrats are tightly clustered at the left end of the scale; all but two fit within the 30-point range between −95 and −65, indicating remarkable in-party agreement. Republicans, however, are spread over a massive 97-point range spanning −6 to +91. This 97-point range among Republicans dwarfs the 34-point gap between the parties. That is, there is more ideological variability among legislative Republicans (a 97-point range) than between the most liberal Republican (at −6) and the most conservative Democrat

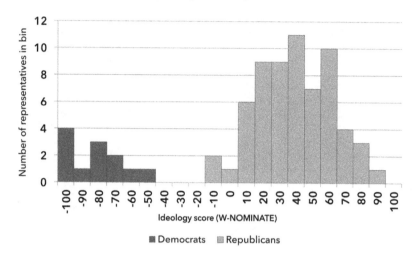

Fig. 17. Distribution of ideology scores in the 2016 Utah House of Representatives. Bars indicate the number of representatives within each bin; bins are ten units wide. Calculated using the w-nominate algorithm from data compiled by the author.

(at −40), a 34-point range. These patterns reveal, once again, how much ideological diversity—and conflict—exists among Utah's supermajority Republicans.

LESSONS FROM THE LEGISLATURE

The Utah Legislature dominates Utah policy. During the frenzied seven-week General Session, legislators pass more bills than the U.S. Congress passes in an entire year. Legislators have crafted careful procedures to handle this flood of bills, but these procedures create power. Taken as a whole, this chapter's findings show that general theories of legislative behavior developed in other contexts, such as from analysis of the U.S. Congress or of other state legislatures, apply well within Utah. Cox and McCubbins (1993, 2005) showed that leaders in the U.S. House use procedural powers to weed out or water down politically difficult bills, a pattern also observed in other state legislatures (Cox et al. 2010). Aldrich and Rohde argued that majority parties display less cohesiveness when they control an overwhelming supermajority of seats (Rohde 1991; Aldrich 1995; Aldrich and Rohde 2000a, 2000b). Curry (2015) found that members of Congress are more likely to follow voting cues from legislative leaders or other colleagues when they have less time to scrutinize and debate bills before voting. Brown and Goodliffe (2017) demonstrated that state legislators nationwide miss votes under predictable circumstances. Though these studies relied on observation of the U.S. Congress or of other state legislatures, this chapter has provided evidence that all these dynamics operate within the Utah Legislature. Utah's may be among the nation's least professionalized state legislatures, yet it has much in common with legislatures elsewhere.

All these findings address only one aspect of a legislator's job: the act of proposing and enacting new laws. Legislators are not only lawmakers, however; they are also representatives. The next chapter continues to address the Utah Legislature, but with a focus on representation: how legislators view their constituents, how organized interests seek to influence legislators, and how campaign contributions change the equation.

CHAPTER FIVE

Representing Competing Voices

Legislators have two roles: Lawmaking and representation. Though their lawmaking activities attract the most attention from the state's political reporters, legislators' behind-the-scenes representational role matters even more since it determines whose voices legislators heed while crafting legislation. Countless interests seek to influence Utah legislators: constituents, party delegates, legislative leaders, organized interests, religious leaders, campaign donors, executive branch officials, activists, and, of course, each legislator's own conscience. If lawmaking involves publicly crafting legislation, then representation involves quietly choosing which of these voices to follow.

Voters evaluate lawmaking and representation differently. Left-leaning voters in Salt Lake City may find little to praise in the conservative body of law produced by the Republican-controlled legislature, for example, yet they may rightfully feel that their Democratic legislators represent them well by voicing progressive concerns—even if those Democratic legislators seldom succeed at passing major laws.[1] Stated more directly, voters apply different standards of judgment to (individual) legislators than to (collective) legislatures (Fenno 1975). Utahns hold the legislature collectively responsible for the body of law actually enacted—that is, for lawmaking—while expecting their individual legislator only to "represent" them faithfully by speaking on their behalf and gaining their trust.

Research has produced ample evidence of this pattern when analyzing the U.S. Congress.[2] For example, a February 2016 poll found that only 27 percent of Americans felt "most members of Congress" deserved reelection, yet a majority (51 percent) of those same respondents said their

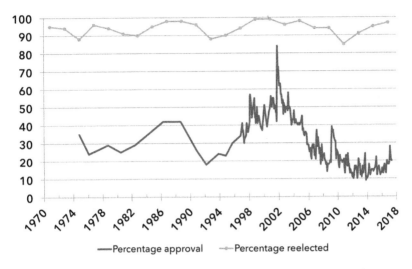

Fig. 18. U.S. congressional approval and reelection rates. Approval ratings come from various Gallup Poll releases posted to Gallup's website. Reelection rates through 2012 from Jacobson (2013, 29–46); subsequent years compiled by the author.

individual representatives deserved reelection.[3] This approval gap produces the almost paradoxical outcome shown in figure 18: voters rarely vote incumbent U.S. representatives out of office even though few Americans say they "approve . . . of the way Congress is handling its job."[4] Americans dislike Congress because they dislike its collective policy output, but they like their individual representatives because they feel individually "represented." Voters evaluate lawmaking and representation differently.

Utah voters evaluate the Utah Legislature similarly. Polling throughout 2012 found that 48 to 58 percent of Utah voters approved of the legislature's performance—higher approval than Congress receives, but still mediocre for a state lacking serious party competition.[5] Regardless, fifty-four of the sixty-one incumbent Utah representatives who sought reelection in 2012 won, an 89 percent reelection rate, with the average incumbent winning 71 percent of the vote.[6] Subsequent elections have brought repeat performances. In 2014 statewide polls in March and October found 57 and 58 percent approval ratings for the legislature, yet sixty of sixty-four Utah House incumbents who sought reelection won, a 94 percent reelection rate.[7] In 2016, 39 percent approved of the legislature in January, yet November brought a 92 percent reelection rate.[8] Utah voters evaluate legislators for their individual representation but the Utah Legislature for its collective lawmaking—and as a result they like their individual legislators more than they like the legislature collectively.

Clearly, then, Utah lawmakers find at least some success in making their constituents feel "represented." This chapter considers representation generally, exploring how legislators balance the many voices competing for their attention. After first asking how constituents influence legislators, I explore how organized interests do, with a special emphasis on the state's most powerful interest: the LDS Church. The chapter concludes with a discussion of campaign contributions, an arena dominated by organized interests but where legislator-to-legislator contributions also play an important role. Like the preceding chapter, this one finds that theories developed elsewhere—such as from examination of the U.S. Congress or of other state legislatures—apply well within Utah.

REPRESENTING CONSTITUENTS

Understanding representation requires understanding how legislators view constituents. At the broadest level anybody who lives within a legislator's district can rightfully be called a constituent—call this the "geographic constituency."[9] For example, each of the seventy-five Utah House districts contains some forty thousand residents. Utah's explosive population growth has inflated these geographic constituencies with time, as shown in figure 19.[10] In fact district populations doubled between 1980 and 2015.

With forty thousand constituents each, Utah's state representatives cannot possibly know every constituent personally. Representatives make these large constituencies more manageable by first prioritizing sympathetic voters over hostile voters and nonvoters. Most Utahns do not vote at all, whether because they are ineligible (because they are minors, felons, or noncitizens) or, more often, because they are simply uninterested in politics. In presidential election years around one-third of Utahns cast a ballot—roughly twelve thousand voters per Utah House district.[11] In midterm years fewer than one-quarter of Utahns cast a ballot—around 7,700 to 8,700 voters per Utah House district.[12] Based on typical election margins, we can estimate that only 5,000 to 5,500 residents within each district actually vote for each winner.[13] Call this the "reelection constituency"—

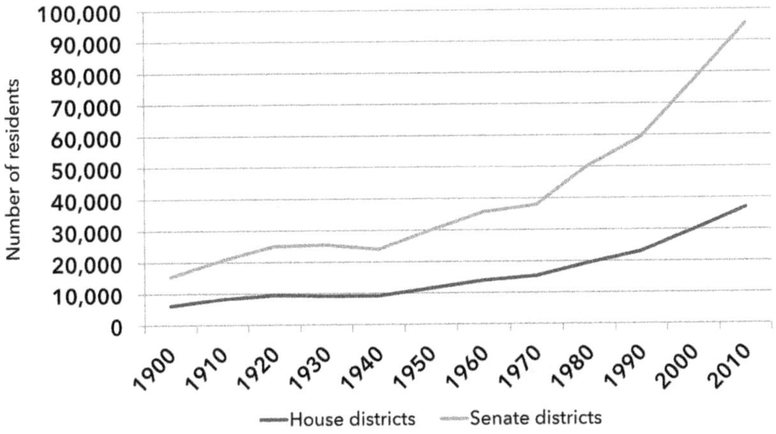

Fig. 19. Constituents per district in each chamber of the Utah Legislature. Calculated by the author from U.S. Census data.

those voters who not only show up on election day but who cast their ballots for the winner. These 5,000 to 5,500 sympathetic voters weigh far more heavily on legislators' minds than hostile voters and nonvoters. Representing the geographic constituency would be nearly impossible; representing the reelection constituency is at least plausible.

Of course giving even five minutes each to these 5,000 to 5,500 sympathetic voters in the reelection constituency would fill eight hours a day, five days a week, for over eleven weeks—an impossible goal for part-time legislators lacking personal staff. With that in mind, legislators further prioritize their most politically active constituents: those who attend party caucuses, make campaign contributions, vote in party primaries, or put up yard signs. Only one in twelve Utahns participates in Republican primary elections, while as few as one in seventy-five attends Republican caucuses, so a Republican candidate can thus narrow his or her focus to only 500 to 3,000 constituents.[14] Call this most energetic group the "primary constituency."

Legislators can view their district through one of three lenses, then. The geographic constituency includes all forty thousand residents of a typical Utah House district. The reelection constituency includes the 5,000 to 5,500 constituents who not only show up for November elections but

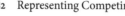

Fig. 20. Voices that most influence Utah legislators, from the author's Utah Legislator Survey.

who also vote for the incumbent. The primary constituency includes anywhere from 500 to 3,000 voters—the legislator's most politically engaged supporters.

Of course the highest priority constituent group is smaller still: the party delegates. Only a few dozen voters per Utah House district serve as Republican (or Democratic) delegates to the party nominating conventions. As detailed in chapter 3, Republican (and Democratic) caucus-goers select these delegates at neighborhood caucus meetings, and then these delegates attend state and county party nominating conventions to choose the year's Republican (or Democratic) nominees. Very few intraparty nomination battles make it out of convention to a primary, making the few dozen party delegates in each Utah House district a legislator's most important constituents—call it the "delegate constituency."

Legislators may speak generically of their "constituents" or of their "district," but typically the context will reveal which of these four constituent groups they have in mind at a given time: the geographic, reelection, primary, or delegate constituency. The Utah Legislator Survey shows that legislators do indeed mentally separate these constituent groups, prioritizing constituents based on their political activity and support. One question

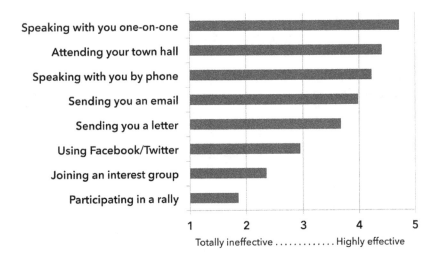

Fig. 21. Ranking effective forms of citizen engagement, from the author's Utah Legislator Survey.

began with this prompt: "Suppose a particular group or individual took a clear position for or against a particular bill. How influential would that position be on your floor vote?" Legislators evaluated each group on a scale ranging from 1 ("not at all influential") to 5 ("highly influential").[15] As shown in figure 20, legislators gave their highest scores to constituents who serve as party delegates; high (but lower) scores to constituents who belong to their party; and very low scores to constituents belonging to the other party. Legislators care about their constituents' views, though they care about some constituents more than others.

Legislators also prioritize constituents who care enough to engage them directly. The Utah Legislator Survey asked, "Suppose a constituent wanted you to know his or her feelings about a particular issue. How effective would each of the following methods be?" Using a scale from 1 ("totally ineffective") to 5 ("highly effective"), legislators showed a clear preference for spoken conversations with constituents, whether in a one-on-one meeting, in a town hall meeting, or in a telephone conversation, as shown in figure 21.[16] Written communication, whether by email or letter, ranked somewhat lower. Indirect communication, whether through social media or participation in rallies, ranked lower still.

Many years ago Richard Fenno (1978) developed the "geographic," "reelection," and "primary" constituency typology based on his careful study of how members of the U.S. House spoke of and interacted with their constituents. Though he developed his model in the U.S. congressional context, the two preceding figures show how well his typology fits Utah legislators, who clearly prioritize constituents differently depending on their party affiliation and political engagement.

All this talk of constituent influence risks obscuring a critical point, though: legislators do not see themselves as mere opinion aggregators, mindlessly polling their constituents and then voting based entirely on their constituents' will. If that were a legislator's role, there would be no need to elect representatives; voters could simply make every decision themselves directly at the ballot box, or pollsters could measure public opinion with the results enacted into law. Instead legislators see themselves as bearing a sacred trust to study the issues more thoroughly than constituents have time for, and then to exercise independent judgment for the benefit of their constituents and of the state as a whole—even if their judgment leads them to cast a vote that some constituents may disagree with.

Edmund Burke, an eighteenth-century British parliamentarian, famously articulated this representational perspective centuries ago: constituent wishes "ought to have great weight" for a representative, and "their opinions high respect," yet a representative's "unbiased opinion, his mature judgment, his enlightened conscience, he ought not to sacrifice" to constituents. Burke continued more firmly, "Your representative owes you, not his industry only, but his judgment; and he betrays, instead of serving you, if he sacrifices it to your opinion" (quoted in Stanlis 1963, 224). With these words Burke contrasted two competing visions of representation, which scholars today label the delegate-trustee trade-off: a "delegate" seeks only to express the will of those who selected her, while a "trustee" aims to exercise independent judgment on behalf of those who empowered her.

Voters may think of their elected officials as delegates, yet most office-holders, like Burke, see themselves instead as trustees.[17] The Utah Legislator Survey asked, "Suppose many of your constituents were urging you to vote one way on a bill, but your own judgment was leading you the other way. How would you vote?" Legislators replied using a scale ranging

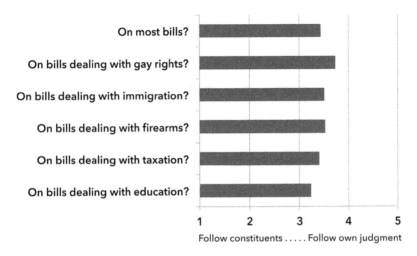

Fig. 22. Constituent influence versus independent judgment, from the author's Utah Legislator Survey.

from 1 ("follow constituents") to 5 ("follow own judgment"), evaluating several types of bill.[18] The results appear in figure 22. Constituent influence clearly matters, but legislators show a modest preference for trustee-style behavior: on "most bills," the average score was 3.4. Here Utah legislators align almost perfectly with legislators elsewhere; when the same question, using the same scale, was put before legislators from five other states, their average was 3.5 (Rosenthal 2004, 44). Utah legislators are especially inclined to follow their own judgment on polarizing issues like gay rights, firearm regulation, and immigration; they are more open to constituent feedback when it comes to education and taxes, though they lean toward their own judgment even in these areas.

On a more practical level, this preference for trustee-style representation also reflects a hard reality: Utah legislators must vote on hundreds of bills each year, only a tiny fraction of which receive any press coverage whatsoever. If voters are unaware of the policies being debated in the legislature, then legislators have little choice but to exercise their own judgment. The Utah Legislator Survey asked, "On what percentage of the bills considered by the Utah Legislature would you estimate that your constituents have an opinion?" As figure 23 shows, Utah legislators esti-

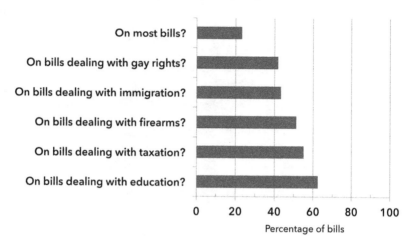

Fig. 23. Percentage of bills on which constituents have an opinion, from the author's Utah Legislator Survey.

mate that constituents have an opinion on only 23 percent of "most bills." Again Utah legislators are similar to legislators elsewhere; in a survey of legislators in five other states using slightly different wording, 92 percent estimated that constituents had an opinion on fewer than one in four bills (Rosenthal 2004, 40). When it comes to specific, high-profile issue areas, Utah legislators give higher estimates—as high as 62 percent for education and 55 percent for tax bills—though it generally remains well under 50 percent. Of special note, legislators show the most desire to follow constituents (in figure 22) on those issues where constituents seem most informed: taxation and education. If constituents fail to express a clear opinion on most bills, legislators have no choice but to rely on their independent judgment. Similar results have been found in surveys of legislators from other states (Rosenthal 2004).

Recognizing how politically disengaged most constituents are, legislators undertake diverse efforts to connect with them. Many mail constituent surveys prior to the annual General Session, email weekly newsletters to constituents during the General Session itself, and hold periodic town hall meetings in the district soliciting constituent comment. Others take less direct actions to engage constituents, such as mailing congratulatory letters to Sterling Scholars and Eagle Scouts. Sometimes, of course, these efforts are more about reminding constituents of the legislator's name and face in hopes of building constituent trust and awareness—with some success, apparently, given that voters generally like their individual legislator far more than they like the legislature as a whole, as shown earlier.[19] But some of these efforts are sincere attempts to learn what constituents want. Despite these efforts, legislators must rely on their own judgment more often than not—partly because they see themselves philosophically as trustees rather than delegates, and partly because constituents fail to express any opinion at all on most bills.

INTEREST GROUPS AND LOBBYISTS

Organized interests compete with constituents for legislators' attention. Unlike constituents, however, organized interests pay attention to every bill potentially affecting them, including bills that constituents never read about in the newspaper. These organized interests work hard to cultivate favorable relations with legislators and other policymakers. After winning her first election, a freshman legislator will suddenly find herself far more popular than before, especially among lobbyists and activists. The sudden attention can feel flattering and overwhelming as birthday cards, dinner invitations, and pleasant greetings come from all quarters. Shrewd legislators recognize that this sycophantic attention comes only by virtue of their political office; upon leaving office it will mostly evaporate.

Many organizations employ a lobbyist or government relations team to monitor pending legislation and maintain friendly relations with policymakers. Lobbyists represent Utah's major corporations, unions, churches, universities, and cities, as well as some citizen activist groups. The public often derides these lobbyists and organized interests as sleazy backroom dealers who use shameful techniques to promote so-called special interests. This derision overlooks a crucial point: in a representative system lawmakers seeking to understand a bill's impacts desire to hear from those most affected by it. That is, policymakers often want to hear what lobbyists think, actively seeking out their opinions. After all, legislators see themselves as trustees tasked with exercising independent judgment on behalf of the entire state, not as delegates who merely funnel constituent opinion. This self-image leads legislators to seek out not only constituent viewpoints but also the viewpoints of so-called stakeholders—those most impacted by a bill.

Two types of lobbyist work the Utah capitol. In-house lobbyists represent a company or association that employs them year-round. Between legislative sessions these in-house lobbyists work full time for their company or association, often as a corporate attorney, public relations manager, or government relations specialist. Contract lobbyists (or consultant lobbyists), on the other hand, advocate on behalf of several paying clients—sometimes dozens. Between sessions these contract lobbyists may work as campaign managers, business consultants, or in other political work.

Utah law requires paid lobbyists of either variety to register with the lieutenant governor's office and disclose the organizations they speak for. In 2016 state records listed 503 registered lobbyists, of whom most (339) represented only one or two organizations, usually indicating an in-house lobbyist.[20] At the other extreme are the contract lobbyists: sixty-four lobbyists disclosed working for ten or more clients, while twenty-three lobbyists disclosed thirty or more. The top ten were Robert Jolley (72 clients), Frank Pignanelli (71), Jodi Hart (70), Paul Rogers (66), Greg Curtis (66), Doug Foxley (66), Jeff Rogers (64), Stephen Foxley (58), Renae Cowley (49), and Michael Ostermiller (43).[21] Of the ten lobbyists with the longest client lists, three served previously as legislators, including former speaker of the house Greg Curtis, former house minority leader Frank Pignanelli, and former representative and senator Paul Rogers. (Former representative Steve Barth falls just outside the top ten.) Critics sometimes call this phenomenon the "revolving door": legislators leave the capitol, only to spin around and reenter as well-paid lobbyists.

Together these 503 registered lobbyists represented 1,378 different organizations, nearly all of which (1,041) had only one or two paid lobbyists speaking on their behalf. At the other extreme, 117 organizations employed teams of five or more lobbyists, usually in-house. Topping the list were the Utah Education Association (18 lobbyists), TransWest Express (15), the Utah Public Employees Association (13), Energy Solutions (13), the Central Utah Water Conservancy District (12), Sandy City (12), the Utah School Employees Association (12), the Utah League of Cities and Towns (12), and a tie between six organizations employing eleven lobbyists each (1-800-Contacts, the Sutherland Institute, the Church of Jesus Christ of Latter-day Saints, the Utah Bankers Association, Rocky Mountain Power, and the Exoro Group). Three decades ago an analysis of Utah's major lobbying forces found that mining and energy interests, public education interests, and banking and finance interests topped the list (Hrebenar et al. 1987); it appears that little has changed.

These registration numbers include only paid lobbyists. Volunteer citizen groups and independent activists may testify in committee hearings and meet with legislators without registering, making it hard to estimate their numbers. Among the most active citizen groups are the Utah Eagle Forum, the Libertas Institute, the Utah Taxpayers Association, Parents for Choice in Education, Utahns against Hunger, Utah Moms for Clean Air, the Southern Utah Wilderness Alliance, Utah Pride, and Voices for Utah Children. Less organized, more fleeting movements have arisen around immigration, autism, and medical marijuana.

Organized interests, including both paid lobbyists and citizen groups, employ different lobbying tactics depending on their access to lawmakers.[22] Those who have already cultivated relationships of trust with legislators rely heavily on so-called insider tactics, while others rely more on outsider tactics. In the popular imagination insider tactics involve lobbyists using bribes or coercion to get legislators to vote against their constituents' interests. The truth is less exciting: legislators usually have preexisting views about how policy ought to look, at least in general terms, and they seek out beneficial relationships with lobbyists for two reasons. First, legislators may already care about a particular industry or interest within the state, so they may ask that interest's lobbyists to provide expert information about how a proposed bill might affect them. Second, they may lack the time to prepare an effective pitch for their bills, so they may ask relevant lobbyists for assistance with developing talking points, identifying potential cosponsors, tracking bills through the legislative process, preparing handouts, and recruiting committee testimony.

Put bluntly, then, insider tactics mostly involve lobbyists and activists helping legislators compensate for their utter dearth of staff support. Nationwide, lobbyists have more influence in states where legislators have less staff, since lack of staff leaves legislators hungry for information and assistance, two things lobbyists are eager to provide (Hrebenar et al. 1987, 115; Berkman 2001; Gray et al. 2015). Not only does the Utah Legislature employ less staff than nearly any other state legislature, but legislators must process hundreds of bills in an unusually short forty-five-day General Session. Lobbyists do, of course, also work to persuade legislators to change their minds, but lobbyists in Utah often succeed simply by identifying already sympathetic legislators and then providing them information and assistance. Indeed a survey of Utah's registered lobbyists found that 81 percent report regularly assisting legislators with the policy process (e.g., by helping prepare bills or providing relevant research), while only 62 percent report regularly working to persuade legislators to change their stance (e.g., by contacting them directly, speaking to reporters, or asking influential constituents to contact legislators).[23]

By contrast, outsider tactics have less to do with filling in for staff than with publicly pressuring legislators toward actions they otherwise oppose. Outsider tactics may include holding rallies, organizing letter-writing campaigns, flooding committee rooms with supporters, hanging signs around the capitol, or taking other actions designed to inspire sympathetic media attention and publicly pressure lawmakers. These pressure tactics sometimes succeed, but legislators often find it easy to ignore them. Moreover even if these outsider tactics do persuade legislators to support a particular stance, actually changing policy requires more than building legislative support; it also requires getting a bill through the difficult legislative process. Given legislators' minimal staff, short session, and enormous bill load, successful lobbying requires the additional step beyond mere persuasion of identifying friendly legislators and working closely with them to craft legislation and shepherd it to passage. That is, the most successful movements employ lobbyists or leaders who can credibly use insider tactics. Outsider tactics alone are seldom enough.

Utah's autism advocates illustrate this point. For several years parents of autistic children asked the Utah Legislature to require health insurance providers to cover early childhood autism interventions. For the first years these advocates relied on classic outsider tactics that repeatedly garnered sympathetic attention, both from the press and from legislators, but failed to produce meaningful policy change. Eventually legislators finally acknowledged autism advocates' years-long effort with some modest policy changes passed in 2010, including a pilot autism treatment program.[24]

Calling these steps inadequate, autism advocates kept pushing. They continued attracting sympathetic press coverage, such as a story about families leaving Utah for states where insurers cover autism, as well as stories about parents unable to fund autism treatment even under the new pilot program.[25] However, autism advocates increasingly realized that these outsider tactics were not enough to deliver the outcomes they sought. When a newly elected senator and physician, Brian Shiozawa, agreed to take up their cause in 2013, autism advocates worked closely with him, adding classic insider tactics to their ongoing outsider pressure campaign. Shiozawa's bill failed to pass before the 2013 General Session concluded. Learning from their mistakes, autism advocates doubled down in 2014. Working again with Senator Shiozawa, autism advocates finally saw their desired legislation pass—and by tremendous margins. Only three representatives (of seventy-five) voted against Shiozawa's SB57, along with only one senator (of twenty-nine).[26]

Legislators acknowledged autism advocates' unusual persistence. One observed that autism bills had been floated for at least six straight years before finally passing; another said, "I do not recall a single group that has been more persistent."[27] Persistence was only part of the formula, though. Autism advocates gained success partly because their relentless outsider tactics eventually turned skeptical legislators into supporters, but mostly because they added insider tactics to their arsenal, working individually with legislators to finally get autism coverage enacted.

If insider tactics are integral to lobbying success, one might reasonably ask why some interests organize themselves more effectively than others. A classic study provides a time-tested answer that begins with a simple observation: some interests are more widely held than others, but larger interests find it harder to organize than smaller ones.[28] To clarify, an "interest" does not necessarily refer to an organized interest group; the homeless are an (unorganized) interest, while the Utah Community Action Partnership is an (organized) interest group that advocates for the homeless. Larger interests find it harder to organize partly because the benefits they seek will be divided among more participants. A hypothetical example illustrates this point: If a $3 million government subsidy will benefit thirty corporations at the expense of three million taxpayers, those thirty corporations stand to gain an average of $100,000 each if the subsidy takes effect—making it very much worth their money to contribute a few thousand dollars each to a trade association that can lobby for the subsidy. However, the three million taxpayers stand to lose an average of only $1 each—making it a waste of their time to spend more than $1 of their time or money organizing to oppose the subsidy. Even setting aside these financial calculations, organizing thirty corporations into a pro-subsidy lobbying group takes far less effort than organizing three million taxpayers into an antisubsidy pro-taxpayer group.

This simple logic explains why narrower interests—trade associations, corporations, unions, and so on—are so much more likely to have enduring organizational structures that can support a paid lobbyist, while broader public movements struggle to recruit volunteers and raise funds. As a result grassroots citizen's groups like those named above—the Eagle Forum, the Southern Utah Wilderness Alliance, Libertas, Utah Pride, and so on—are often outnumbered by narrower interests that can organize more easily.

UTAH'S MOST POWERFUL INTEREST

Only one Utah interest combines broad grassroots support with tremendous organizational strength: the Church of Jesus Christ of Latter-day Saints. As I noted earlier, more than half of Utahns self-identify to pollsters as Mormon, and even more appear on LDS membership rolls. At the same time the LDS Church has a uniquely hierarchical polity; ecclesiastical authority flows unambiguously from Church headquarters in Salt Lake City down to congregations around the globe (Prince and Wright 2005; Quinn 1994, 1997). This unusual combination of organizational strength and grassroots support allows the Church to influence policy using both insider and outsider tactics.

As for insider tactics, the Church's organizational strength enables it to hire full-time government relations personnel who engage in traditional insider lobbying; on issues Church leadership cares about, its lobbyists—jokingly called the "home teachers" within the capitol—can approach legislators directly.[29] One former legislator (and former Mormon), Carl Wimmer, accuses the Church of using lobbying tactics so aggressive they border on "political bullying": "It killed me to know that this time the 'bully' was my own [former] church." Though conceding that "they rarely want things badly enough to engage openly," Wimmer claims, "If the Church wants something in Utah politics, they get it."[30] Another former legislator, Chris Herrod, agrees, though in gentler language, revealing that Church lobbyists would state that their instructions came "directly from the top," or from "the brethren," to leverage ecclesiastical authority.

Other legislators push against Wimmer's "bullying" narrative, arguing that LDS lobbyists have no more influence than other interests. Senator Curt Bramble has said, "I view the LDS Church in the political context as the same as any other interested observer that wants to make their position known." His colleague, Senator Scott Jenkins, is more direct: "Never has this happened with me." Former representative Stephen Sandstrom, who passed anti-immigration legislation opposed by the Church, claims LDS lobbyists "made very clear to me that they respected what I was doing as a representative and they wanted me to do what I felt was right." Except Wimmer, who has disaffiliated from the LDS Church, all these legislators are Mormon.

Regardless of whether LDS lobbyists use tactics that are too heavy-handed, they clearly get results on those occasions when they choose to take a stance. For example, LDS lobbyists have consistently worked against any effort to relax Utah's famously strict liquor laws; they have resisted sales of liquor-by-the-drink (Magleby 2006) and of alcoholic sweets, or "alcopops."[31]

As for outsider tactics, the Church can also call on its broad membership to agitate for specific policy changes. Most famously, Mormons responded vigorously to pleas from Church leadership to support California's Proposition 8 in 2008 to prohibit same-sex marriage, "tipping the scale" toward passage.[32] High-level LDS leaders have issued similar calls to oppose gambling (Campbell and Monson 2007), alcohol liberalization (Magleby 2006), the Equal Rights Amendment (Magleby 1992; Quinn 1997), and other policies (Campbell et al. 2014).[33]

At times the Church combines these insider and outsider strategies. In 2011, as legislators considered punitive anti-immigration bills, the Church lobbied hard for a more compassionate, comprehensive approach. It supplemented this inside lobbying with public statements referencing specific bills.[34] Those statements moved public opinion significantly, particularly among self-identified "very active" Mormons who also identify as "strong Republicans." Prior to the Church's statements, a poll asked Utahns to place their support for a particular anti-immigration bill on a 5-point scale. After the Church statements, the same people were polled again; "very active" Mormons who were also "strong Republicans" changed their answers by an average of 1.05 points away from enforcement and toward compassion, a tremendous change for a 5-point scale.[35] When the Church's favored immigration bill (HB116) eventually passed—a compassionate bill rather than an enforcement bill—Church leaders showed their approval by dispatching a high-level authority, the presiding bishop, to attend the governor's bill signing.

More often than not, though, LDS leaders need not say anything at all—not publicly, and not through their lobbyists. In recent years around half of legislative Democrats and nearly all legislative Republicans have been Mormon; because the Legislature has been over 80 percent Republican, the net membership is around 90 percent LDS.[36] Moreover many of these legislators have served as lay leaders of their local congregations, making them intimately familiar with official Church teachings.[37] As a result LDS culture alone is sufficient to produce policy outcomes favorable to LDS interests. A study in the 1980s attributed this outcome to "anticipatory decision-making," with faithful Mormons throughout state government trying to anticipate "how the church would react to a proposed new policy" (Hrebenar et al. 1987, 115).

This "anticipatory decision making," wherein officials seek to apply Church principles even when they have not been approached directly, arises not only in the Utah Legislature but also among local officials. In 2010 researchers at Brigham Young University and the University of Utah partnered with the Utah League of Cities and Towns and the Utah Association of Counties to field the Utah Elected Officials Survey, a poll administered to hundreds of city and county officeholders. Though this study will be discussed in greater detail in chapter 9, it contained an experiment that bears discussion here. A few months before the survey was fielded, the LDS Church had issued a surprise November 2009 endorsement of a proposed Salt Lake City ordinance that would prohibit housing and employment discrimination against gays and lesbians. After Salt Lake City enacted the ordinance, several other local governments followed suit. In the Utah Elected Officials Survey, one-quarter of respondents were assigned to a control group that received this question: "One issue that some local governments have addressed is an ordinance protecting people against discrimination in housing and employment based on sexual orientation. Would you favor or oppose your local town or city council passing this kind of non-discrimination ordinance?"

Three treatment groups, each consisting of one-quarter of respondents, saw a few additional words added to this question. For the first treatment group, the question asked, "Would you favor or oppose your local town or city council passing this kind of non-discrimination ordinance, *such as the one recently endorsed by the LDS Church?*" (emphasis added). For the second treatment group, the treatment phrase was "such as the one recently passed by the Salt Lake City Council"; for the final treatment group, the phrase was "such as those recently passed by seven cities and counties in Utah." Respondents in all groups then evaluated this nondiscrimination ordinance on a scale from 0 (strongly oppose) to 100 (strongly favor).

In the control group the average score was 54. In the latter two treatment groups (referencing Salt Lake City and other cities), this average did not move significantly—perhaps because these local officials had already heard that other cities had been adopting nondiscrimination laws, or perhaps because they did not care. But the LDS treatment language did have an effect, raising the average evaluation from 54 to 61. Surely the effect would have been larger if the LDS endorsement had not already been so well publicized; officeholders in the control group who were already aware of the LDS endorsement would have previously adjusted their views, after all. This significant finding shows how eager local officials are to apply their religious values to the policy realm.

Because officeholders engage in anticipatory decision making, LDS values influence policy even when the Church says nothing. Of the Church's lobbying efforts, the ACLU of Utah's director concedes, "They're not keen on direct lobbying." Another lobbyist, a non-LDS former Democratic legislator, calls the LDS Church "unreasonably cautious. . . . We never said, 'Please don't say anything,' it was always, 'Can't you say more?'" The Catholic diocese's full-time lobbyist, who works the legislature throughout each annual session, calls the LDS Church "determined not to interfere," adding, "I don't even know the name of their lobbyist" (all preceding quotes from Magleby 2006). To expand Wimmer's words from earlier, "They rarely want things badly enough to engage openly. The church is very selective regarding the legislation they engage. . . . Because most of Utah's legislators are LDS members, the majority of legislation already aligns with the LDS Church position without their influence." Even as Wimmer accused Church lobbyists of using bullying tactics, he acknowledged that "during the three terms [six years] I served in the Utah House of Representatives, I was only approached twice by the LDS lobbyists for a vote."[38] The state's most powerful interest, then, exerts influence more through cultural dominance than through direct lobbying or explicit public appeals.

CAMPAIGN CONTRIBUTIONS

Candidates for state or local office in Utah can accept unlimited donations to fund their reelection efforts. One recent candidate for governor received $650,000 from a single donor—his boss—comprising 69 percent of the candidate's total receipts.[39] Utah law requires only that candidates disclose all contributions and expenditures publicly and that they use campaign funds only for approved purposes.[40]

Research focused on the U.S. Congress has shown that organized interest groups tend to make unsolicited campaign contributions in a nonpartisan manner to legislators whose committee assignments or leadership positions make them relevant to the interest group's particular policy concerns. That is, most campaign donors give to incumbents of both parties. They make these contributions not to influence election results but to gain favor with key legislators. In this way contributions buy access, not officeholders (Francia et al. 2003).

An examination of Utah legislators' campaign finance disclosures reveals similar patterns. During the 2012 election cycle, for example, candidates for the Utah House and Senate reported $5.9 million in aggregate campaign contributions; the total rose to $6.7 million in 2014, an average of $56,000 per Utah House race and $176,000 per Utah Senate race. Due to their unique control over the legislative process, however, legislative leaders (of both parties) received contributions far above these averages. Two-term speaker of the house Rebecca Lockhart announced her retirement that year, so access-minded donors piled contributions on two potential successors: House Majority Leader Brad Dee, who received a total of $261,566 from 286 separate donations for his utterly uncompetitive District 11 race, and Greg Hughes, who received $161,812 from 197 separate donations in his equally uncompetitive District 51 race. Their fellow leadership aspirant

Jim Dunnigan received $161,768 from 116 donations for his uncontested District 39 race. (Ultimately house Republicans chose Hughes as speaker and Dunnigan as house majority leader.) Over in the Senate, President Wayne Niederhauser raked in $323,223 from 387 donations for his lopsided District 9 race, followed by Majority Whip Stuart Adams with $234,088 from 263 donations. Senate Democratic leaders also shared in the largesse, with Minority Whip Karen Mayne receiving $300,483 from 397 donations for her lopsided District 5 race and Minority Leader Gene Davis receiving $197,710 from 230 donations for his uncontested District 3 race.[41]

If campaign contributors were concerned about influencing elections, they would target legislators in competitive races, not legislative leaders in uncompetitive or uncontested races (Francia et al. 2003). These patterns present clear evidence that most donors seek postelection lobbying access, not regime change. As further evidence, most of these contributions came from organized interests, not from individual constituents. Organized groups gave $297,076 to Senate President Niederhauser (92 percent of his 2014 total), $197,519 (66 percent) to Senate Minority Whip Mayne, $178,938 (76 percent) to Senate Majority Whip Adams, $128,460 (79 percent) to future speaker Hughes, and $79,550 (49 percent) to future house majority leader Dunnigan.

No single industry dominates this campaign contribution game. Utah's biggest donors—to all Utah races, including nonlegislative races—are the Utah Association of Realtors (165 donations in 2014), Energy Solutions (151), Reagan Outdoor Advertising (143), CenturyLink (106), Micron (102), Workers Compensation Fund of Utah (102), Pacificorp (94), Utah Hospitals and Health Systems Association (91), Utah House Republican Elections Committee (82), and Education First (79). All these organizations (except the Utah House Republican Elections Committee) gave mostly to incumbents of both parties, with only a small minority of their donations going to challengers or open-seat candidates. In the U.S. Congress organized interests give to incumbents of either party because they are less interested in influencing elections than in currying favor with whoever wields power—that is, in creating opportunities for insider lobbying tactics (Francia et al. 2003). The evidence presented here reveals the same pattern within the Utah Legislature.

Congressional research has also found that U.S. representatives contribute to their colleagues' campaigns to advance their own leadership ambitions, as well as to promote party loyalty once in leadership (Cann 2008). Again the same pattern arises among Utah legislators.[42] In 2012 contenders for vacant Senate Republican leadership positions contributed to seven (Niederhauser), ten (Jenkins), and four (Adams) legislative colleagues; Niederhauser ultimately became senate president and Adams became majority whip, forcing Jenkins, previously the senate majority leader, out of leadership.[43] Meanwhile two contenders for the vacant house minority leader position contributed to twenty-one (Brian King) and fourteen (Jennifer Seelig) fellow candidates; ultimately King chose not to run for leadership, clearing the way for Seelig.[44]

In 2014 house Republicans pursuing leadership vacancies contributed to twelve (Greg Hughes), twenty-six (Don Ipson), fourteen (Jim Dunnigan), and eleven (Brad Wilson) colleagues; Hughes became speaker, Dunnigan became house majority leader, and Wilson became house majority assistant whip. Aspirational house Democrats contributed to nineteen (Rebecca Chavez-Houck), eighteen (Brian King), and fourteen (Patrice Arent) colleagues; King became house minority leader, Chavez-Houck became minority whip, and Arent became minority caucus manager. The senate had no open leadership races in 2014, yet existing leaders shored up support anyway: President Niederhauser gave to four colleagues, Majority Leader Ralph Okerlund gave to five, and Majority Whip Adams gave to four. In addition former senate majority leader Jenkins gave to five colleagues.

Legislators can and do rise to leadership without making contributions to their peers. Still, three of four house Republican leaders, three of four house Democratic leaders, and three of four senate Republican leaders contributed to their peers' campaigns in 2014. Of the eleven legislators who gave to a significant number of their peers that year, nine wound up in leadership; only two (Representative Ipson and Senator Jenkins) received no apparent return on their investment. Advancing to legislative leadership might not require contributing to colleagues' campaign funds, yet those contributions do not seem to hurt.

WHOSE VOICE IS HEARD?

Utah legislators feel pressure from all directions: from constituents, including the geographic, reelection, primary, and delegate constituencies; from organized interests, including in-house lobbyists, contract lobbyists, and citizen groups; from fellow legislators, especially legislative leaders; from their own judgment; from their religious sensibilities; and from other sources not considered here, such as the executive branch. Legislators do care about constituent opinion, especially their most politically active constituents, but they see themselves as trustees tasked with exercising independent judgment rather than as mere opinion aggregators, so they also seek input from stakeholders affected by bills—that is, from organized interests.

Organized interests with sufficient access to legislators rely more on insider tactics that help legislators compensate for their lack of staff than on outsider tactics that seek to pressure legislators publicly; in turn, organized interests seek to enhance their legislative access through campaign contributions. Legislators seeking to rise within their chambers employ the same technique, raising money so they can pass it on to fellow legislators. Legislators are especially open to hearing from these other voices—that is, from organized interests, from fellow legislators, from the executive branch, and so on—when their constituents seem to have no preference about a particular bill. And more often than not that is exactly what legislators perceive.

These dynamics affirm representational patterns found in studies of the U.S. Congress and of other state legislatures. Fenno (1978) identified U.S. representatives' layered views of their constituencies and originated the "geographic," "reelection," and "primary" constituency terminology; Rosenthal (2004) measured legislators' delegate-trustee attitudes in five state legislatures; Nownes (2006) described insider and outsider lobbying tactics; Berkman (2001) and Gray et al. (2015) reported that state legislators rely more on lobbyists when they lack staff support; Olson (1965) explained why larger interests are less likely to organize than narrower ones; Francia et al. (2003) asked who gives to congressional campaigns and what they seek in return; and Cann (2008) found that U.S. representatives aspiring to congressional leadership donate aggressively to their colleagues' campaigns. This chapter has presented evidence that Utah legislators and interests behave consistently with all these other studies.

Perhaps Utah's greatest deviation from the research literature's expectations is the outsized role of the LDS Church; Olson (1965) to the contrary, the LDS Church enjoys the unusual combination of broad-based grassroots support and a strong hierarchical organization. Though the Church seldom lobbies for a specific bill or mobilizes its membership to oppose a specific policy, those actions it does pursue are unusually effective. Moreover this LDS dynamic has remained constant for decades; even thirty years ago a study of lobbying in Utah found the same general pattern as reported here, in which the LDS Church influences policy more through its cultural dominance (via "anticipatory decision-making") than through direct appeals (Hrebenar et al. 1987). Otherwise, though, Utah legislators interact with constituents, organized interests, campaign contributors, and one another in the same ways that legislators elsewhere do.

CHAPTER SIX

Legislating at the Ballot Box

On January 26, 2007, Representative Steve Urquhart introduced HB148 onto the Utah House floor. Dubbed the "Parent Choice in Education Act," HB148 would create the nation's first statewide school voucher program, allowing Utah children to attend private schools at state expense.[1] After narrowly passing the Utah House by a single vote on February 2, the bill moved to the Utah Senate, where it passed more comfortably on February 9. Three days later Governor Jon Huntsman signed HB148 into law—only seventeen days after the bill's introduction. Jubilant supporters nationwide hailed "Utah's revolutionary new school voucher program," the "most comprehensive school choice program in the nation."[2] The national school choice movement saw HB148 as the first "of several such state laws" to be enacted, proof "that this can now be passed" everywhere.[3]

Public education advocates watched their world implode. They had fought to stop the bill of course: house and senate committees had heard passionate testimony against HB148 from the Utah Education Association, the Salt Lake City Board of Education, the State Board of Education, the Park City School Board, the Utah League of Women Voters, the Utah School Boards Association, the Utah Superintendents Association, the American Federation of Teachers, the Utah Parent Teacher Association, the Utah Superintendent of Education, and the Utah School Employees Association. Those committees approved the bill despite this organized opposition. When the governor signed HB148, the battle was lost forever.

Or so it seemed. Jilted public education advocates unearthed a rarely used, mostly forgotten provision in the Utah Constitution. Unlike the U.S. Constitution, which vests "all [federal] legislative powers" within the

"Congress of the United States" alone (Article I, §1), Utah's Constitution vests the "Legislative power of the State" jointly in the "Legislature of Utah" and in "the people of the State of Utah" (Article VI, §1). Of course this language does not mean that a citizen can walk into the legislature and vote freely on bills. Instead it empowers voters to enact new legislation (by initiative) or veto it (by referendum) at the ballot box.

Taking voucher proponents by surprise, the Utah Education Association announced its intention to place HB148 before voters using Utah's referendum process. From the day the governor signed HB148, Utah law gave opponents only forty-five days to collect 92,781 signatures from registered voters hoping to overturn it.[4] With support from the National Education Association, the Utah Education Association began its petition drive on March 1, 2007, and submitted 124,218 valid signatures on April 12, easily qualifying for the ballot and delaying implementation of HB148 until voters could weigh in. Those 124,218 signatures set a Utah record, marking the first successful referendum petition in thirty-three years.[5] As voucher opponents celebrated, even HB148's proponents acknowledged their foes' strength. The executive director of Parents for Choice in Education, the main agitator for HB148, remarked, "When you have that many PTA moms and teachers and other government employees working on this, it's not hard to gather enough signatures to get on the ballot."

A ferocious public campaign ensued, attracting hefty out-of-state donations on both sides.[6] Finally voters issued their judgment on November 6, 2007. Only 38 percent of Utahns voted to keep the new school voucher program, with 62 percent rejecting it. This bruising defeat in a fiercely Republican state not only killed vouchers in Utah but stalled the conservative-led school choice movement nationwide. Kim Campbell, president of the Utah Education Association, joyously declared, "With the eyes of the nation upon us, Utah has rejected this flawed voucher law."[7]

Utahns showed near-universal opposition to vouchers, rejecting HB148 in all twenty-nine counties and in 102 of 104 legislative districts—even in districts represented by ardent voucher supporters, such as HB148's sponsor, Representative Urquhart, and House Speaker Greg Curtis.[8] Utah Democrats promised to remind voters at the next election "that their legislators are not representing their values."[9] Keeping this promise, Democrats picked up two seats a year later, including the seat held by Speaker Curtis.[10]

This chapter completes the portrait of Utah's lawmaking processes by exploring the direct role that citizens can play through initiatives and referendums. Though few initiatives and referendums appear on Utah ballots, the mere presence of these processes changes how the legislature operates. The unexpected and overwhelming success of the antivoucher referendum in 2007 enhanced these effects, making legislators wary of new citizen revolts. Before exploring those broader effects, however, I begin with a brief description of the powers and processes available to Utah voters.

DIRECT DEMOCRACY IN UTAH

The school voucher episode illustrates how Utah voters can take policy into their own hands, power known generically as direct (as opposed to representative) democracy. Various states confer any of five common direct democracy powers on their voters: direct initiatives, indirect initiatives, legislative referendums, popular referendums, and recalls. In general, initiative processes enable citizens to enact a new law; referendums allow them to veto a recently passed law; and recalls allow them to remove an official before his or her term expires (Magleby 1984). Voters in Utah enjoy all these powers except the recall.

In referendums voters consider a law already passed by the Utah Legislature. Utah's constitution provides for two distinct types of referendum: legislative and popular. A legislative referendum occurs when the legislature voluntarily sends a proposal to voters for ratification. Though some states use legislative referendums for diverse purposes, Utah uses them only to ratify proposed amendments to the constitution. Because proposed amendments must first win support from two-thirds of legislators in each chamber before appearing on the ballot, they are rarely controversial on election day; most amendments pass easily as a result. By contrast, a popular referendum occurs when voters gather signatures to prevent a bill passed by the legislature from taking effect, as happened with the 2007 voucher law. Popular referendums, called "people's vetoes" in some states, arise far less frequently than legislative referendums but produce far more controversy, for obvious reasons. The 2007 referendum petition marked Utah's first successful popular referendum since voters overturned a land use bill in 1974.[11]

With initiatives, by contrast, voters propose a new law without the legislature's prior involvement. Utah's constitution provides for both direct and indirect initiatives. In a direct initiative a citizen writes a law and gathers signatures to qualify for the ballot. If voters approve the law on election day, the proposal becomes law, bypassing the legislature entirely. In an indirect initiative a citizen writes a law and gathers signatures, but a successful petition does not place the proposal on the ballot; instead a successful petition compels the legislature to hold an up-or-down vote on the proposal as originally written.[12]

Three of these direct democracy mechanisms—popular referendums, direct initiatives, and indirect initiatives—require signature-gathering drives. Utah's constitution and statutory code impose strict procedural requirements on this process.[13] Once the petitioners formally declare their intentions to the lieutenant governor—for initiatives, a step that includes publishing the initiative's exact language and holding public hearings throughout the state—they may begin gathering signatures. Qualifying a direct initiative or popular referendum requires gathering a number of signatures equal to 10 percent of the votes cast in Utah's most recent presidential election. For an indirect initiative the threshold falls to 5 percent. Petitioners must also meet dispersion requirements to demonstrate broad support. Initiative petitions must meet the 5 percent (indirect) or 10 percent (direct) threshold not only statewide but also in twenty-six of Utah's twenty-nine state senate districts; popular referendum petitions must meet the 10 percent threshold not only statewide, but also in fifteen of Utah's twenty-nine counties.

Roughly half the American states—mostly those in the West—have direct democracy provisions in their state constitutions. Many, including Utah, impose such stringent requirements that few petitions qualify for the ballot. By contrast, California and Oregon stand out for their relatively simple requirements. Qualifying a direct initiative in Oregon requires fewer actual signatures than in Utah, even though Oregon's population is over one-third larger; qualifying a direct initiative in California requires five times more signatures than in Utah, but California's population is more than thirteen times larger.[14] Predictably more initiatives qualify in California and Oregon than in Utah and other western states, as shown in table 3, with an astounding seventy-six direct initiatives qualifying in

Table 3. Initiative use in western states, 2004–16

STATE	QUALIFIED	ENACTED
Arizona	22	9
California	76	32
Colorado	39	16
Idaho	2	0
Montana	15	12
Nevada	14	10
Oregon	43	14
Utah	1	0
Washington	22	13
Wyoming	0	0

Note: Only even-year direct initiatives included. Data from Ballotpedia.org, a project of the Citizens in Charge Foundation. All contiguous western states included except New Mexico, which lacks a direct initiative process.

California alone during these thirteen years. Meanwhile voters in Idaho, Utah, and Wyoming—states with high qualification barriers—seldom see initiatives on their ballots. Clearly not all initiative procedures are created equal (Bowler and Donovan 2004; Hicks 2013).

Initiatives and referendums, like item vetoes and nuclear warheads, can influence policy without being used. The mere threat of an initiative influences policymakers, to the point that policy outcomes reflect public opinion more closely in initiative states than elsewhere (Arceneaux 2002; Gerber 1996, 1999; Matsusaka 2010; Phillips 2008).[15] Evidently legislators heed constituent concerns more closely when they know constituents can simply take policy into their own hands. Some have labeled the initiative's deterrent effect "the gun behind the door" (Lascher et al. 1996). The initiative has the greatest deterrent effect where qualification requirements are simpler, of course; initiatives pose less threat to lawmakers where initiatives seldom qualify (Gerber 1996).

Even in Utah, though, where initiatives rarely qualify for the ballot, the "gun behind the door" effect still occurs in limited circumstances. It grew especially strong following the 2007 voucher referendum, when voters' overwhelming rebuke embarrassed many lawmakers and made them wary of future direct democracy drives. One year later, during the 2008 general elections, allegations of ethical improprieties fouled a few of Utah's electoral contests. Remembering the successful school voucher referendum, activists immediately began planning an initiative to impose stricter ethics rules on candidates and officeholders. Legislators, still scarred by the school voucher fight, took these grumblings seriously. Seeking to head off the initiative, legislators enacted a series of ethics reforms during the legislature's 2009 General Session. Voters had flexed their muscles with the 2007 referendum; as a result the mere threat of a 2009 ethics initiative caused the legislature to pass an ethics bill it would not otherwise have considered, a classic example of the "gun behind the door" effect.

The story does not end there, though. Claiming that the legislature's reforms did not go far enough, a new group, Utahns for Ethical Government (UEG), drafted a far stricter ethics initiative that created an independent ethics commission and a strict code of officeholder conduct. In late September 2009 UEG began gathering signatures for the November 2010 ballot. Officeholders fretted publicly that UEG's initiative went too far; Utah's governor, the state Republican Party, and various legislators announced their opposition to it. Still the petition attracted thousands of signatures and showed no sign of slowing when the legislature convened for its 2010 General Session. With one eye on UEG's petition, legislators passed several additional ethics bills, going much further than their 2009 reforms, including a proposed constitutional amendment establishing a legislatively controlled ethics commission. None of these bills went as far as UEG's initiative, but the legislature hoped its actions would dampen voter enthusiasm for UEG's petition.[16] The gambit paid off. UEG's signature drive sputtered, and initiative backers ultimately collected fewer than 80,000 signatures, well short of the 94,552 required.[17] No ethics initiative appeared on the ballot, yet the "gun behind the door" pushed the legislature to take actions it would have otherwise avoided, even if those actions fell short of UEG's proposal.[18]

Reformers next turned their attention to Utah's nomination system. For decades Utah's major political parties had used the caucus-convention system to select their general election candidates. To review, Republican voters would attend local precinct caucuses each spring, where they would choose a handful of delegates to attend the Republican state or county conventions; at the convention those delegates would meet Republican candidates and ultimately nominate one candidate per office. If the delegates deadlocked—a rare occurrence—the top two candidates for a particular office would move from the party convention to a Republican primary election, where Republican voters would break the tie. Democrats used the same system. Fearing that this nomination system empowered ideological extremists and therefore produced unrepresentative policy outcomes (see chapter 3), a wide coalition of moderate Utah Republicans, including former governor Mike Leavitt, formed Count My Vote (CMV) to agitate against the caucus-convention system in favor of direct primaries. Many elected officials opposed CMV, preferring the caucus-convention system that had placed them in office. Finding no support in the legislature, CMV organizers filed an initiative and began gathering signatures to qualify for the ballot. By the time the Utah Legislature convened for the 2014 General Session, CMV had gathered more than 40,000 of the roughly 100,000 signatures required and had raised $800,000 to finish its petition drive.[19] All signs pointed to the initiative's eventual success.

Legislators hatched a plan familiar from the 2010 UEG ethics reform campaign: to forestall an even more stringent initiative, they would propose a bill meeting the initiative effort partway, in hopes of killing the initiative altogether. In 2014 the legislature passed SB54. Unlike the CMV petition, SB54 did not mandate direct primaries; it would allow political parties to keep their caucus-convention system under certain conditions. However, SB54 also created a second track to the ballot: any candidate could bypass his or her party's caucus-convention system and appear automatically on a primary election ballot by submitting sufficient signatures. Thus SB54 created a dual track to a Republican (or Democratic) primary election: a Republican (or Democratic) candidate could either prevail in the caucus-convention system or simply gather voter signatures. CMV organizers agreed with legislators to cease gathering signatures if SB54 passed, preferring a sure legislative outcome to the initiative process's uncertainty. SB54 passed comfortably through both chambers, though many legislators emphasized they were voting for it only to avoid what they saw as an even worse outcome. CMV organizers did not get everything they wanted, but the "gun behind the door" worked: legislators enacted a reform they never would have considered if not for the threat of an initiative.

Of course the "gun behind the door" sometimes misfires, as an episode from longer ago illustrates. In the 1990s a nationwide movement successfully enacted term limits in several states, usually by direct initiative. That movement soon stormed into Utah, qualifying an initiative for the November 1994 ballot that would have imposed a strict eight-year term limit on state and county officeholders, including state legislators. Legislators, unsurprisingly, opposed this petition. Before voters had the chance to vote on this initiative, however, legislators passed a term-limit law of their own during the 1994 General Session: HB305 enacted a more modest twelve-year limit. With this law in place, legislators urged voters to reject the initiative's too-strict eight-year limit. Trusting the legislature's good faith, voters did so.

For the next nine years it seemed the "gun behind the door" had worked. As with the UEG and CMV petitions that would come later, the threat of an initiative had compelled legislators to enact legislation they would otherwise have opposed. The tide shifted in 2003, though. That year the legislature passed a new bill, SB240, repealing the 1994 term-limit law. Because twelve years had not yet passed since 1994, no officeholders were ever termed out. Some voters complained about what they saw as the legislature's duplicity, but the 1990s term-limit fervor had waned enough that no new initiative materialized. In the case of term limits the "gun behind the door" failed.

On balance, though, Utah's experience with direct democracy has affirmed the "gun behind the door" logic, at least when it comes to provoking legislative action on a specific issue. Initiatives and referendums are hard to qualify in Utah, making the initiative's deterrent effect weaker than in California and Oregon (Bowler and Donovan 2004). However, when serious movements arise, legislators actively seek to meet proponents halfway to prevent far-reaching initiatives from making the ballot. The initiative's deterrent effect grew even more powerful after the embarrassing 2007 voucher referendum, prompting both advocates and legislators to take the initiative more seriously. Though Utahns never saw an ethics bill or a primary election bill on their ballots, the UEG and CMV initiative drives nevertheless spurred legislators into action on these issues. In Utah, as in other states with direct democracy provisions, the mere threat of an initiative changes public policy (cf. Arceneaux 2002; Gerber 1996, 1999; Matsusaka 2010; Phillips 2008).

CHAPTER SEVEN

The Most Powerful Governor

Utahns love their governors—at least, they love to reelect them. No incumbent governor has lost in November since Democrat Herbert Maw lost after two terms to Republican J. Bracken Lee in 1948. And other than the special case of Olene Walker (discussed below), no governor has lost an intraparty renomination battle since Lee lost his Republican primary in 1956.[1] When incumbent governors run, they win—over and over again.

Governor Calvin Rampton (Democrat, 1965–77) coasted to reelection twice, becoming Utah's first three-term governor. His handpicked successor, Scott Matheson (Democrat, 1977–85), served two terms before he too retired. Next came Norm Bangerter (Republican, 1985–93), whose first term was marked by natural and economic disasters: the Great Salt Lake's flood, shutdowns at Kennecott Copper and Geneva Steel, and general economic recession. Though Bangerter's solutions to these problems proved controversial and expensive, including a $55 million project to pump the Great Salt Lake's excess water into the west desert and a $230 million proposed tax increase, he nevertheless won reelection in an unusual three-way race in 1988.[2]

When Bangerter retired, Mike Leavitt (Republican, 1993–2003) succeeded him. Like Rampton, Leavitt won reelection not once but twice. Still popular late in his third term, Leavitt resigned to accept a presidential appointment. His lieutenant governor, Olene Walker, became the state's first (and only) female governor, in November 2003. She used her new position to press an early reading program through the Utah Legislature and veto a bill experimenting with school vouchers, angering Republican activists. Only six months after she assumed office, Republican delegates at the state convention refused to nominate her for a full term, nominating Jon Hunstman instead. Walker became the only sitting governor to be forced out since 1956.[3]

Emerging from this intraparty battle, Huntsman (Republican, 2005–9) soon reached unprecedented popularity. Only two years into his first term he had 77 percent approval, including 68 percent among Democrats.[4] After coasting to reelection in 2008, he enjoyed an inconceivable 90 percent approval rating in January 2009.[5] Later that year, however, Huntsman resigned to accept an appointment as ambassador to China.[6] His lieutenant governor, Gary Herbert, assumed office in August 2009. In a special November 2010 election voters formally granted Herbert the privilege of completing Huntsman's four-year term, giving him 64 percent of the vote over his Democratic opponent. In November 2012 Herbert won a full four-year term in his own right (with 68 percent of the vote), followed by another easy reelection victory in November 2016 (with 67 percent). Herbert thus matches Rampton's and Leavitt's records of winning three gubernatorial elections.

Other than Walker's special case, then, Utah voters have not removed a sitting governor for over half a century. Governors themselves choose when to leave office. Most take their time—and why would they hurry? After all, American governors have "the best job in politics" (Rosenthal 2013), with many tools at their disposal empowering them to pursue their goals (see Beyle and Ferguson 2008; Kousser and Phillips 2012). This chapter argues that Utah governors' unusual longevity stems from their unusual power. That is, Utah's institutional environment gives its governors unusual advantages when compared to governors elsewhere.

Existing research has identified five key features of gubernatorial power that vary significantly across the fifty states: the size of the plural executive, the strength of the gubernatorial veto, the governor's tenure potential, the governor's budgetary role, and the governor's appointment power (Beyle and Ferguson 2008). Combined these five features suggest that Utah governors possess more institutional authority than any other American governor. No governor is a dictator, of course, and previous chapters have already demonstrated the legislature's jealous defense of its own prerogatives. Still, Utah governors' unusual strength contributes to their unusual longevity.

UTAH'S PLURAL EXECUTIVE

The federal Constitution creates a unitary executive branch where all powers are ultimately vested in a single person, the president of the United States. Every cabinet officer, agency director, bureaucrat, and executive branch employee answers ultimately to the president alone, who bears final responsibility for the federal government's executive operations. To remind all of this authority, President Harry S. Truman famously kept a sign on his desk declaring, "The buck stops here."

Only three states have followed this unitary model in their own executives. The remaining states, including Utah, have adopted a plural executive, in which voters separately elect various members of the executive branch. At the extreme, North Dakota's plural executive includes twelve separately elected executives. Utah employs a more modest plural executive, consisting of five constitutional officers. Utahns elect a governor (jointly with a lieutenant governor), an attorney general, a treasurer, and a state auditor. Each of these constitutional officers answers only to the voters. Other than the lieutenant governor's subservience to the governor, none of these constitutional officers outranks the others; the governor can neither command nor dismiss the attorney general, treasurer, or auditor.

Each constitutional officer has a defined executive role. The attorney general handles the state's legal matters, provides legal counsel to offices throughout the executive branch, and manages the state's prosecutorial efforts, which includes broad authority to investigate possible corruption or malfeasance anywhere in Utah's government. The treasurer serves as chief financial officer, managing and investing Utah's public funds. Only the legislature can enact the budget that spends state money, but the treasurer oversees the collection, investment, and disbursement of these funds. The state auditor conducts financial audits and performance reviews of state agencies. The auditor can also independently assess whether state and local government agencies are in compliance with existing statutory law. The lieutenant governor serves as the state's chief election officer, charged with administering and certifying the state's elections and other official acts. (Prior to 1976 a separately elected secretary of state conducted these functions.) The governor holds all other executive powers not specifically delegated by the constitution to one of these other offices. Voters elect the governor on a joint ticket with the lieutenant governor, who succeeds the governor in the event of death or resignation.

Plural executives weaken governors by cultivating a class of politicians with the experience and talent necessary to challenge the governor's reelection attempts. In the forty-seven states with plural executives, gubernatorial candidates routinely come from within the executive branch itself. From 1998 through 2010, 61 percent of open gubernatorial elections—that is, elections in which the incumbent governor did not seek reelection—featured at least one major party nominee who had previously served as an elected executive.[7] Plural executives serve as something of a farm team, patiently waiting their opportunity to advance to the governor's mansion. Some of these plural executives refuse to wait; during this same period 16 percent of incumbent governors seeking reelection faced a major party challenge from another elected executive.[8] Of course larger plural executives threaten governors' electoral ambitions more than smaller ones.

Plural executives also weaken governors by limiting their policy domain—and once again, larger plural executives limit governors more than smaller ones. In Utah neither the treasurer nor the auditor plays significant policy roles; only the attorney general's control over legal matters seriously cuts into the governor's authority. As such, most executive responsibilities remain under the governor's control, including the departments of Agriculture, Commerce, Corrections, Environmental Quality, Financial Institutions, Health, Insurance, Natural Resources, Public Safety, and Technology. The governor also commands the state militia (Utah's branch of the National Guard) and directs diverse boards and commissions. On balance, then, Utah's relatively small and weak plural executive leaves more power to the governor than most American governors enjoy.

A STRONGER VETO

The U.S. Constitution grants the president authority to veto bills passed by Congress, and all American governors enjoy the same authority to veto bills passed by their respective state legislatures. However, vetoes vary from state to state in two key ways. First, they vary in their override potential. Just as Congress can override a presidential veto with a two-thirds supermajority, most states (including Utah) set the override threshold at two-thirds. Some set it lower, at three-fifths or even one-half.

Second, vetoes vary in their scope. All governors have full veto (or "package veto") authority, the only type enjoyed by the U.S. president—that is, the authority to reject a bill in its entirety. But most governors also enjoy item veto authority, or the authority to reject portions of a bill while signing other portions into law.[9] Article VII of Utah's constitution (as amended in 1980) grants the governor item veto authority, but only with respect to appropriations bills; Utah governors can remove any expenditure from a budget bill while signing the rest of the budget into law. (Utah's legislature can override an item veto with the same two-thirds majority that overrides a full veto.)

Utah governors seldom exercise their full and item veto powers, as shown in figure 24. From 1998 through 2003 Mike Leavitt exercised a total of thirty-five vetoes, including thirty-two full vetoes and three item vetoes, only one of which was overridden; in 2004 Olene Walker issued seven vetoes (five full, two item), with two overridden; from 2005 through 2009 Jon Huntsman issued thirteen vetoes (nine full, four item), with none overridden; and from 2010 through 2017 Gary Herbert issued twenty-nine vetoes (twenty-two full, seven item), with only two overridden. Put differently, Leavitt vetoed only 1.6 percent of the bills placed before him, Walker vetoed 1.9 percent, Huntsman 0.7 percent, and Herbert 0.8 percent. Utah governors seldom veto bills.

Like nuclear weapons and ballot initiatives, vetoes do not need to be used to have an effect: they are so difficult to override that legislators prefer to avoid them in the first place. Utah's governors exercised eighty-seven vetoes (seventy-two full, fifteen item) between 1998 and 2016, yet the legislature overrode only five. Even bills that pass easily through the legislature seldom overcome a gubernatorial veto. In 2012, for example, the legislature enacted HB363 to restrict sex education programs in Utah's public schools. On its way through the legislature, HB363 won by nearly veto-proof majorities—60 percent in the house and 66 percent in the senate. After public outcry led Governor Herbert to veto HB363 a few weeks later, however, legislators had little desire to reconsider it; they never so much as attempted an override vote.[10] Even vetoes largely overlooked by the public can be hard to override. In 2015 the legislature passed the relatively obscure SB278 with 72 percent support in the house and 83 percent in the

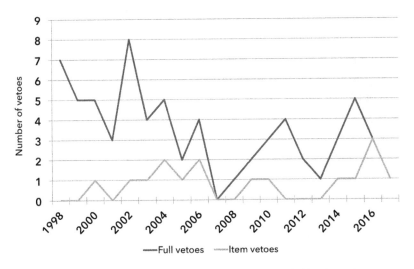

Fig. 24. Full and item vetoes cast by Utah governors. Compiled by the author.

senate, exceeding the 67 percent override requirement, yet legislators did not attempt to override Herbert's subsequent veto.

Recognizing the difficulty of overriding a veto, legislators avoid them by paying careful attention to the governor's preferences when first crafting their legislative agenda (Kiewiet and McCubbins 1985; Matthews 1989; Cameron 2000)—or, in the case of item vetoes, when crafting the annual budget (Brown 2012; but see Carter and Schap 1990). As a result vetoes influence policy more at the beginning of the legislative process (when legislators first decide how ambitiously to push their policy goals) than at the end (when governors decide whether to issue vetoes). Even if a way-ward legislator decides to push an idea the governor opposes, legislative processes empower a variety of committee chairs and legislative leaders to kill proposals they prefer not to waste time on—and given the short legislative session's severe time constraints, few legislative leaders want to waste time on proposals the governor plans to veto. Thus the governor's veto power strengthens his position when negotiating with legislators, and his item veto—a power that U.S. presidents covet—strengthens the governor further.

UNLIMITED TENURE POTENTIAL

At the 1787 Constitutional Convention, America's founders hotly debated how long the U.S. president would serve. After narrowly voting down life terms, delegates initially agreed to award the president a seven-year term without the possibility of reelection; by the time delegates settled on a four-year term without term limits, they had already considered terms of twenty, fifteen, eight, seven, and six years (see Madison 1920). Given how carefully the founders deliberated presidential term lengths, we can marvel that gubernatorial term lengths vary so little among the states. Nationwide forty-eight states (including Utah) have adopted four-year gubernatorial terms; only Vermont and New Hampshire differ, having two-year terms. Despite the ubiquity of four-year terms, however, American governors nevertheless vary widely in their so-called tenure potential—that is, their potential to remain in office indefinitely. Even among governors with four-year terms, two factors combine to influence tenure potential: term limits and election timing. Utah governors fare well on both dimensions.

Term limits have straightforward effects: governors have no choice but to leave office if their state constitution prohibits another run. Governors in thirty-six states are subject to some sort of term limit, usually a two-term maximum (Council of State Governments 2015, table 4.9). Responding to citizen pressure, Utah's legislature reluctantly enacted a twelve-year term limit for all state officials in 1994, but legislators repealed the limit only nine years later (in 2003), before anybody had been termed out. As a result Utah remains one of only fourteen states without gubernatorial term limits.

Without term limits Utah governors can run as many times as they can win—and the unusual timing of gubernatorial elections helps them win. Few voters pay much attention to politics outside of campaign season. Even in campaign season voters show far more interest in the highest profile races, largely ignoring down-ballot contests (Brown 2011). Recognizing voters' limited interest in politics, most states avoid holding their gubernatorial elections concurrently with presidential elections, which tend to dominate political news and voter attention so thoroughly that voters pay little attention to other races—even gubernatorial races—in presidential years. Only nine states (including Utah) hold their gubernatorial elections in presidential years; the remaining states elect governors in midterm years (thirty-four states), odd years (five states), or biennially (two states).

Holding gubernatorial elections in presidential years reduces media coverage and voter attention to gubernatorial campaigns. Incumbent governors provide a steady stream of favorable press releases and photo ops to state media throughout their terms. Their challengers have only a brief campaign period to rebut these positive narratives. If challengers' rebuttals must compete with presidential races for media space, voters are unlikely to hear them. Campaign messages matter in gubernatorial campaigns (Carsey 2000), yet Utah voters do not hear them. Thus Utah's decision to hold gubernatorial elections in presidential years strengthens incumbent governors by making it harder for challengers to get their message to voters.[11]

As evidence for these claims, consider how top-of-the-ticket races influence voter turnout nationwide. Holding other variables constant, a typical state sees turnout of 58.3 percent in presidential years and 35.6 percent in midterm years. This tremendous 22.7-point jump in turnout reflects voters' greater interest in and awareness of presidential elections. More to the point, though, states that hold gubernatorial elections in midterm years see a 6.6-point jump in turnout over the 35.6 percent baseline; states that hold gubernatorial elections in presidential years see no jump whatsoever over the 58.3 percent baseline. When a gubernatorial race is held in a midterm year, these results suggest that voters will turn out specifically to participate in that race, presumably because they have heard enough about the gubernatorial candidates to be interested in the contest. When a gubernatorial race is held in a presidential year, however, voters are not drawn to the gubernatorial race specifically but rather turn out solely to participate in the presidential election.[12] The case is not clear-cut, but this suggestive evidence implies that Utah's incumbent governors benefit from the unusual timing of the state's gubernatorial elections. During the brief campaign period local media are so preoccupied with the presidential campaign that gubernatorial challengers struggle to get their campaign messages through.

Presidential-year elections strengthen incumbent governors by complicating challengers' efforts to reach voters; off-year elections weaken incumbent governors by giving their opponents an easier opportunity to attack the incumbent's record. Moreover term limits weaken governors by limiting their time in office. Utah is one of only four states—along with

North Dakota, Washington, and Wisconsin—to combine presidential-year elections with unlimited terms.[13] Together these features boost Utah governors' tenure potential dramatically. Utah governors can seek reelection as many times as they like, and many do. Other than Olene Walker's unusual case, every governor since 1956—including George Dewey Clyde, Calvin Rampton, Scott Matheson, Norm Bangerter, Mike Leavitt, and Jon Huntsman—has left office voluntarily. Voters simply do not remove Utah governors from office.

BUDGETARY INFLUENCE

Governors nationwide have more influence over budgets than statutory policy (Kousser and Phillips 2012).[14] On paper Utah governors have so little budget authority that this claim may seem surprising. As do most state constitutions, Utah's grants the legislature sole authority to craft and enact each year's budget, specifying which programs the state will provide and how much it will spend on them. Every state service—including public universities, highways, aid to needy families, public schools, state parks, law enforcement, courts, water projects, environmental monitoring, and wildlife management—depends on the state's multibillion-dollar annual budget.

The governor plays an official role only at the beginning and end of the annual budget process. First, the governor releases a gubernatorial budget proposal prior to the legislative session that serves as a starting point for the year's budget negotiations. Utah law requires the governor to provide a (potentially confidential) draft budget to legislative staff at least thirty days before the legislature's annual session begins, with a final (public) budget proposal delivered within the session's first three days (see Utah Code §63J-1-201, 2016). In practice governors release their budget proposals publicly several weeks before each year's legislative session so they can drive the public dialogue. If revenues are down due to recession, the governor's proposal starts the dialogue about where cuts should happen. If revenues are up, the governor's proposal starts the dialogue about whether to cut taxes, save the extra money for a rainy day, or invest in new programs. By requiring the governor to submit a budget proposal each winter, Utah law empowers the governor to set the budget narrative. Once the governor has submitted a budget proposal, he plays no formal role in the budgeting process until it ends, at which point the governor decides whether to exercise item veto authority to strike individual programs from the budget.

Governors thus play a formal role only at the beginning and end of the budgeting process. During the intervening weeks the legislature has full authority to shape the budget as it pleases. However, the governor has a tremendous resource advantage over the legislature that gives him or her an outsized role throughout the legislative budgeting process. Understanding and formulating a multibillion-dollar state budget requires incredible time and expertise. The governor works year-round and full time managing the state, supported by a large personal staff. When it comes to the budget, the governor's most important assistance comes from the Governor's Office of Management and Budget, where a small army of analysts, economists, and advisers assist the governor in carefully assembling the year's budget proposal and keeping an eye on the legislature's budget hearings.[15] By contrast, Utah's legislators convene for only forty-five calendar days each year, or thirty-three working days. Individual legislators have far less time than the governor to study the budget. Moreover individual legislators have no personal staff to assist them during the legislative session (other than a single intern); instead they rely on a well-trained but small shared staff housed in the Office of the Legislative Fiscal Analyst.

Putting all this together points to the governor's major budget advantage over the legislature: the governor works full time and is backed by a large personal staff, while legislators work part time with no personal staff. Not all states have such a stark contrast between legislative and executive resources. In many states legislators serve year-round with large support staffs.[16] Resource disparities between governors and legislatures stand out as perhaps the most important indicator of gubernatorial budget power (Kousser and Phillips 2012), and Utah's executive-legislative resource gap stands out as one of the nation's largest. As a result Utah governors have more influence over the annual budget than most of their peers—and more than their limited formal role implies.

APPOINTMENT POWER

Subject to U.S. Senate approval, the U.S. president appoints the entire executive cabinet, every federal judge, every federal agency's director, and every other top-level actor in the federal executive branch. States do not generally grant their governors the same broad authority over appointments. For one thing, most states have a plural executive, which naturally restricts the governor's ability to appoint cabinet-level officials. But many states, including Utah, go further in these restrictions.

In particular, few governors get to shape their state's judiciary. At the federal level the president fills all federal judicial vacancies by sending any nominee he or she chooses to the U.S. Senate for confirmation. By contrast, most states either elect judges directly or use complicated appointment schemes designed to minimize partisan influence on the courts. Utah falls into the latter group. When vacancies arise in Utah's state courts, the Judicial Nominating Commission sends a short list of potential appointees to the governor, who must choose a nominee from the Commission's list, subject to Utah Senate confirmation. Like most American governors, Utah's have limited opportunity to shape the judiciary.

The governor's appointment authority is similarly restricted with the many independent boards and commissions charged with regulating various aspects of state policy. Utah governors fill hundreds of positions on these regulatory boards and advisory commissions, but in most cases the governor's appointment power faces severe statutory constraints. For example, no more than four of the seven appointees to the Alcoholic Beverage Control Commission may belong to the same political party (see Utah Code §32B-2-201, 2016). As a more complex example, Utah's Air Quality Board includes nine members serving staggered four-year terms subject to detailed appointment rules: one member must be a physician, engineer, or scientist "not connected with industry"; two must represent state or local government agencies; one must represent the mining industry; one must represent the fuels industry; one must represent the manufacturing industry; one must represent an environmental advocacy group or related organization; one must be a "representative from the public who is trained and experienced in public health"; and no more than five may belong to the same political party (see Utah Code §19-2-103, 2016). The Utah Marriage Commission's seventeen members must include social workers, psychologists, physicians, family therapists, legal professionals, scholars, two members of the Utah Senate, two members of the Utah House, and a handful of others (see Utah Code §62A-1-120, 2016). The Political Subdivisions Ethics Commission's seven members must include a former mayor or city councilor, a former judge, a former school board member, two members of the public, and a few others (see Utah Code §11-49-201, 2016).

Utah's government includes almost four hundred boards and commissions.[17] Some have regulatory authority, like the Alcoholic Beverage Control Commission and the Air Quality Board; some can censure elected officials, including the Political Subdivisions Ethics Commission; many serve only an advisory role, such as the Marriage Commission and the Constitutional Revision Commission. Detailed rules limit the governor's appointment power with respect to most of these boards.

Perhaps the only area where the governor has unbridled appointment authority is within the executive cabinet. The governor can appoint the directors of each department, subject to senate approval (except for those departments led by independently elected plural executives). With the exception of cabinet appointments, however, the governor's appointment authority is severely limited. Because these sorts of limitations are common across the fifty states, however, they place Utah's governor at no particular disadvantage compared to governors elsewhere. In this area Utah's governor is merely average.

ASSESSING UTAH'S GUBERNATORIAL POWERS

This chapter has considered five major ways that American governors vary in their formal powers. First, some governors enjoy unitary executive authority or a small plural executive, while others share authority with a large plural executive; second, some governors have only a package veto with easy legislative override requirements, while others have item veto authority and supermajority override rules; third, some governors have short terms, limited terms, or off-year elections that reduce their tenure potential, while others have unlimited tenure potential; fourth, some governors have tremendous advantages in budget negotiations owing to resource advantages over their legislatures, while others face more powerful legislatures; and fifth, some governors enjoy broader appointment power than others.

These five features of gubernatorial power—plural executives, veto strength, tenure potential, budget authority, and appointment authority—separate strong from weak governors. Beyle and Ferguson (2008) constructed an index from these five powers that places Utah's governor among the top seven most powerful nationwide.[18] Utah's score is driven up by its relatively small plural executive, its unlimited tenure potential, and its item veto with a supermajority override. Note that Beyle and Ferguson's scores do not account for the governor's resource advantage over the legislature, a consideration shown elsewhere to be critical (Kousser and Phillips 2012). On this dimension Utah's legislature ranks at the bottom, with only four state legislatures having fewer legislative resources.[19] Combining Utah's high rank (#7) in gubernatorial power with its low rank (#46) in legislative capacity suggests that the governor enjoys the most favorable position of any in the nation. Some of these dimensions of gubernatorial power—especially tenure potential—contribute directly to the longevity of Utah's governors. Others contribute only indirectly by increasing governors' ability to deliver on their promises and demonstrate active leadership.

CHAPTER EIGHT

Judges and Courts

American courts labor in obscurity. Voters know nearly nothing about them—not even about the U.S. Supreme Court, the nation's most visible judicial body. Recent polls show that only 47 percent of Americans know that U.S. Chief Justice John Roberts is generally considered a conservative; only 33 percent know that three of the nine justices are women; and only 28 percent choose Anthony Kennedy when asked to select the justice who has most often been the U.S. Supreme Court's swing vote.[1] Voters know even less about their state courts, even when they are asked far simpler questions. Nationwide only 53 percent of voters know their state has its own constitution, the most basic yet critical piece of legal information imaginable; only 51 percent can accurately say whether their state elects or appoints its judges; and only 41 percent know that their state supreme court can strike down legislative acts for violating the state constitution (see National Center for State Courts 2009).

Perhaps we should not expect voters to know these possibly trivial facts about their state courts—but perhaps we should. Because most legislating happens in the state legislatures, most judicial activity happens in state courts. Collectively the fifty American state legislatures pass one hundred times more laws per year than Congress[2]—and collectively the fifty American state court systems hear one hundred times more cases than the federal court system.[3] Moreover voters who know little about their courts are more likely to question the state court system's overall legitimacy, saying that "it might be better to do away with [their state supreme court] altogether" if the court issues unpopular decisions, or that the "state's highest court gets too mixed up in politics" (see Cann and Yates 2016). By contrast, the more Americans know about their state courts, the more they trust them (Cann and Yates 2016).

As it happens there is much to appreciate about Utah's judicial branch. This chapter argues three points. First, Utah's entry-level courts manage a tremendous caseload each year while provoking very few appeals, reflecting efficient judicial organization and reliance on specialized courts. Second, although Utah's appellate courts do engage regularly in judicial review, Utah's brief but frequently updated constitution reduces pressure on the state supreme court to invalidate state actions; as such, the Utah Supreme Court does not attract the accusations of judicial activism that so often dog the U.S. Supreme Court. Third, Utah's merit-based method of selecting judges reduces ideological conflict on the courts, promoting legal expertise in its place. As a result Utah Supreme Court rulings display high levels of judicial consensus, and Utahns exhibit high confidence in their courts. These three claims affirm findings from the broader literature on judicial politics.

UTAH'S ENTRY-LEVEL COURTS

Those who break federal laws get charged by a federal prosecutor before a federal judge in federal court; those who break state laws get charged by a state prosecutor before a state judge in state court. Federal judges play no role in Utah's judicial system, just as the U.S. Congress plays no role in the Utah Legislature and the U.S. president plays no role in Utah's executive. Utah employs a three-tiered judiciary, beginning with entry-level courts (district courts, juvenile courts, justice courts, and so on), then an intermediate Utah Court of Appeals, and finally the Utah Supreme Court.

Cases begin in Utah's entry-level district courts, sometimes generically called trial courts.[4] The legislature has divided the state into eight judicial districts, headquartered in Logan, Ogden, Salt Lake City, Provo, St. George, Richfield, Price, and Vernal. Each district employs several judges working across several courtrooms, though only a single judge hears any given case. These are the courts depicted in television dramas, with a single judge moderating the clash between prosecutors and defense attorneys and a jury rendering the final verdict, though only a fraction of the caseload involves criminal trials—14 percent in FY2014. District courts also hear domestic cases (divorce, visitation, paternity, child custody),

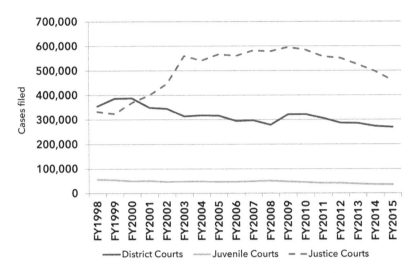

Fig. 25. Case filings in Utah's entry-level courts. Compiled by the author from reports posted at *Utah Courts*, utcourts.gov.

civil cases (debt collection, small claims, civil rights violations, wrongful termination), probate matters (adoption, inheritance, name changes), torts (malpractice, personal injury), traffic offenses (speeding tickets, parking violations), and other judgments (enforcing liens and child support). In FY2014 Utah's various district courts heard 273,492 cases—one case for every ten Utahns—a total that includes 37,484 criminal cases, 79,721 civil cases, 20,595 domestic cases, 20,011 traffic and parking cases, and 115,681 other cases.[5]

Other entry-level courts labor alongside these district courts to relieve the case pressure or provide specialized services. For example, all eight judicial districts house a separate juvenile court to hear cases involving suspects younger than eighteen; in FY2014 these courts heard 36,078 cases statewide. In addition many counties and cities create local justice courts to efficiently address minor cases; these justice courts heard 496,953 cases in FY2014, nearly all of which (397,258, or 79.9 percent) involved traffic and parking offenses. As shown in figure 25, these justice courts handle the bulk of Utah's caseload.

To promote rehabilitation, judicial districts have created additional specialized courts to divert needy populations from Utah's standard criminal justice system. For example, youth courts place young offenders before a volunteer panel of their teenage peers. These panels negotiate contracts with offenders that may require them to raise their grades, perform community service, or take other positive steps. Offenders who meet their contract's terms avoid being tried in the standard juvenile court, which generally imposes more austere sentences, such as incarceration, fines, and placement in foster care.[6] Likewise drug courts offer low-level drug offenders a chance to avoid prison if they receive treatment (at their own expense), pass regular drug tests, check in often with a judge, and show other efforts toward rehabilitation. Those who meet all program conditions avoid having a conviction placed on their record; those who fail face incarceration.[7] Mental health courts take a similar approach toward offenders suffering from mental illness.[8]

Utah's district courts form the foundation of the state court system, though these parallel courts—juvenile courts, justice courts, youth courts, drug courts, and mental health courts—relieve much of the caseload pressure. Together these courts serve as Utah's entry-level courts, establishing the facts of each case—that is, establishing whether a wrong was committed, whether a penalty should be imposed, and so on. These entry-level courts alone have a caseload exceeding that of the entire federal court system.[9] In 2015, 281,608 civil cases and 80,081 criminal cases were filed in federal district courts nationwide, a total of 361,689 filings. More than twice as many cases—806,523—were filed during FY2014 in Utah's district courts, juvenile courts, and justice courts. Less than 1 percent of the U.S. population resides in Utah, yet Utah's entry-level courts hear 2.2 cases for every case heard in federal court. State courts and state laws matter.

JUDICIAL REVIEW AND THE UTAH CONSTITUTION

On appeal, cases originally heard in these entry-level courts proceed to the Utah Court of Appeals, housed in Salt Lake City. Seven judges sit on this court, though only three hear any particular case. In the Utah Court of Appeals there are no citizen juries, no cross-examination of witnesses, no presentations of physical evidence, nor any of the other dynamics familiar from courtroom dramas; those determinations of fact are the purview of Utah's district courts and other entry-level courts. Instead the Utah Court of Appeals considers questions about the proper interpretation of the law and the fair application of judicial procedures. Very few cases are actually appealed. In FY2014 the Utah Court of Appeals issued only 301 rulings, suggesting that only 0.04 percent of lower-level cases were appealed.[10]

On final appeal cases proceed from the intermediate Utah Court of Appeals to the Utah Supreme Court, the state's highest court.[11] The five justices appointed to this court choose from among themselves a chief justice to serve a four-year term. The chief justice presides not only over the Utah Supreme Court but also over the state's Judicial Council, which meets monthly to adopt uniform administrative rules for the state's courts and set standards for judicial performance.

In the Utah Supreme Court all five justices hear every case; if a justice recuses himself or herself from a particular case due to a potential conflict of interest, the remaining four judges will invite a lower court judge to sit on the case as a temporary fifth justice. The Utah Supreme Court hears far fewer cases than the Utah Court of Appeals, issuing only seventy-six decisions in 2014—implying that less than 0.01 percent of lower-level cases make it all the way to the Utah Supreme Court. Like the Utah Court of Appeals, the Utah Supreme Court does not consider physical evidence or make judgments about guilt. Rather it engages in judicial review, ensuring that lower courts applied the law correctly and followed appropriate rules of procedure. The court may also consider whether the underlying state law that led to a district court conviction violates the Utah or U.S. Constitution in any way.

The Utah Supreme Court is the court of final appeal for all interpretations of Utah law and of the Utah Constitution. Federal courts, including the U.S. Supreme Court, do not interpret state constitutions. Cases do not move from the Utah Supreme Court to the U.S. Supreme Court except in the rare circumstance when petitioners can persuade the U.S. Supreme Court that a particular case has a federal nexus—that is, that a Utah law or a provision of the Utah Constitution violates some superior provision in U.S. law or in the U.S. Constitution.

State supreme courts strike down fewer laws than does the U.S. Supreme Court despite hearing a similar number of cases. Since 1990 the U.S. Supreme Court has heard an average of 100.4 cases per year, declaring in 7.9 cases per year that some state or federal action violates the U.S. Constitution.[12] The nation's fifty state supreme courts have similar caseloads, averaging from 55 to 216 cases per year, yet the median state supreme court declares laws unconstitutional in only 1.3 cases per year. The Utah Supreme Court remains even more restrained than its peers, declaring laws unconstitutional in only 0.5 cases per year despite having a fairly typical overall caseload.[13]

The Utah Supreme Court flexes its judicial review muscles less often partly because the Utah Legislature works to keep the Utah Constitution manageable. Nationwide state constitutions vary tremendously in length (from 8,500 to 375,000 words), age (from 27 to 233 years), and amendment rate (from 0 to 28 amendments adopted over twenty years), and nationwide state supreme courts strike down laws more often in states with longer, younger, or less frequently updated constitutions (Brown forthcoming). These three variables operate independently. First, longer constitutions inevitably contain dense, restrictive policy detail, limiting policymakers' statutory flexibility and compelling state courts to enforce narrow boundaries on state policy actions.[14] Second, constitutions that receive fewer amendments often fail to address major issues of the day, leaving policymakers with ambiguous authority to address current societal needs; by contrast, regularly updated constitutions ensure that state governments have clear authority to address modern concerns.[15] And third, younger constitutions may contain fragile logrolls and lack clear judicial precedents, creating an uncertain legal environment and therefore increasing judicial invalidations of state actions.[16]

Compared to other state constitutions, Utah's is brief (17,849 words, the 33rd percentile among the states) and regularly amended (nineteen amendments over the past twenty years, the 78th percentile). As for age, Utah's 1896 constitution lies nearly on the 1890 median. Though Utah's constitution does not stand out for its age, its brevity and amendment rate help explain why the Utah Supreme Court strikes down laws less often than do other state supreme courts. Simply put, Utahns have kept the Utah Constitution current while avoiding the trap of making it too restrictive. As a result the Utah Supreme Court has one of the lowest invalidation rates of any state supreme court—and far lower than the U.S. Supreme Court's.

MERIT AND CONSENSUS

Federal judges at all levels are appointed at the president's pleasure; after confirmation by the U.S. Senate, they serve for life, regularly handing down momentous decisions. In the nation's highest court, U.S. Supreme Court justices vote in predictable ways, with Republican-appointed justices routinely disagreeing with their Democratic-appointed colleagues along measurable ideological lines.[17] As a result federal nominations have become high-profile, deeply partisan affairs. Even when voters dislike their party's presidential nominee, they may vote for him or her anyway to avoid losing control of the U.S. Supreme Court nomination process.[18]

Hoping to eliminate these sorts of ideological rifts within its state courts, in 1940 Missouri created the nation's first merit-based judicial selection system. Nearly half the states have since mimicked Missouri's innovation, including Utah, which adopted a merit-based selection plan in 1984.[19] Broadly speaking, merit-based judicial selection systems have two key features: first, judges are nominated not by the governor alone but by an expert bipartisan or nonpartisan nominating commission that sends a short list of approved names to the governor; second, judges must stand periodically for uncontested retention elections, in which voters indicate whether each individual judge should remain on the bench or be replaced.

To implement the merit plan, the Utah Constitution establishes several judicial nominating commissions. The statewide Appellate Court Nominating Commission handles vacancies in the Utah Supreme Court and in the Utah Court of Appeals; separate nominating commissions within each of the state's eight judicial districts handle vacancies within their respective district courts and juvenile courts. The governor appoints each of these commissions, subject to restrictions spelled out in the Utah Code. For example, the governor appoints seven members to the statewide Appellate Court Nominating Commission, but no more than four of these commissioners may belong to the same political party. The governor must draw two of these commissioners from a list of six nominees provided by the Utah State Bar, but no more than four commissioners may be members of the Bar. The governor selects the Commission's chair from among its membership. In addition the chief justice of Utah's supreme court appoints a nonvoting member of this Commission from among the court's membership. These complicated restrictions seek to ensure that each nominating commission is balanced in terms of partisanship, legal expertise, and judicial independence. When a vacancy arises in one of the state's appellate courts, the Appellate Court Nominating Commission sends a list of seven approved names to the governor. After the governor chooses a name from this list, the Utah Senate confirms the appointment.[20]

Once appointed, Utah's judges stand for occasional retention elections, where voters indicate whether each judge should remain in office or be removed. Voters do not choose between two candidates competing for a judicial vacancy; rather they simply check "yes" or "no" to retain each judge. Under the Utah Constitution a judge's first retention election occurs at the first general election held after three or more years of judicial service. Subsequent retention elections are held every ten years for appellate judges and every six years for district court judges. If the careful appointment procedure nevertheless places an unqualified or overly ideological judge on the bench, these retention elections provide a remedy; if voters remove a judge, the process starts over again, with the relevant nominating commission sending a new list of approved names to the governor.

Among the fifty states Missouri-style merit systems are the single most common judicial selection method. Most remaining states leave it to voters to elect judges directly, though a handful follow the federal model, allowing the governor to appoint judges subject to the state senate's confirmation (Council of State Governments 2015, table 5.6). These differences have provoked a vigorous research literature contrasting elected and merit-based judiciaries (Davis 2005; Bonneau and Hall 2009, 2017). In general, evidence suggests that elected judges write less scholarly judicial opinions (Goelzhauser and Cann 2014; Leonard and Ross 2016), give special courtroom consideration to their campaign donors (Cann 2007), rule more harshly on crime (Huber and Gordon 2004; Gordon and Huber 2007), and have more rulings overturned on appeal (Owens et al. 2015)—but also that elected judges are more productive (Choi et al. 2007) and more responsive to citizen preferences (Brace and Hall 1997, 2001; Brace and Boyea 2008).

Utah's merit system was designed to reduce ideological conflict and promote neutral judicial expertise in its place—and evidence suggests that it has succeeded. Unlike the U.S. Supreme Court, the Utah Supreme Court rarely issues divided opinions. To the contrary, most of the Utah Supreme Court's decisions are unanimous, with all five justices signing the majority opinion—or at the least, signing a concurring opinion. Figure 26 illustrates the trend since 1997. In a typical year, nine in ten Utah

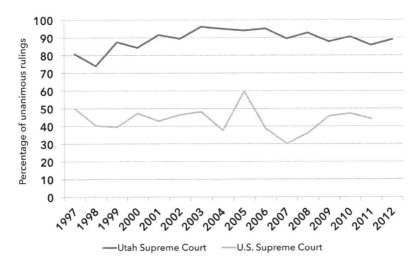

Fig. 26. Unanimity in the Utah and U.S. Supreme Courts. Compiled by the author.

Supreme Court rulings are unanimous; this is true of fewer than half of the U.S. Supreme Court's rulings.[21]

Of course Utah's Supreme Court operates in an overwhelmingly Republican state, which may predispose the courts toward greater consensus. However, for the first three years in figure 26 four of the Utah Supreme Court's five members were Democratic appointees left over from the Rampton and Matheson administrations. In 2000, two of these Democratic appointees retired and were replaced (under the merit plan) by appointees of a Republican governor, creating a court with two Democratic and three Republican appointees. By 2003 only one Democratic appointee remained on the bench—Christine Durham, appointed by Governor Matheson in 1982—alongside four Republican appointees. The court's 2000–2003 partisan transition did not expose sharp divisions; to the contrary, unanimity remained just as common during this period, a robust testament to the merit plan's ability to mute partisan squabbling on the state's highest court.

Nor is it the case that Utah Supreme Court justices simply defer to one another, lazily preferring not to take the time to think through each individual case. To the contrary, even those judges who agree with the court's verdict routinely make the effort to release concurring opinions articulating their own views. Over the period covered in figure 26, Thomas Lee authored an opinion in 43 percent of cases he participated in, Michael Zimmerman in 33 percent, Richard Howe in 29 percent, Daniel Stewart in 27 percent, Christine Durham in 26 percent, and Leonard Russon in 26 percent.[22] Clearly Utah Supreme Court justices take their work seriously.

Having ruled out partisanship and indolence as causes of the Utah Supreme Court's frequent unanimity, only one conclusion remains: the justices simply find more to agree on than do justices on the U.S. Supreme Court. Of course it may be unfair to compare unanimity on a five-member court to that on a nine-member court, since it is easier to get five people than nine to agree on anything. However, the pattern persists even when we use a more robust measure: the percentage of justices voting with the majority. For this comparison, the Utah court's smaller size works against it; a single dissent produces an 80 percent majority in Utah's five-member court but an 89 percent majority in the nine-member federal court. Nevertheless this measure still reveals tremendous agreement on Utah's court. For the period shown in figure 26, the average decision issued by the Utah Supreme Court found 97 percent of justices joining the majority, compared to 82 percent for the U.S. Supreme Court.

Even during periods of partisan transition, then, Utah's judges show far more agreement and far less partisan division than federal judges. Perhaps for this reason voters have never removed a Utah Supreme Court judge standing for retention, and they have removed only a small handful of lower court judges. To be sure, Utah is not the only state with high levels of consensus on its state supreme court. Data from the State Supreme Court Data Project show that 83 percent of state supreme court rulings in the median state are decided unanimously, a level approaching Utah's recent rates.[23] Nationwide, judicial consensus rates are higher in states (like Utah) using merit-based appointment than in states that elect their judges (Arceneaux et al. 2007); this difference is especially stark in states (like Utah) with low political competition (Choi et al. 2007).

A RESPECTED JUDICIARY

In 2016 a fifty-state study found that Utahns have more favorable views of their state supreme court than residents of almost any other state. Respondents answered a battery of questions to measure the popular "legitimacy" of each state supreme court; for example, one question asked whether the "state's highest court gets too mixed up in politics," and another asked whether the state's highest court should have less authority "to decide . . . controversial issues" (Cann and Yates 2016, 26). Utahns rated their state supreme court more favorably than respondents in forty-six states; only Washington, Connecticut, and California earned higher marks. Though the study found that evaluations were generally more favorable in states (like Utah) with a merit-based nomination system (Cann and Yates 2016, 45), Utah nevertheless stands out for its unusually high score.

This chapter began by showing that Utah courts labor in obscurity. Like Americans in other states, Utahns know little about the court system's structure or operations. Many lack even the most basic understanding of the court's role, unaware that Utah has its own constitution and that the Utah Supreme Court can strike down laws that conflict with it. Despite public ignorance, Utah's judicial branch operates smoothly. I have argued, first, that Utah's entry-level courts handle a tremendous caseload well enough to provoke very few appeals, reflecting competent organization and specialized courts. Second, I have argued that the brief but regularly updated Utah Constitution simplifies the Utah Supreme Court's work by providing proper legal authority for the elected branches to act, thereby reducing the court's need to engage in frequent judicial review. As a result the Utah Supreme Court hears fewer cases presenting difficult constitutional questions. Third, I have argued that Utah's merit-based judicial selection system successfully reduces partisanship and contention on the bench, promoting consensus in judicial rulings and raising popular esteem for the state's courts.

CHAPTER NINE

Local Governments

On September 30, 2014, the Salt Lake City Council passed an ordinance requiring businesses with drive-through windows to serve bicyclists, part of the city's "agenda of walkability and alternative transportation."[1] Salt Lake City's Democratic majority may support these progressive goals, but their city council governs only at the pleasure of the state's Republican legislature, which views matters differently. Claiming "the city overreached," a Republican legislator from Taylorsville, Representative Johnny Anderson, prepared legislation to preempt Salt Lake City's action.[2] As enacted during the 2015 General Session, Anderson's HB160 prohibits local governments from "requir[ing] a business that has a drive-through service . . . [to] allow a person other than a person in a motorized vehicle to use the drive-through service." Local governments statewide now lack authority to regulate nonvehicular drive-through traffic.

This drive-through spat marked but one in a long series of disagreements between Utah's Republican legislature and Salt Lake's Democratic city council. In October 1993 the city council enacted sweeping new firearms restrictions; the Utah Legislature responded with a state law prohibiting any local government from passing any ordinance relating to firearms.[3] In 2011, as residents of Salt Lake City's Yalecrest neighborhood pressed the city to designate their area a "historic district" to slow demolitions of century-old structures, a Republican legislator (and real estate developer) from another city passed SB243 to impose a moratorium on new municipal historic districts.[4] In each of these cases the legislature's action preempted Salt Lake City's.

There are exceptions of course. In 2009 Salt Lake City's Democratic mayor proposed an ordinance prohibiting employers and landlords from discriminating on the basis of sexual orientation. Conservatives throughout Utah blasted the proposal. Provo's *Daily Herald* published an editorial calling on the legislature to preempt Salt Lake's "crazy quilt gay agenda" should the city council proceed: "If [the mayor's] ordinance prevails in Salt Lake City, state lawmakers should immediately pass a statewide preemption statute covering discrimination, just like the statute that applies to firearms." The *Herald* continued, "Only the Legislature should be allowed to write law with respect to basic civil rights."[5]

The *Herald* did not get its wish. When the Salt Lake City Council held a final vote on the mayor's proposal a few weeks later, a spokesperson for the state's dominant religion, the Church of Jesus Christ of Latter-day Saints, surprised everybody by reading an official statement of support: "The city has granted common-sense rights that should be available to everyone, while safeguarding the crucial rights of religious organizations."[6] This statement split legislative Republicans; some still favored preempting Salt Lake City's action, while others sought to follow the Church's lead by passing a statewide nondiscrimination statute. The two sides stalemated for five years, until a new Church statement propelled a statewide nondiscrimination law to passage in early 2015.[7]

Even Republican-leaning cities complain about the legislature's micromanagement of municipal policy. In early 2010, for example, the legislature passed HB381, prohibiting municipalities from requiring landlords to bring their old rental properties into compliance with updated city codes. Under HB381 rental properties would need to conform to requirements in place only when they were first rented out. Though this bill was described in legislative floor debate as an innocuous technical clarification, its backers were consciously targeting the city of Provo, which had recently undertaken efforts to compel improvements in certain dilapidated rental units. Frustrated landlords, having lost their battle in Provo City Hall, worked quietly with a sympathetic legislator to preempt Provo's actions. Legislators did not learn the bill's true purpose until it had already passed. At that late moment one legislator from Provo regretted voting for the bill: "We made a mistake. . . . All the bills early on [in the session] are really just technical bills. This was buried in those, and it just got by us." A Provo community activist gave a more blunt assessment: "The very same Legislature that thinks it's terrible for the federal government to tell states how to run things passed two laws that now micromanage a city's zoning and tells cities how to run things."[8]

All these episodes illustrate a single point: the Utah Legislature has absolute authority to preempt any action taken by any local government. Though the Republican-leaning legislature uses that authority most often against Democratic-leaning Salt Lake City, the legislature can lawfully direct it anywhere—even against a Republican stronghold like Provo. With that in mind, this chapter begins by reviewing more carefully the legal status and authority of Utah's local governments as political subdivisions of the state. I then discuss the structure and operations of Utah's three main political subdivisions: counties, municipalities, and districts. Following these descriptive sections I present data from a survey of Utah's local officials to develop an argument about how they understand their role as local representatives. For the most part this analysis produces results similar to those in the discussion of legislative representation; that is, local officials care about constituent views but mostly find themselves governing as trustees rather than delegates. This survey of local officials also shows, once again, the unique influence of the LDS Church.

UNITARY GOVERNANCE AND DILLON'S RULE

Local governments provide ground-level services to citizens, with a focus on the basics: law enforcement, land use regulation (zoning, redevelopment, and eminent domain), and public works (parks, utilities, libraries, and roads). However, Utah's constitution does not formally endow local governments with any independent authority. That is, the state of Utah does not have a federal relationship with its local governments. Internally Utah—like every other American state—is unitary, with all authority vested solely in the state government. The Utah Legislature has absolute authority to create, modify, overrule, or remove any local government at any time. If it chose, the Utah Legislature could dissolve every local government and govern everything centrally from the capitol. Doing so would introduce massive inefficiencies in government administration, of course, but the legislature unambiguously has this right. Utah's local officials derive their authority not from the voters who elect them but from the state government.

Perhaps to emphasize this unitary relationship, the Utah Legislature refers generically to all counties, municipalities, and districts as "political subdivisions" of the state—language suggesting that local governments have no authority beyond what the state government delegates. All American states have this same absolute authority over their political subdivisions, a legal concept sometimes known as "Dillon's rule." The name references John Forrest Dillon, a nineteenth-century Iowa judge and legal scholar who wrote, "[Local governments] owe their origin to, and derive their powers and rights wholly from, the legislature. . . . As it creates, so may it destroy. If it may destroy, it may abridge and control."[9]

That said, Utah's local governments nevertheless enjoy more legal discretion than local governments elsewhere to adopt ordinances tailored to local needs. Outside Utah many state courts apply the narrowest possible reading of local government authority and freely strike down ordinances treading into new policy areas—areas where the state government has not yet delegated express authority.[10] In Utah, however, state courts have taken a broader view of local government authority. In 1980 the Utah Supreme Court ruled that the state's grant of general welfare powers to county and city governments authorizes them to adopt ordinances reasonably related to county or city goals, even where the legislature has not granted express authority, a principle known in Utah as "Hutchinson's rule."[11] To be clear, Hutchinson's rule does not restrict the legislature from preempting municipal actions; rather it authorizes local governments to enter new policy areas without explicit prior legislative delegation.

Taken together Hutchinson's (Utah-specific) rule and Dillon's (generally applicable) rule move most oversight of Utah's local governments to the legislature rather than the courts. Under Hutchinson's rule Utah courts view most local ordinances as presumptively permissible, even if those ordinances reach beyond those powers expressly delegated by the legislature. But under Dillon's rule the Utah Legislature retains full power to modify local governments' delegated authority at any time. In other states Salt Lake City's 1993 firearms restrictions, 2009 nondiscrimination ordinance, and 2014 drive-through ordinance might have met their end in state court for reaching too far beyond the authority granted by the legislature to municipal governments—a possibility made unlikely in Utah, though, by Hutchinson's rule. Instead it falls to the legislature to decide whether to adopt statutory language specifically forbidding municipalities from taking these sorts of actions. Laws restricting local government authority are known as preemption laws; the legislature preempted Salt Lake City's actions on firearms and drive-throughs, but not on nondiscrimination.

Dillon's rule gives the Utah Legislature absolute authority to preempt any local ordinance. In practice political concerns deter the legislature from exercising this power too often. After all, local governments are led by elected officials who can claim a popular mandate for ordinances they enact. Moreover Utah legislators' frequent harangues against federal intervention in state affairs arms local officials with abundant rhetorical ammunition against state intervention in local affairs. Utah's local governments employ powerful lobbying groups to make these arguments: the Utah League of Cities and Towns, the Utah Association of Counties, and the Utah Association of Special Districts. Utah legislators overrule local governments at their own risk.

FORMS OF LOCAL GOVERNMENT

Broadly speaking, local governments nationwide generally adopt one of three common forms of government: mayor-council, council-manager, and commission. Cities generally favor the first two forms, with 34 percent of cities nationwide using the mayor-council system and 55 percent using the council-manager system.[12] Commissions are more common among counties; twenty-three of Utah's twenty-nine counties are led by commissions.[13]

A mayor-council system follows the presidential form of government seen in Washington DC and in Utah's capitol, with separately elected legislative and executive branches. Just as the U.S. president and Utah governor hold executive powers while the U.S. Congress and Utah Legislature hold legislative powers, mayor-council systems vest executive power in a mayor and legislative power in a separately elected city council. Mayors in this system typically work full time and enjoy hefty administrative and budget authority as the city's chief executive, though some mayors work only part time and appoint a full-time city manager instead. These mayors often hold veto power over council decisions, subject to a council override. The mayor's responsibilities may include hiring and firing city employees, drafting an annual budget for council consideration, and overseeing the city's daily operations.

The more common council-manager system follows the parliamentary form of government seen in many European nations, in which a single elected body holds all legislative and executive powers but delegates its executive authority to a hired agent. In parliamentary nations that agent is the prime minister; in council-manager cities that agent is the city manager (or city administrator). This appointed city manager receives delegated authority to hire and fire city employees, draft an annual budget for council consideration, and oversee the city's daily operations. Legally executive authority resides with the part-time city council, not the city manager, and is exercised by the manager only at the council's pleasure.

City councils play the same basic role in both these systems, meeting regularly to consider new city ordinances, approve an annual budget, or take other legislative actions. Just as the U.S. House of Representatives selects a speaker to preside, city councils have a presiding councilor, sometimes chosen by the council itself, sometimes chosen by voters. In mayor-council systems the presiding councilor is usually called the council chair or council president; in council-manager systems the presiding councilor is usually called the mayor.

Both systems have a mayor, then, but the mayor's role differs drastically in each. In a mayor-council system voters elect the mayor separately as a chief executive officer, analogous to a U.S. president or state governor; in a council-manager system, voters or the council itself selects the mayor, who serves merely as presiding councilor, analogous to the speaker of the house. Mayors in a mayor-council system typically serve as full-time executives; mayors in a council-manager system typically play no executive role, with executive authority delegated instead to a city manager selected by the council as a whole. For these reasons mayor-council systems are sometimes called "strong mayor" systems, while council-manager systems are sometimes called "weak mayor" systems.

The commission system lacks a mayor and council. Instead voters elect several commissioners to a small governing board that holds both executive and legislative powers. The commission meets to exercise legislative powers by majority vote, such as adopting new ordinances or approving an annual budget. Each commissioner also holds executive power, though; typically each commissioner will hold a specific executive portfolio, such as responsibility for public works, health, emergency services, or utilities. In a commission system, then, individual commissioners hold partial executive authority while the commission collectively wields legislative authority.

Each American state has its own constitution declaring its powers and structure. Local governments do not generally have their own constitution, however. (When they do, it is called a "charter.") Instead Utah law declares the powers available to each type of government—that is, to a county, to a municipality, or to a district. State law also specifies the structure that each local government will adopt. Utah law provides one menu of structural options for counties, another for municipalities, and another for districts. We will consider each in turn.

COUNTIES

Utah's twenty-nine counties provide general services such as running jails, surveying property lines, issuing deeds and titles, recording birth certificates and wedding licenses, distributing vaccinations, and assessing property values for tax purposes. In unincorporated areas—that is, areas lacking a city or town government—counties provide additional services, such as law enforcement, fire protection, public parks, utilities, and land use planning.

Counties choose their form of government from a brief menu declared in Utah law. They may choose a commission government with three commissioners; an "expanded commission" government with five or seven commissioners; a mayor-council structure consisting of a county mayor (statutorily termed a county executive) and a county council; or a council-manager form consisting of an elected county council that hires a county manager.[14] By default all counties are assigned the three-commissioner form unless they take action to switch to one of the permissible alternatives. As a result twenty-three of Utah's counties have three-member commissions. Of the rest, two (Cache and Salt Lake) have adopted the mayor-council form, and four (Grand, Morgan, Summit, and Wasatch) have adopted the council-manager form. (Because Salt Lake County uses the mayor-council form, Utahns take care to differentiate between the Salt Lake County mayor and the Salt Lake City mayor.)

Utah law requires counties to supplement their core government—that is, their commission, mayor-council, or council-manager system—with several separately elected executives: an assessor, attorney, auditor, clerk, recorder, sheriff, surveyor, and treasurer. Less populous counties can consolidate two positions into a single officeholder, potentially vesting these eight executive offices in as few as four actual officeholders.[15] For example, twenty-one counties combine the clerk's and auditor's duties, the most common consolidation. Only Salt Lake County actually elects all eight county offices separately without any consolidation. Of the rest, eleven counties consolidate these eight offices into seven officeholders; eighteen consolidate them into six; and the remaining three consolidate them into four or five officeholders. All county officers are elected to four-year terms, with half a county's officers standing for election every two years.

MUNICIPALITIES

Municipalities—cities and towns—are general-purpose local governments with defined territorial jurisdictions. Utah contains 244 incorporated cities and towns; only ten have fifty thousand or more residents, while sixty-eight have fewer than five hundred.[16] As with counties, state law delegates certain powers to municipal governments and provides a menu of structural options.[17] Only nine Utah cities use the mayor-council ("strong mayor") system, and they tend to be Utah's older, larger cities: Salt Lake City, Provo, Sandy, Logan, Murray, Ogden, Taylorsville, South Salt Lake, and Marriott-Slaterville. Even fewer cities retain the council-manager ("weak mayor") system, being grandfathered in after the legislature eliminated this option in 2008: Orem, Holladay, Cottonwood Heights, West Jordan, West Valley City, Tremonton, and Brian Head.

The neighboring cities of Provo and Orem provide clear examples of these two very different forms of government. Provo's mayor holds all executive powers and works full time managing the city's government. The mayor has no formal role in city council meetings, just as the governor has no role in the Utah Legislature and the U.S. president has no role in Congress. However, Provo's mayor wields a veto over council decisions, which the council can override. By contrast, Orem's mayor is merely the ranking member of the city council. Unlike Provo's mayor, Orem's mayor participates actively in every city council meeting, conducting each meeting and participating in votes. Orem's mayor has no veto—only a vote—and, like other council members, works only part time. The Orem city council delegates its executive authority to a full-time city manager to oversee daily affairs. Provo has a mayor-council system; Orem has a council-manager system.

As it happens, only 16 of Utah's 244 cities have adopted one of these two archetypal forms of government that are so common nationwide. Of the remaining 228 cities, 227—93 percent—use hybrid structures unique to Utah known as the "five-member council" (102 cities) and the "six-member council" (125 cities). In both systems the mayor serves as chair of the city council, presiding at all council meetings. In the five-member system the mayor participates in all votes, while in the six-member system the mayor votes only to break ties and in other limited circumstances, detailed below; the two forms are otherwise the same. However, mayors in these systems also serve as the city's chief executive officer.

Mayors in the five- and six-member council systems are unusually strong, then. Council-manager mayors preside only over the legislative body, while mayor-council mayors preside only over the executive apparatus; by contrast, mayors in these unique Utah hybrids preside over both. Utah law provides some flexibility in how these mayors manage the executive branch, though. These mayors may appoint members of the city council to administer one or more city departments, which verges on the commission form of government; alternatively mayors may hire a full-time city manager to wield executive power on the mayor's behalf, which verges on the council-manager form.[18]

Utah law provides one additional structural option for municipal governance: crafting an original charter rather than adopting one of the forms of local government approved by the legislature. Article XI, Section 5, of Utah's constitution guarantees any Utah municipality this right, subject to certain restrictions. Only one Utah city has taken advantage of this provision, however: Tooele adopted a home rule charter in 1965, creating its own customized municipal government.[19] Though nothing stops other cities and towns from following Tooele's lead, Utah's other 243 municipalities have chosen from the legislature's menu.

Cities vary in other important ways beyond their executive and legislative structure, of course. Of particular note are municipal electoral systems. Utah's larger cities, including Salt Lake City, Ogden, Provo, Sandy, and Murray, use district-based electoral systems, where the city is divided into districts of equal population, and each district elects a single council member.[20] Most other Utah cities use at-large systems, where an entire slate of council members is elected in a single citywide election. State law allows cities to choose whether to use district-based or at-large elections, though it requires that all councilors serve four-year terms.

Counties and municipalities are general-purpose governments. That is, they provide a wide variety of basic services within their jurisdictions under broad grants of state authority. By contrast, special districts are single-purpose governments. Utah law allows for the creation of two types of special district: special service districts and local districts.[21]

Special service districts are created by existing city or county governments to provide a specific service that does not align neatly with a single city's or county's boundaries. The city or county governments that create special service districts appoint members to a governing board to administer the district's functions. For example, recognizing that their residents regularly travel from one community to the next, several Wasatch Front cities and counties created the Utah Transit Authority, a special service district that provides a regional transit system. Northern Utahns also rely heavily on another special service district, the Central Utah Water Conservancy District, which delivers water from the Uintah Basin to consumer counties along the Wasatch Front using a network of canals, tunnels, and reservoirs. As special service districts, the Utah Transit Authority and Central Utah Water Conservancy District are stand-alone government entities, with governing boards appointed by their member governments.

Local districts are created by citizen petition rather than by existing governments. Citizens can petition to create a local district to provide a specific service that existing governments choose not to provide. For example, if a particular county maintains only a handful of public cemeteries, all of which are far from some isolated rural community, residents of that community might petition to create a cemetery district. If successful, the newly created cemetery district would gain authority to assess a property tax on those living within the district boundaries (or use some other funding mechanism) to pay for the creation and ongoing maintenance of a local cemetery. Those living outside the district would not pay the tax, nor would they be entitled to the cemetery's services.

Special service districts and local districts are known collectively as special districts. According to the Utah Association of Special Districts, Utah has 238 local districts and 157 special service districts, a total of 395 special districts. These special districts provide cemeteries, water and sewer service, irrigation, emergency services, mosquito control, public transit, parks, roads, animal control, hospitals, snow removal, garbage collection, erosion control, public lighting, and other core services.[22]

School districts are not special districts, but they bear superficial similarities: they are single-purpose governments with clearly defined geographic boundaries. However, they are governed under different sections of state law, producing somewhat different structures. For example, all school districts are led by locally elected school boards, which govern local schools subject to limits established by state law and the State Board of Education. Some school districts have geographic boundaries that align with a particular city (such as the Provo City School District and the Salt Lake City School District), even though the school district is a separate government entity from the city government. Many school districts have boundaries unrelated to city boundaries, however, such as the Alpine School District, which covers the northern half of Utah County, and the Jordan School District, which serves southwestern Salt Lake County.

REPRESENTATION IN LOCAL GOVERNMENTS

Utah's local officials tend to be older and more educated than the general population and are more likely to be white, Republican, and male. These patterns are not unique to Utah; nationwide, elected officials overrepresent political and demographic majorities, as well as skewing older and male.[23] Among Utah's local officeholders, half are fifty-five or older, nearly two-thirds hold college degrees, three-quarters are male, and nearly all (97 percent) are white. These figures come from the Utah Elected Officials Survey, a 2010 poll of Utah officeholders administered jointly by the Utah League of Cities and Towns, the Utah Association of Counties, and scholars at the University of Utah and Brigham Young University.[24]

Table 4. Demographic profile of Utah's local officials, in percentages

	ELECTED OFFICIALS	UTAH VOTERS	UTAH POPULATION
College degree	62	58	31
55 or older	49	45	18
Male	76	48	50
White	97	94	86
LDS	85	67	55
Republican	75	62	43
Democratic	12	27	9
Independent	10	11	46

Source: Calculated by author from data in Hall et al. (2010). Other sources given in text.

Table 4 juxtaposes these statistics alongside Utah voters and the Utah population generally.[25]

Despite these demographic differences, local elected officials nevertheless value citizen input. In the Utah Elected Officials Survey, 76 percent placed "the opinions of city or town residents" among the two most important influences on their votes, followed by "my beliefs . . . in general" (51 percent), "the opinions of neighborhood or community organizations" (24 percent), "the opinions of local business leaders" (21 percent), "the opinions of other council members" (13 percent), "the opinions of city . . . staff" (13 percent), and "the opinions of local developers" (2 percent). On the whole 81 percent of local officials believe that "citizens' opinions are considered" before "the city makes major decisions."

At the same time local elected officials lament that poor attendance at city council meetings and other public hearings renders those meetings less useful than they otherwise might be. Though 86 percent call public hearings "an effective way for community residents to participate," and 82 percent feel that public hearings lead to better decisions, only 17 percent believe that "opinions expressed at public hearings are . . . an accurate reflection of how most community residents feel." Instead 44 percent complain that "special interests are too influential at public hearings." Still, 73 percent of these local officials say, "[I] have changed my mind . . . because of something a community resident said at a public hearing."

Recognizing the shortcomings of public hearings, local elected officials prefer one-on-one interactions with their constituents. When asked for "the single most effective way" for constituents to communicate with them, 91 percent preferred direct communication: 46 percent favoring a phone call, 33 percent preferring an email, and 12 percent recommending constituents personally visit the official's office. Only 7 percent named public hearings as "the single most effective way" for constituents to communicate with them.

These findings from the Utah Elected Officials Survey mirror the results from the Utah Legislator Survey presented in chapter 5. Like the legislators, local officeholders want to hear from constituents and prefer one-on-one conversations, whether in person, over the phone, or by email. Like legislators, however, local officeholders also see themselves as trustees rather than delegates. That is, they see themselves not as mere aggregators of constituent opinion but as independent actors tasked with studying difficult policy issues and making a good decision on behalf of the community and their constituents. The Utah Elected Officials Survey presented officeholders with a 5-point scale anchored by two competing statements about their "relationship with their constituents": elected officials should "do what their constituents want, even if it conflicts with what the elected official thinks is right" (often called delegate-style representation), or they should "do what they think is right, even if it conflicts with what their constituents want" (i.e., trustee-style representation). The results appear in figure 27. Only 19 percent chose the first two points on the scale, while 56 percent chose the latter two points; the rest chose the midpoint. Local officials, like statewide legislators, lean toward trustee-style representation.

As they make their decisions, many local officials conduct their business with scant staff support. When asked how much in-house staffing capacity their city or county had in several areas, 47 percent report high capacity for legal counsel, 52 percent report high capacity for financial accounting,

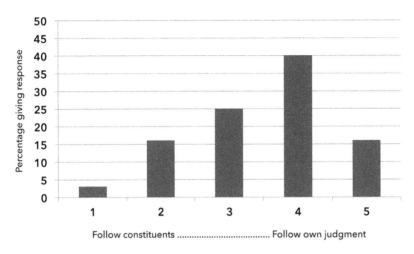

Fig. 27. How local officials understand their role. Calculated by the author from data in Hall et al. (2010).

and only 29 percent report high capacity for policy analysis.[26] At the other extreme 32 percent report inadequate capacity for legal counsel, 18 percent report inadequate capacity for financial accounting, and 32 percent report inadequate capacity for policy analysis. Many local officials, especially in Utah's smaller communities, govern on the fly without expert assistance.

Nevertheless Utah's cities and counties successfully deliver core services to their residents, starting with the basics: emergency services, roadways, land use planning, public utilities, and so on. Many go much further, providing public parks, recreation centers, high-speed Internet service, sports leagues, libraries, parades, and festivals. Nearly all (98 percent) local elected officials report regularly attending public hearings as part of their official duties, and—as noted earlier—most (76 percent) local officials place higher priority on constituents' opinions than on any other influence. If there is a central lesson to draw from the Utah Elected Officials Survey, then, it is that Utahns exert far more influence on their local elected officials than they may think. Research conducted nationwide supports this conclusion: American cities generally succeed at producing policy outcomes consistent with residents' desires—and it does not matter much whether cities use a mayor-council, council-manager, or commission form of government (Trounstine 2010; Tausanovitch and Warshaw 2014).

CHAPTER TEN

A Multibillion-Dollar Budget

In December 2015 Governor Gary Herbert unveiled a $14.8 billion budget proposal for FY2017. His proposal included $561 million growth in state spending, with $422 million of this increase directed toward public (K–12) education and higher education. To Herbert this $422 million increase for education was merely "a good start," but "not enough": "My plan is to invest another billion over the next five years into public education." House Speaker Greg Hughes received Herbert's budget proposal with aplomb: "We have different roles. . . . The [legislature], as it's designed with all its committee hearings, with the independent scrutiny that each lawmaker provides, will most likely come up with something" different.[1] In the end, though, the legislature more than endorsed the governor's education goals in the final budget, exceeding his proposed education increase by $23 million. Combined with increases from preceding years, the FY2017 budget included $1.7 billion more education funding than the FY2012 budget only five years earlier. Herbert praised the legislature, declaring, "We have reason to be very optimistic about the future . . . because of the funding that we're putting into education." David Crandall, chair of the Utah State Board of Education, concurred: "We're pleased. . . . It's a significant increase."[2]

Despite this growth, though, Utah continues to rank last nationwide in per pupil public education funding, falling behind all other states and the District of Columbia year after year.[3] Utah spends $6,555 per K–12 pupil, only 63 percent of the median state's $10,401 per pupil. Utah's neighbors vary widely. Idaho barely exceeds Utah, with $6,791 per pupil; Wyoming ranks near the top, at $15,700 per pupil (2.4 times Utah's rate); Montana's

$10,625 per pupil sits near the median. In fairness, per pupil spending is an educational input, not an output, and Utah's last-place spending does not necessarily indicate last-place performance. Stressing this point, State School Superintendent Brad Smith has urged Utahns to focus on improving Utah's middling ranking for student performance (twenty-seventh) rather than its abysmal ranking for per pupil spending.[4] Responding to this perspective, however, Governor Herbert has said, "It's not all about the money, but it is some about the money."[5]

Though the specific dollar amounts change, these same arguments recur over and over again in the legislature. Every year the budget process features battles over whether to increase Utah's lowest-in-the-nation per pupil spending, and every year the budget process provokes arguments about whether increased spending will actually produce improved outcomes. But these recurring battles over public education funding are only one piece of the state's overall budget puzzle, a puzzle that must be assembled anew every year. Every December the governor submits a budget proposal for the coming fiscal year, and every March the legislature enacts a final budget. No single task occupies so much of the legislature's time as formulating the annual budget, and no bill passed by the legislature impacts Utahns as much as the annual budget bills do. The people and dollar amounts may change, but the underlying disputes endure.

This chapter addresses Utah's budget politics. Utah's budget is a moving target; over just a few years the budget can shift significantly in both size and substance. As such, I avoid delving too deeply into the fleeting details of the current budget situation other than providing illustrative figures. Instead I discuss the size and composition of the budget generally, followed by a discussion of the state's budgeting process. In doing so I illustrate how the institutions discussed in previous chapters interact on the single largest matter of practical governance.

BUDGETARY TRENDS

No organization in Utah has a larger operating budget than the state government—and the state's budget grows nearly every year. In FY2003 the budget authorized only $7.5 billion in total spending. As shown in figure 28, the budget doubled over the next fifteen years, with $16.2 billion authorized for FY2018. The budget might have grown even faster during

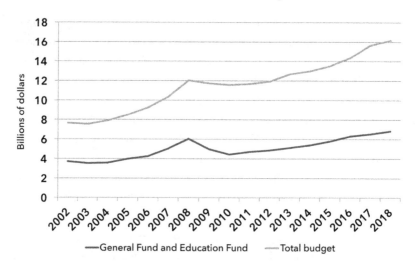

Fig. 28. Size of Utah's annual budget in billions of dollars. Compiled by the author.

these years if the unusually severe Great Recession had not forced steep cuts beginning in FY2008. Indeed most budgetary growth occurred in the four years immediately prior to the Great Recession, with 52 percent growth from FY2004 to FY2008. The budget grew more modestly after the recession, rising 38 percent over the seven years from FY2011 to FY2018.

Utah's tremendous budgetary growth does not reflect naked government expansion so much as underlying growth in the state's economy and population. In fact when calculated as a percentage of the state's overall economy, the budget has remained fairly constant and possibly even shrunk since FY2002. As shown in figure 29, state spending accounted for 10.0 percent of state GDP in FY2002, falling as low as 8.7 percent in FY2006, rising as high as 10.3 percent in FY2008, and finally stabilizing around 9.2 to 9.4 percent in subsequent years.[6] Utah's Republican-led legislature rarely increases tax rates, so state revenue growth reflects mostly economic growth.

Utah receives most of its revenue from general sales taxes, personal income taxes, and transfers from the federal government, though it also generates some revenue from specialized sales taxes (on gasoline, tobacco, and other products), corporate franchise taxes, mineral and energy royalties, the state liquor monopoly, and several other minor sources. Many

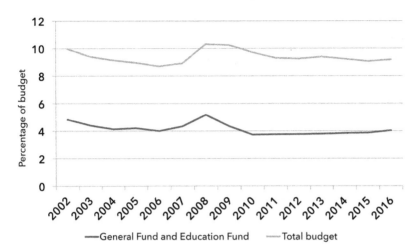

Fig. 29. Utah's state budget as a percentage of its gross domestic product. Calculated by the author.

of these revenue sources must be used for certain purposes; for example, income taxes may be spent only on education, gasoline taxes may be spent only on transportation projects, and federal funds provided by Congress are earmarked toward Medicaid and other uses. Utah tracks these earmarked purposes by depositing revenues into designated funds: the Education Fund, the Uniform School Fund, the Transportation Fund, Enterprise Funds, Capital Project Funds, and others. Most sales taxes are unrestricted and therefore appear in the state's General Fund.

Lawmakers have the most discretion over the General Fund (fueled mostly by sales tax) and the Education Fund (fueled mostly by income tax), making them the most politically important funds.[7] The Education Fund pays for public (K–12) school programs (accounting for 75 percent of FY2018 Education Fund expenditures), state colleges and universities (14 percent), public school administration (3 percent), and various other expenses. The General Fund pays for health services (accounting for 21 percent of FY2018 General Fund expenditures), other social services (22 percent), prisons and courts (18 percent), state colleges and universities (13 percent), the legislature's own operating expenses (1 percent), and many minor programs. These two funds account for only part of the state budget's massive growth over the past fifteen years, though, as shown in figures 28 and 29. As a result they have declined as a percentage of the total, from 50 percent in FY2008 to 42 percent in FY2018, with 15 percent from the General Fund and 27 percent from the Education Fund.[8]

These two major budget funds are rivaled only by federal transfers. Temporary federal stimulus funds helped maintain state spending levels during the Great Recession, preventing sharp cuts in the General Fund and Education Fund from excessively impacting the total budget. In FY2010, near the end of the Great Recession, these stimulus funds caused federal funds to peak at 32 percent of Utah's budget before returning to normal levels (26 to 28 percent of the budget) by FY2013. Federal money funded 27 percent of Utah's FY2018 budget; these federal transfers combined with the General Fund and Education Fund to account for 69 percent of Utah's FY2018 revenues—well within the typical range. Nearly half these federal transfers support Utah's Medicaid program. Most of the rest goes to freeway construction and other infrastructure or to state-federal social programs like the Children's Health Insurance Program and Temporary Assistance to Needy Families.

When all state and federal funds are brought together into a single overall budget picture, Utah's three largest expense categories are social services (dominated by Medicaid), accounting for 34 percent of authorized FY2018 spending; K–12 public education, accounting for 31 percent of authorized spending; and higher education, accounting for 11 percent (see Stevenson et al. 2017, 4). These three budget categories sum to 76 percent of Utah's spending. Other major spending categories are transportation (10 percent), state-level law enforcement (7 percent), and debt service (2 percent). These percentages from the FY2018 budget represent the continuation of long-term patterns. Year after year education and social services dominate state spending.

UTAH'S BUDGET PROCESS

Utah budgets on a fiscal year running from July 1 of one year to June 30 of the next, a schedule that allows the legislature to work out the new budget during its January–March General Session, then have it take effect a few months later. Fiscal years are numbered by the year's end; FY2020 spans July 1, 2019, through June 30, 2020. Like many states—but unlike the federal government—Utah's constitution requires a balanced budget.

That is, the legislature may not authorize spending that exceeds expected revenues. Therefore each year's budgeting process begins with legislative and gubernatorial staff collaborating to estimate expected tax revenues for the coming fiscal year based on current tax rates and economic trends.[9] To comply with the balanced budget requirement, the final budget may not authorize spending exceeding these staffers' "consensus revenue estimates" unless it also enacts a tax increase or other revenue enhancement to cover the cost.

Utah's constitution grants full budgetary authority to the legislature, subject only to the governor's veto (or item veto). Nevertheless the legislature has, by statute, conferred additional budgetary authority on the governor: Utah law requires the governor to deliver a draft budget to the legislature at least thirty days before the annual General Session and to publicly release a final budget by the General Session's third day (see discussion of Utah Code §63J-1-201, 2016 in chapter 7). (In practice governors generally release their proposal publicly by the first deadline.) Standing atop the entire state apparatus, the governor takes this opportunity to review state programs and recommend changes—recommendations that the legislature may heed or ignore.

Once the legislature convenes in its General Session, it divides the budget by policy area into several separate bills, sending each portion to a relevant appropriations subcommittee, where a handful of representatives and senators meet jointly.[10] Typically these appropriations subcommittees begin by carrying over all ongoing expenditures from the previous year's budget and stripping out one-time expenditures—that is, expenditures that were authorized for only a single year, such as construction projects and pilot programs. These subcommittees may also receive orders from legislative leadership to cut a certain percentage from their total budget, especially during recession years. Legislative rules require each subcommittee to send these pared-down "base budgets" back to the floor for a vote by the General Session's tenth day (see JR4-5-201). If, for some reason, the legislature failed to agree on a "real" budget by the end of the General Session, these austere base budgets would take effect.

Appropriations subcommittees then spend the remainder of the General Session reworking these base budgets into final budgets, conducting frequent public hearings to consider new programs and evaluate existing ones. Most budgeting work happens in these bicameral appropriations subcommittees, not on the house or senate chamber floor. As the General Session ends, each appropriations subcommittee sends its final proposal to the Executive Appropriations Committee (EAC), which consists of the leadership teams from both parties and both chambers. This high-level committee has complete authority to rewrite any portion of the budget. Ostensibly this authority empowers the EAC to ensure that the final budget package complies with the state's balanced budget requirement; in practice, of course, this authority also enables legislative leaders to ensure that the budget reflects their own priorities, as discussed in chapter 4. The EAC seldom holds public hearings, conducting most of its work informally behind the scenes. The 2017 General Session was typical: the EAC held only two public meetings in the session's final weeks—a five-minute meeting and a twenty-minute meeting—during which it summarily adopted thick packets of consolidated budget amendments negotiated privately in advance.

Legislative rules require voting on the general and education budget bills by the General Session's forty-third day and on all remaining budget bills by the forty-fifth (and final) day (see JR4-5-202 and JR4-5-203). These deadlines leave little room for floor debate in the short session. Of course by the time these budget bills arrive on the floor, the complete budget is so massive that genuine floor debate is mostly impossible anyway. Because of this most floor discussion of the budget bills is of the perfunctory and self-congratulatory variety. Budget bills routinely pass their floor votes by near-unanimous majorities.

In good years the budget process ends with these final floor votes held in March, which set state spending levels for the next fiscal year, starting nearly four months later on July 1 and ending nearly sixteen months later on June 30. In practice, however, even the best-trained economists cannot perfectly forecast tax revenues four to sixteen months in advance. The state budget relies heavily on income taxes and sales taxes, both of which are highly elastic with respect to economic growth and decline. If the economy grows faster than expected, then staffers' revenue estimates will underestimate actual tax revenues, and the state will find itself spending less than it earns; these excess revenues will simply be held in state accounts until the legislature enacts legislation to spend them. But if the economy slows, then staffers' estimates will overestimate revenues, and the state will find itself spending money it does not have—a far more serious problem.

To stay ahead of these possibilities, legislative and executive staff release updated consensus revenue estimates throughout the year. During the 2008 General Session, for example, the legislature enacted an optimistic budget for FY2009 (spanning July 2008 to June 2009) that anticipated continued economic growth. By late summer 2008, however, economists began noticing the first signs of the Great Recession, and plummeting tax revenues forced stark revisions to FY2009 consensus revenue estimates. Governor Jon Huntsman called the legislature into a special session in September 2008 to slash $350 million from the budget less than three months after it had taken effect. Unfortunately the economy continued its decline, so legislators revisited the budget once again during the next General Session, cutting another $300 million. If the legislature had not made these midyear cuts, state agencies would have been statutorily obligated to spend the full amount originally budgeted, plunging the state into deficit.

IMPLICATIONS OF UTAH'S BUDGET PROCESS

The federal government has shut down fourteen times since 1981 as a result of the U.S. Congress failing to enact a budget on time, most recently in February 2018.[11] Sometimes Congress has failed to pass a budget at all due to House-Senate disagreements; at other times the president has vetoed a congressional budget. Either way, the result is the same: shutdown. Utah, like many states, has never experienced a state government shutdown. Although Utah's budgeting process differs from the federal process in many ways, three key differences make a shutdown less likely in Utah than nationally.

First, Utah's legislative rules require adopting base budgets within the first ten days of the General Session. Congress has no such procedure, so congressional failure to enact a budget results in a complete government shutdown, while a legislative failure to enact a final budget results only in reversion to the (austere) base budgets. Although base budgets cut considerable spending compared to a regular budget and would cause real economic pain for many Utahns, the base budgets are sufficient to keep most government functions running.

Second, Utah's governor has item veto authority, while the U.S. president has only a full veto (or "package veto"). In 1981 President Ronald Reagan kept his promise to veto the federal budget if it did not include at least $8.4 billion in cuts, triggering the nation's first federal shutdown. Had he enjoyed item veto power, he could have simply vetoed portions of the budget he did not like and allowed the rest to pass into law, producing the desired $8.4 billion in cuts on his own. Lacking item veto power, he chose shutdown instead.

Third, Utah's balanced budget requirement takes the most difficult budgeting question off the table: how much to spend. Staffers' consensus revenue estimates dictate the maximum amount that legislators can allocate; allocating more requires explicitly changing Utah's tax laws to adjust state revenues. In Congress, by contrast, spending levels need not match revenues, complicating the budget process by injecting disagreements about the total size of the federal government into the already complicated budgeting process.

These three differences make budget stalemates far less likely in Utah than in Washington. If conflicts within the legislature prevent passage of a budget, the base budgets will kick in to prevent a shutdown; if conflicts arise between the legislature and the governor, the governor's item veto authority can resolve the standoff more gracefully than a package veto; and the balanced budget requirement focuses budget politics on how to spend existing money rather than on how much to spend.

CHAPTER ELEVEN

Different People, Similar Processes

In 1961 the renowned actor Robert Redford bought his first two acres behind Utah County's Mount Timpanogos, an investment that would later grow into the Sundance Mountain Resort and the Sundance Film Festival. Early on, his environmental and liberal activism caused frustrated locals to burn him in effigy—not once, but twice. He reflects on those years with aplomb: "The politics of the state are very conservative, and I'm not conservative."[1]

Redford's observation elides the difference between Utah's Republicanism and the Republicanism found elsewhere. Daniel Elazar (1966) once suggested that political competition revolves around different axes in different parts of the country because of varying political subcultures. Elazar described a "moralist" political culture that spread from New England across the northern plains to the Pacific coast, an "individualist" political culture that spread due west from the Mid-Atlantic states, and a "traditionalist" political culture in the Old South built on antebellum nostalgia. Elazar's formulation has received its share of criticism and revision over the years (e.g., Nardulli 1990; Lieske 1993, 2012; Rice and Sumberg 1997; Miller et al. 2006). Still, he reminds us that Republicanism can mean different things to different Republicans. Today's Republican Party brings together market deregulators, moral crusaders, defense hawks, nativists, libertarians, states' rights activists, and many others into a sometimes uncomfortable coalition.

That coalition became especially uncomfortable in 2016, when Republican nominee Donald Trump's caustic rhetoric roiled his party; even the Republican speaker of the U.S. House, Paul Ryan, walked back his support for Trump's candidacy, as did several other prominent Republicans. In the

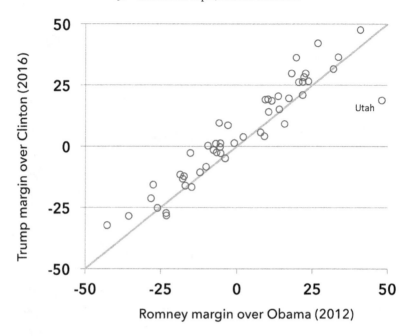

Fig. 30. Republican presidential vote shares in Utah and other states, 2016 versus 2012. Compiled by the author.

end Republican voters stuck with their party and placed Trump in the White House—but less so in Utah. Utah's Mormons are usually among the most reliable Republicans, but Trump won only 47 percent of the overall vote in a state that had given 73 percent of its votes to Republican nominee Mitt Romney in 2012 and 72 percent to George W. Bush in 2004.[2] According to the 2016 Utah Colleges Exit Poll, Trump received only 70 percent support among Utah's self-identified "strong Republican," "very active Mormon" voters.[3] True, 70 percent is still a supermajority, yet these same "strong Republican," "very active Mormon" voters gave 100 percent support to Romney in the 2012 exit poll and 100 percent to Bush in the 2004 exit poll, making themselves the nation's most loyal Republican bloc.[4] Clearly Trump underperformed dramatically among this bloc.

But here is the key point: only in Utah did Trump fail to consolidate the Republican vote. Figure 30 plots Republican vote margins in the 2016 presidential election (Trump) against the 2012 election (Romney). Trump fared better than Romney in states appearing above the diagonal reference line and worse in states appearing below it. In the average state Trump's 2016 margin versus Clinton was 4.9 percentage points higher than Romney's 2012 margin versus Obama—enough growth to secure victory. But in Utah Trump's margin was 29 percentage points *lower* than Romney's. After Utah the next largest shift away from the Republican candidate was a mere 7-point shift in Texas, followed by a 5-point shift in California. Something strange happened in Utah.

This book has detailed many ways that Utah's unique religious heritage continues to influence its politics today, and these results from the 2016 election provide yet another example. Trump lagged in Utah because he activated precisely those cleavages that make Utah's Mormon Republicans most different from Republicans elsewhere. From the day he announced his candidacy in June 2015, Trump took a belligerent tone against Muslim refugees from the Syrian conflict, even proposing that the United States prohibit Muslim immigrants from entering the country. Mormons remember well their forebears' nineteenth-century persecutions; there was even a time, in 1879, when U.S. Secretary of State William Evarts sought to prohibit Mormon immigrants from entering the country. Trump's anti-Muslim rhetoric provoked a rare rebuke from LDS headquarters. In a December 2015 statement Church leaders quoted to Mormons what Joseph Smith had said in 1843: "If it has been demonstrated that I have been willing to die for a 'Mormon,' I am bold to declare before Heaven that I am just as ready to die in defending the rights of a Presbyterian, a Baptist, or a good man of any denomination; for the same principle which would trample upon the rights of the Latter-day Saints would trample upon the rights of the Roman Catholics, or of any other denomination who may be unpopular and too weak to defend themselves."[5]

Trump's virulent anti-Mexican rhetoric, sexually charged comments, two failed marriages, extravagant lifestyle, and generally abrasive persona alarmed Mormons as much as his proposed Muslim ban. It did not help that few Utahns matched his blue-collar, Rust Belt–centric core constituency. Together these concerns caused Trump to receive less support in Utah's Republican caucus (14 percent) than in any other state's Republican primary.[6] After securing the nomination Trump continued struggling to bring Mormon Republicans to his side, even acknowledging in August 2016 that he had a "tremendous problem" in Utah.[7]

This is not a book about Trump or the 2016 election, of course, but a book about Utah politics. I began with a simple two-part thesis: Though Utah's institutions operate similarly to institutions elsewhere, Utah's voters are different, having been profoundly shaped by a unique religious and territorial history. Early Mormons were driven out of Missouri after Governor Lilburn Boggs issued his 1838 "extermination order"; LDS Church founder Joseph Smith was assassinated in 1844 in an Illinois prison despite the governor's personal promise of protection; deciding no peace was possible, Smith's successor, Brigham Young, led the Mormons far from American civilization into the Great Basin in 1847; the U.S. government sent the army to forcibly reassert its authority over the Mormons in the 1857 Utah War; and for the next several decades Mormons faced off against the federal government over polygamy and theocracy, finally reaching an accommodation in the 1890s. Chapter 1 reviewed this history. Chapter 2 showed how it continues to feed Utahns' simmering suspicion of federal authority even today. Chapter 3 explained how this history eventually gave rise to Utah's modern Republican supermajority—but with a peculiar brand of Republicanism, one deeply intertwined with Mormonism itself. And chapter 5 explored the LDS Church's policy impact, demonstrating that the Church influences policy less through direct lobbying and public appeals than by structuring cultural mores.

Not all Utahns are Mormon, of course. As chapter 3 also revealed, non-Mormon Utahns moved left in the 1970s and 1980s as Mormon Utahns moved right. Eventually they moved not only ideologically, but also physically (cf. Tiebout 1956). Increasingly, non-Mormons have become clustered most heavily in Salt Lake City, Park City, and Moab. In the nineteenth century these served as the centers of Utah's mining boom, hosting significant non-Mormon populations;[8] though no longer associated with mining, these cities remain non-Mormon centers. These cultural islands are as different from Utah as Utah is from the nation, to the point that *The Advocate*, a gay and lesbian news magazine, even ranked Salt Lake City the "gayest city" in America because of its high "per capita queerness."[9] In 2008 Democrat Barack Obama lost to Republican John McCain in all twenty-nine Utah counties—except the three counties containing these cities. In 2016 Democrat Hillary Clinton lost to Republican Donald Trump in all twenty-nine counties—except two of these three counties, losing the third (Moab's Grand County) by only four votes. Outside these islands Utah remains overwhelmingly Mormon and Republican.

Trump's Utah struggles serve as a stark reminder of Utah's unique political subculture. As this book has shown, however, Utah's political institutions mostly operate like institutions elsewhere despite these differences. Chapter 4 argued that Utah's citizen legislature operates like state legislatures elsewhere, except that its unusually short session and unusual lack of staff support mean that legislative leaders can exploit their procedural authority even more than legislative leaders elsewhere. Chapter 5 demonstrated that elected officials represent constituents and organized interests similarly to officeholders elsewhere, favoring trustee- over delegate-style representation, and also that organized interests employ familiar outsider and insider tactics. Chapter 6 found that the threat of an initiative can spur legislative action, just as has been observed in other states, though the threat is somewhat weaker in Utah than in states like California and Oregon, where qualifying an initiative is easier. Chapter 7 relied on widely used measures of gubernatorial power to argue that Utah's unusually strong governorship continues to promote Utah governors' unusual longevity in office. Chapter 8 claimed that Utah's merit system of selecting judges and its brief but regularly updated constitution reduce ideological conflict in the courts. Chapter 9 reviewed Utah's local governments, concluding that local officeholders behave similarly to their peers elsewhere. And chapter 10 showed that Utah's different branches interact in familiar ways to produce an annual budget.

Utah presents a study in contrasts. On the one hand, its political institutions fall well within the national mainstream; political scientists experienced with American politics generally can observe Utah's legislature, executive, courts, and local governments without having their assumptions significantly challenged. But on the other hand, Utahns themselves create a unique political subculture, and the LDS Church's cultural dominance unquestionably influences Utah policy. In short, Utahns are unique, but Utah is not.

FOR POLITICAL NEWCOMERS

The preceding section summarizes this book's major scholarly conclusion: Utah may have a different political subculture, yet its political institutions are familiar. I pause now to consider another set of lessons from this book, lessons applicable to those reading this book in hopes of getting involved in politics. After two terms as president, Theodore Roosevelt spent several months touring Africa and later Europe. In France he gave his "Citizenship in a Republic" speech on April 23, 1910, offering these memorable words: "It is not the critic who counts; not the man who points out how the strong man stumbles, or where the doer of deeds could have done them better. The credit belongs to the man who is actually in the arena, whose face is marred by dust and sweat and blood . . . who at the best knows in the end the triumph of high achievement, and who at the worst, if he fails, at least fails while daring greatly, so that his place shall never be with those cold and timid souls who neither know victory nor defeat."

Democratic politics is not a spectator sport. If citizens fail to engage their government, then consciously or not they abdicate their rights to vote and "to petition the Government for a redress of grievances," choosing to be governed rather than to govern themselves. Thankfully Utah's elected officials care more deeply about their constituents than voters may think, as shown especially in chapters 5 and 9. Still, constituents too often limit their own influence by misunderstanding how elected officials understand their role. To put it bluntly, voters see officeholders differently than those officeholders see themselves. In the 2010 Utah Colleges Exit Poll, 52 percent of Utah voters felt that elected officials should "do what their constituents want, even if it conflicts with what the official thinks is right"; only 27 percent said officeholders should "do what they think is right, even if it conflicts with what their constituents want." Officeholders, however, take precisely the opposite view. Thus voters see officeholders as delegates who should carefully follow constituent opinion, but officeholders see themselves as trustees who should study issues and then exercise independent judgment.

Voters who wish to influence elected officials must see officeholders as they see themselves: as trustees, not delegates. Erroneously thinking they are addressing delegates rather than trustees, many citizens speaking for the first time in a city council meeting or other public hearing make the mistake of simply stating their stance on an issue and expecting elected officials to fall in line. Because elected officials see themselves as trustees rather than delegates, however, they wish to be persuaded rather than given mere marching orders. In addressing trustee-minded officeholders, citizens have greater influence when they eschew impassioned pleading in favor of statistical, constitutional, statutory, historical, or even anecdotal evidence. Government bodies hold frequent public meetings to which they invite residents to speak, and outside these meetings voters can telephone and write to officeholders. In all these venues concrete evidence has more sway on trustee-minded officeholders than an emotional plea or a threatened loss of electoral support.

As the stakes rise and organized interests get involved, citizen activists should remember the lessons of chapter 5: officeholders need not only persuasion but assistance. For this reason citizens engaging major issues or higher-level officials often benefit from contributing to or volunteering with an organized interest they agree with so that the organization can pool resources to engage officeholders and prepare handouts, talking points, and media guides.

More often than not, however, entering the arena requires no more than writing to or telephoning an elected official, attending a city council meeting or other public hearing, or showing up to a politician's town hall meeting. On Twitter officeholders engage Utahns directly, often using the #utpol (Utah politics) and #utleg (Utah Legislature) hashtags; on Facebook many officeholders maintain pages for more personal interaction. Those looking to deepen their involvement can run for party delegate at neighborhood caucuses, volunteer on a campaign, or join an advocacy group. Through it all, constituents will find greater success if they see officeholders as they see themselves: as trustees.

Each year America's fifty state legislatures pass one hundred times as many bills as Congress, and America's fifty state court systems hand down one hundred times as many rulings as the federal court system. City and county governments add countless additional ordinances to these totals. It is America's state and local governments that foster economic growth, police crime, educate children, combat poverty and homelessness, fight fires, license businesses, inspect restaurants, provide water and electricity, build airports, and create robust communities. Fortunately Utah's state and local governments are as accessible as they are essential. Every Utahn can attend local city or county meetings, and four in five Utahns live within an hour's drive of the state capitol and can easily observe the legislature's deliberations. Government "of the people, by the people, for the people" cannot exist without the people.

Appendix 1

Utah's capitol stands, fittingly, on Capitol Hill, though the hill once had other names. Salt Lake City's first settlers called it Prospect Hill. After large powder stores were built there in the 1860s, it became Arsenal Hill. On April 5, 1876, two teenage boys tending cattle near the powder cache were seen to shoot a rifle at some birds. One of their shots apparently went astray, starting a chain reaction that detonated forty tons of gunpowder. The boys died, the blast shattered most windows in the city, and boulders rained down blocks away, killing a young child playing outside and a woman pumping water. One reporter described the scene as "a column of smoke and debris as grand as Vesuvius ever belched forth."[1]

At the cost of these four lives and extensive property damage, the explosion also cleared prime real estate. In 1888 Salt Lake City ceded twenty acres on Arsenal Hill to the state for a future capitol. In 1909, thirteen years after Utah achieved statehood, the legislature approved a Capitol Commission to oversee the new building's construction. Construction spanned 1912 to 1916. Financial constraints prevented the new state from fulfilling all aspects of the architect's plan, but the state nevertheless acquired a beautiful classical home. After a small tornado caused modest damage in 1999, inspections revealed the capitol's vulnerability to an earthquake or other disaster. Renovations spanning 2004 to 2008 not only provided seismic retrofitting but also fleshed out the architect's original vision, constructing elements that were financially out of reach a century earlier.

Today the capitol complex includes four rectangular buildings around a central square featuring a large oblong fountain. The capitol building itself lies to the south. It holds the house and senate chambers, the Utah Supreme Court's historic chambers, the governor's suite, several legislative committee rooms, offices for legislative leaders and committee chairs, and suites for Utah's other executives: the lieutenant governor, attorney general, state auditor, and treasurer.

To the west stands the house building, where rank-and-file representatives have offices. This structure also houses legislative support offices, including the Office of Legislative Research and General Counsel, the Office of the Legislative Fiscal Analyst, the legislative intern workroom, and several committee rooms. To the east stands the senate building, where rank-and-file senators have offices. This building also houses several conference rooms and other support facilities. Room numbers start with W (for "west") in the house building and E (for "east") in the senate building. To the north stands the nondescript State Office Building, constructed between 1959 and 1961. Executive agencies and the legislative auditor general occupy this building.

Appendix 2

DATA TABLES

The tables in this appendix contain information drawn from historical records and the U.S. Census. Table 5 draws on archived legislative journals to list Utah's governors, speakers of the house, and senate presidents since statehood, with shading indicating Republican control. Tables 6, 7, and 8 draw on the U.S. Census to provide demographic profiles of Utah and its twenty-nine counties. Table 9 illustrates Utah's continuing movement toward the Republican Party by presenting county-level Republican vote shares from the 1988, 2000, and 2012 presidential elections.

Table 5. Utah's governors and legislative leaders since statehood

YEAR	GOVERNOR	HOUSE SPEAKER	SENATE PRESIDENT
1896	Heber Wells	Presley Denny	George M. Cannon
1897	Heber Wells	John M. Perkins	Aquila Nebeker
1899	Heber Wells	William Roylance	Aquila Nebeker
1901	Heber Wells	William Glasmann	Abel Evans
1903	Heber Wells	Thomas Hull	Edward Allison
1905	John Cutler	Thomas Hull	Steven Love
1907	John Cutler	Harry Joseph	Steven Love
1909	William Spry	Edward Robinson	Henry Gardner

1911	**William Spry**	**Edward Robinson**	Henry Gardner
1913	**William Spry**	**William Seely**	Henry Gardner
1915	**William Spry**	L. R. Anderson	W. Mont Ferry
1917	Simon Bamberger	John Tolton	James Funk
1919	Simon Bamberger	Charles Richards	James Funk
1921	**Charles Mabey**	**Edward Callister**	Thomas McKay
1923	**Charles Mabey**	**William Seegmiller**	Thomas McKay
1925	George Dern	**William McKell**	**Alonzo Irvine**
1927	George Dern	**S. M. Jorgensen**	**Alonzo Irvine**
1929	George Dern	**David Stein**	**Hamilton Gardner**
1931	George Dern	**James Hacking**	**Ray Dillman**
1933	Henry Blood	I. A. Smoot	J. Francis Fowles
1935	Henry Blood	Walter Granger	Herbert Maw
1937	Henry Blood	Joseph Jensen	Herbert Maw
1939	Henry Blood	Heber Bennion Jr.	Ira Huggins
1941	Herbert Maw	Sheldon Brewster	Wendell Grover
1943	Herbert Maw	W. R. White	Grant McFarlane
1945	Herbert Maw	W. R. White	Dexter Farr
1947	Herbert Maw	**Rendell Mabey**	Alonzo Hopkin
1949	J. Bracken Lee	Ed McPolin	Alonzo Hopkin
1951	J. Bracken Lee	Clifton Kerr	J. Francis Fowles
1953	J. Bracken Lee	**Merrill Davis**	**Mark Paxton**
1955	J. Bracken Lee	**Charles Peterson**	**C. Taylor Burton**
1957	**George Clyde**	**Jaren Jones**	Orval Hafen
1959	**George Clyde**	Sheldon Brewster	Sherman Lloyd
1961	**George Clyde**	Ernest Dean	Thorpe Waddingham
1963	**George Clyde**	**Charles Welch Jr.**	Reed Bullen

1965	Calvin Rampton	Kay Allen	Bruce Jenkins
1967	Calvin Rampton	**Franklin Gunnell**	Haven Barlow
1969	Calvin Rampton	**Lorin Pace**	Haven Barlow
1971	Calvin Rampton	Richard Howe	Haven Barlow
1973	Calvin Rampton	**Howard Nielson**	Haven Barlow
1975	Calvin Rampton	Ronald Rencher	Ernest Dean
1977	Scott Matheson	**Glade Sowards**	Moroni Jensen
1979	Scott Matheson	**James Hansen**	Miles "Cap" Ferry
1981	Scott Matheson	**Norm Bangerter**	Miles "Cap" Ferry
1983	Scott Matheson	**Norm Bangerter**	Miles "Cap" Ferry
1985	**Norm Bangerter**	**Robert Garff**	**Arnold Christensen**
1987	**Norm Bangerter**	**Glen Brown**	**Arnold Christensen**
1989	**Norm Bangerter**	**Nolan Karras**	**Arnold Christensen**
1991	**Norm Bangerter**	**H. Craig Moody**	**Arnold Christensen**
1993	**Mike Leavitt**	**Rob Bishop**	**Arnold Christensen**
1995	**Mike Leavitt**	**Mel Brown**	**Lane Beattie**
1997	**Mike Leavitt**	**Mel Brown**	**Lane Beattie**
1999	**Mike Leavitt**	**Martin Stephens**	**Lane Beattie**
2001	**Mike Leavitt**	**Martin Stephens**	**Alma "Al" Mansell**
2003	**Mike Leavitt, Olene Walker***	**Martin Stephens**	**Alma "Al" Mansell**
2005	Jon Huntsman	**Greg Curtis**	John Valentine
2007	Jon Huntsman	**Greg Curtis**	John Valentine
2009	Jon Huntsman **, Gary Herbert	David Clark	**Michael Waddoups**
2011	Gary Herbert	Rebecca Lockhart	**Michael Waddoups**
2013	Gary Herbert	Rebecca Lockhart	Wayne Niederhauser

| 2015 | **Gary Herbert** | **Greg Hughes** | **Wayne Niederhauser** |
| 2017 | **Gary Herbert** | **Greg Hughes** | **Wayne Niederhauser** |

* Olene Walker, Utah's first female governor, served for one year following Mike Leavitt's appointment to George W. Bush's presidential cabinet (November 2003), until her successor, Jon Huntsman, took office following the November 2004 election.

** Shortly after winning reelection in 2008, Huntsman accepted Barack Obama's request to serve as ambassador to China. Gary Herbert took office in August 2009.

Note: For speakers and senate presidents, only the first person to assume office following November elections is listed; those who filled vacancies midyear are omitted. Bold indicates Republican control.

Source: Compiled by author from legislative journals.

Table 6. Utah's changing demographic composition

INDICATOR	1990 UTAH	1990 USA	2010 UTAH	2010 USA
Population	1,722,850	248,709,873	2,763,882	308,745,538
Area (mi²)	82,170	3,794,101	82,170	3,794,101
Population / mi²	21.0	65.6	33.6	81.4
Median age	26.3	32.9	29.2	37.2
Under 20 years old	40.0%	28.7%	34.8%	27.0%
Over 64 years old	8.7%	12.6%	9.0%	13.0%
White alone	91.2%	75.6%	80.4%	63.7%
Black alone	0.6%	11.7%	0.9%	12.2%
Asian/Pacific alone	1.9%	2.8%	2.8%	4.8%
Native American alone	1.3%	0.7%	1.0%	0.7%
Hispanic (any race)	4.9%	9.0%	13.0%	16.3%
Average household size	3.15	2.51	3.10	2.58
Average family size	3.67	3.03	3.56	3.14

Source: U.S. Census data.

Table 7. Population, area, and density of Utah's counties

COUNTY	POPULATION	AREA (MI²)	POPULATION PER MI²
Beaver	6,629	2,590	3
Box Elder	49,975	5,746	9
Cache	112,656	1,165	97
Carbon	21,403	1,478	14
Daggett	1,059	697	2
Davis	295,332	299	988
Duchesne	18,607	3,241	6
Emery	10,976	4,462	2
Garfield	5,172	5,175	1
Grand	9,225	3,672	3
Iron	46,163	3,297	14
Juab	10,246	3,392	3
Kane	7,125	3,990	2
Millard	12,503	6,572	2
Morgan	9,469	609	16
Piute	1,556	758	2
Rich	2,264	1,029	2
Salt Lake	1,029,665	742	1,388
San Juan	14,746	7,820	2
Sanpete	27,882	1,590	18
Sevier	20,802	1,911	11
Summit	36,324	1,872	19
Tooele	58,218	6,941	8
Uintah	32,588	4,480	7

Utah	516,564	2,003	258
Wasatch	23,530	1,176	20
Washington	138,115	2,426	57
Wayne	2,589	2,461	1
Weber	231,236	576	401

Source: U.S. Census data, 2010.

Table 8. Racial and ethnic composition of Utah's counties, in percentages

COUNTY	WHITE	BLACK	HISPANIC	NATIVE AMERICAN
Beaver	89.0	0.2	10.8	1.1
Box Elder	91.8	0.3	8.3	0.8
Cache	89.1	0.6	10.0	0.6
Carbon	92.3	0.4	12.4	1.2
Daggett	95.9	0.4	3.1	0.8
Davis	90.0	1.2	8.4	0.5
Duchesne	89.2	0.2	6.0	4.5
Emery	93.9	0.2	6.0	0.7
Garfield	94.1	0.4	4.5	1.6
Grand	89.0	0.3	9.6	4.1
Iron	90.7	0.5	7.7	2.2
Juab	95.9	0.2	3.7	0.9
Kane	95.7	0.2	3.7	1.5
Millard	87.6	0.1	12.8	1.0
Morgan	97.5	0.2	2.4	0.2
Piute	94.7	0.1	7.0	0.3

Rich	97.0	0.0	4.2	0.7
Salt Lake	81.2	1.6	17.1	0.9
San Juan	45.8	0.2	4.4	50.4
Sanpete	90.4	0.8	9.4	1.1
Sevier	94.9	0.2	4.5	1.1
Summit	90.5	0.4	11.5	0.3
Tooele	90.7	0.7	11.4	1.0
Uintah	86.6	0.4	7.1	7.7
Utah	89.4	0.5	10.8	0.6
Wasatch	90.4	0.3	13.5	0.5
Washington	89.7	0.6	9.8	1.4
Wayne	94.8	0.1	4.2	0.5
Weber	85.2	1.4	16.7	0.8

Source: U.S. Census data, 2010. Totals may exceed 100 because the census allows respondents to mark multiple racial categories.

Table 9. County-level partisan trends, 1988–2012

COUNTY	% GOP 1988 (G. H. W. BUSH)	% GOP 2000 (G. W. BUSH)	% GOP 2012 (ROMNEY)	CHANGE, 1988–2012
Beaver	61	75	86	+25
Box Elder	82	83	90	+8
Cache	79	83	85	+6
Carbon	35	53	69	+34
Daggett	67	75	81	+14
Davis	75	77	82	+7
Duchesne	72	82	91	+19

Emery	56	77	87	+31
Garfield	80	91	86	+6
Grand	60	61	54	-6
Iron	78	85	87	+9
Juab	61	77	88	+27
Kane	82	85	77	-5
Millard	76	85	91	+15
Morgan	74	82	91	+17
Piute	70	82	90	+20
Rich	73	83	92	+19
Salt Lake	60	61	60	0
San Juan	63	60	59	-4
Sanpete	72	83	90	+18
Sevier	77	85	91	+14
Summit	60	57	52	-8
Tooele	57	66	76	+19
Uintah	75	83	91	+16
Utah	79	86	90	+11
Wasatch	63	72	77	+14
Washington	81	82	84	+3
Wayne	69	83	84	+15
Weber	65	66	73	+8

Source: Calculated by author from official election canvasses. Percentages shown are the Republican share of the two-party presidential vote, ignoring minor parties.

NOTES

INTRODUCTION

1. Hillary Clinton, "Exclusive: Hillary Clinton: What I Have in Common with Utah Leaders," *Deseret News* (Salt Lake City UT), August 10, 2016. For reactions, see Cristiano Lima, "Clinton Opens Campaign HQ in Utah," *Politico*, August 22, 2016; Dora Scheidell and Brittni Strickland, "Former President Bill Clinton Visits Utah for Hillary Clinton Campaign," *Fox 13 Now*, August 11, 2016; Rebecca Shabad, "Hillary Clinton Reaches Out to Mormon Voters in Effort to Win Utah," *CBS News*, August 10, 2016.

2. Questions placed by the author on the March 2013 Utah Voter Poll, an instrument described later in this chapter. With 1,054 respondents, the margin of error was ±3 percent.

3. Citations for these statistics are given in relevant chapters.

4. In their defense the same can be said of many states' residents, though ignorance of state politics rises in states like Utah, where elections are less competitive and where the ideological divisions between parties are less stark (Lyons et al. 2013).

5. These were multiple-choice questions; the results would have been poorer still with an open-ended format.

6. Utahns cast 1.13 million ballots in the 2016 presidential race but only 1.03 million in the seventy-five state house races. Of these, 0.34 million ballots were straight-ticket ballots, in which voters merely chose a party without viewing any candidate names. Thus of the 0.79 million voters who manually selected a name in the presidential race, only 0.69 million selected a name in a Utah House race, a roll-off rate of 12 percent. On ballot roll-off as an indicator of voter ignorance and apathy, see Brown (2011).

7. See Utah Education Network, "Social Studies Core," n.d. uen.org/core /socialstudies/.

8. See Piacenza (2015). Chapter 4 reviews other estimates of Utah's Mormon population, some of which produce higher figures.

9. See Adam R. Brown, "Research about the Utah Legislature," n.d. adambrown .info/s/utleg.

10. Margin of error calculations assume a 50–50 split among respondents; as opinions grow more lopsided, the margin of error approaches zero.

11. See "Utah Colleges Exit Poll," exitpoll.byu.edu. The exit poll's methods are discussed in Grimshaw et al. (2004). The Utah Voter Poll has been discontinued and no longer has an online presence; archived data are held by the Center for the Study of Elections and Democracy at Brigham Young University.

1. A CHURCH AND A STATE

1. See especially Alexander (2007), Carter (2003), Farmer (2008), Lyman (1986), May (1987), Peterson and Cannon (2015), Powell (1994), Verdoia and Firmage (1996), Walker et al. (2011), and Whitley (2006). For general information, see Utah State Historical Society (n.d.). Citations are not provided in this chapter for general claims that appear in most or all of these sources, only for specific quotations or lesser-known historical claims.

2. These are the people formerly known as Anasazi, a Navajo epithet meaning "our enemies' [the Pueblos'] ancestors" but now known more respectfully as the Ancestral Puebloans. Their descendants are today's Pueblo peoples (the Hopi, Zuni, and Pueblo tribes).

3. It is not clear whether the Shoshone, Ute, Paiute, and Goshute peoples conquered the Fremont, absorbed them, or resettled lands abandoned due to drought (Alexander 2007, 39). Alexander provides a map of each tribe's settlement patterns (40).

4. This paragraph draws particularly on Carter (2002) and Farmer (2008, 27–29).

5. As practiced among Utah's tribes, the Spanish-Indian slave system involved abducting children and adolescents from other tribes and selling them to merchants who brought them to Mexican settlements for baptism and then slave labor. Farmer (2008) and Carter (2003) discuss this slave trade as practiced among the Timpanogos, as well as the cultural conflict that ensued when the Timpanogos later tried to involve Mormon settlers.

6. An Illinois census counted 11,057 Nauvoo residents in 1845 (Leonard 1992). Converts from Europe and elsewhere continued to arrive in the months following Joseph Smith's assassination. Estimates of the city's peak population prior to the 1846 exodus vary widely but reach as high as 15,000 (Black 1995; Leonard 1992). Meanwhile Hoyt (1933, 50) places Chicago's population at 12,000 in 1845 and 14,000 in 1846.

7. Whether Young actually spoke the famous words "This is the right place" when entering Salt Lake Valley remains underdetermined, but Farmer (2008, 40) suggests Young set out without deciding which valley to settle.

8. See Carter (2003) and Farmer (2008, 41) on Bridger's warning and its impact on Young.

9. For vivid accounts of these clashes, see Carter (2003) and Farmer (2008).

10. Farmer (2008) provides a detailed account of this changing cultural geography and the new population's forgetting—partly willful, partly not—of the Timpanogos expulsion.

11. Because of this rash decision, some label this conflict "Buchanan's Blunder" (Aird 2011; Bailey 1978; Farmer 2008, 97; Poll and Hansen 1961). See also Greg Bradsher, "From Buchanan's Blunder to Seward's Folly," posted November 26, 2013, to the blog of the National Archives, https://text-message.blogs.archives .gov/2013/11/26/from-buchanans-blunder-to-sewards-folly-sort-of/.

12. Each side's tactics are detailed in Poll and Hansen (1961).

13. Many details surrounding this event, including clarity about who exactly ordered it, have been lost to history. See Alexander (2007, 129–34), Farmer (2008, 96), or May (1987, 99–100) for brief accounts. For a thorough account, see Walker et al. (2011). These works also provide accounts of the Utah War generally. For the Church's perspective, see Church of Jesus Christ of Latter-day Saints, "Peace and Violence among 19th-Century Latter-day Saints," May 2014, https://www .lds.org/topics/peace-and-violence-among-19th-century-latter-day-saints.

14. The following paragraphs summarize information found in Whitley (2006). Claims about the Bingham Canyon's mine size and output draw additionally on Rio Tinto Kennecott, "Kennecott Utah Copper's Bingham Canyon Mine: Teacher Guide," 2009, http://www.kennecott.com/library/media/TeacherGuide.pdf.

15. For more on the dissident Godbeites who founded the *Mormon Tribune*, as well as the origin of the Liberal and People's Parties generally, see Alexander (2007, 170–74).

16. The first women to cast a ballot in the United States did so in Utah, after the territorial legislature enfranchised women in 1870. (Wyoming granted women suffrage shortly before Utah, but Utah held the first actual election featuring women voters.) Twenty-three-year-old Seraph Young, Brigham Young's niece, is credited as the first woman to vote in a U.S. election; a large painting depicting her in the polling place adorns the chambers of the Utah House of Representatives.

17. Woodruff's statement appears as "Official Declaration 1" in *The Doctrine and Covenants of the Church of Jesus Christ of Latter-day Saints*, a canonized volume published by the Church.

18. For the Church's perspective, see Church of Jesus Christ of Latter-day Saints, "Plural Marriage in the Church of Jesus Christ of Latter-day Saints," October 2014, https://www.lds.org/topics/plural-marriage-in-the-church-of-jesus-christ -of-latter-day-saints.

19. It is the FLDS, not the AUB, that regularly receives critical press coverage owing to allegations of underage marriage and welfare fraud. The FLDS president, Warren

Jeffs, has been imprisoned since 2007 (first in Utah, but in Texas since 2011) for his involvement in coerced underage marriages (*BBC News*, "US Polygamy Sect Leader Sentenced," November 20, 2007; also Lindsay Whitehurst, "Warren Jeffs Gets Life in Prison for Sex with Underage Girls," *Salt Lake Tribune*, August 10, 2011). Several FLDS leaders and adherents were arrested in February 2016 on suspicion of committing a vast welfare fraud conspiracy (Erin Alberty, Jessica Miller, and Nate Carlisle, "Polygamous Church Leaders and Members Indicted," *Salt Lake Tribune*, June 9, 2016).

20. On these efforts to integrate into the national party system, see Alexander (2007, 201).

21. See Grover Cleveland, "Proclamation 382: Admitting Utah to the Union," January 4, 1896, http://archives.utah.gov/research/exhibits/Statehood/presproc.htm.

22. Almost. A constitutional amendment proposed as HJR12 in the Utah Legislature's 1945 Regular Session and later ratified by Utah voters made minor changes to the public lands provision, allowing the state to tax some of these lands under certain circumstances. Otherwise these four constitutional ordinances remain unchanged.

23. Representative Mike Noel ran HB99 during the 2017 General Session of the Utah Legislature to stiffen state laws against polygamy. When FLDS and other polygamists testifying against the bill sought to point out their common heritage, he lashed out, "The fact that individuals come up [to the legislature] and testify they are FLDS Mormons insults me and bothers me. They are an apostate group and they are no part of my religion" (quoted in Nate Carlisle, "LDS Church Has Been Brought into Polygamy Debate at Utah Legislature," *Salt Lake Tribune*, March 1, 2017). To the FLDS, AUB, and other polygamist offshoots, of course, the modern LDS Church's abandonment of polygamy is equally heretical.

24. For section-by-section commentary, see White (2011).

25. These claims about the Utah Constitution draw on data described in the introductory chapter. Readers may visit the author's website to view the raw text of all amendments and compare the Utah Constitution at different points in time: adambrown.info/s/utconst.

26. All comparisons in this paragraph draw on an original twenty-year (1994–2013) dataset covering all fifty states described in Brown (2015).

27. Utah's constitution also differs in another important way: it has never been replaced. Utah remains only one of nineteen states to retain its original constitution. Only twenty states have a constitution younger than Utah's—even though only five states were created after Utah. Perhaps Utah's preference for amending rather than replacing its constitution grows out of the four irrevocable ordinances mandated in the 1894 Enabling Act, which could complicate wholesale

replacement. This preference may also reflect a general nationwide shift against replacement. After all, most twentieth-century replacements happened before 1970, when Utah's constitution was still relatively young; the most recent state to replace its constitution did so in 1986.

28. Utah poll administered by the author to a representative sample of 402 Utah adults (weighted for age and gender) via Google Consumer Surveys, June 14–16, 2016. Wording: "Off the top of your head, do you happen to know whether your state has its own constitution?" Response options: "Yes, my state has its own constitution" (39.5 percent), "No, my state does not" (8.4 percent), "I don't know" (52.1 percent). Margin of error ±5.6 percentage points. Using the same wording, a national poll pegged awareness of state constitutions at 53 percent (National Center for State Courts 2009).

2. A STATE AND A NATION

1. On Roberts, see Peterson and Cannon (2015, 18); on Smoot, see page 24 in the same volume.

2. From Dieter Uchtdorf's "Faith of Our Father" address at the Church's April 2008 General Conference.

3. The 67 percent figure includes other federal lands, particularly Defense Department lands; see Gorte et al. (2012).

4. Author's calculation based on 2010 U.S. Census data. The percentages here reflect the population and land area of Weber, Davis, Salt Lake, and Utah counties.

5. See generally Riker (1975) and Hanson (2008).

6. Some writers employ more colorful terms, such as "marble cake" and "layered cake" federalism, to describe how much overlap there is between state and federal authority (Grodzins 1966; Hanson 2008; Donovan et al. 2013).

7. This interpretation originates in *McCulloch v. Maryland* (1819). As an interesting aside, it was President James Madison's policy being challenged (and ultimately upheld) in this decision. For his leading role in organizing the Constitutional Convention, crafting the actual Constitution, and advocating its ratification, Madison is often revered as the "father of the Constitution."

8. Quoted from the majority opinion in *United States v. Carolene Products Co.* (1938). This logic gave rise to the "rational basis" test used by federal judges to adjudicate the constitutionality of many congressional actions. See also Ellis (2007).

9. See generally Ellis (2007).

10. The U.S. government adjusts these matching rates regularly. Utah's low per capita income results in an unusually generous match. Updated rates appear in the Federal Register but are found more easily at Kaiser Family Foundation, "Federal

Medical Assistance Percentage (FMAP) for Medicaid and Multiplier," n.d., http://kff.org/medicaid/state-indicator/federal-matching-rate-and-multiplier/.

11. From Herbert (2016, 30).

12. See Skowronek (1982) and Ellis (2007).

13. For critical arguments against federal expansion from Utah's most vocal anti-federalist, see Ivory (2011) and Ken Ivory, "Here Is Why Utah Should Acquire Its Federal Lands," *Deseret News* (Salt Lake City UT), March 11, 2012.

14. Their video manifesto was uploaded February 25, 2010, as "Revolution Media: Patrick Henry Caucus," youtu.be/U5legitZhpo.

15. In 2013, HB160 replaced the requirement to seek advance authorization with a weaker requirement to simply report in advance on what actions would be taken, what specific sections of the Affordable Care Act required those actions, and what the cost would be. In 2015, SB18 moved this language in the Utah Code from §63M-1-2505.5 to §63N-11-106 without otherwise changing it.

16. HB234S1 also prohibited state agencies from complying with the REAL ID Act. At risk of federal sanction, the Utah Legislature repealed those prohibitions in SB25 two years later.

17. Debate over the meaning and questionable historicity of the neologism "compound Constitutional republic" appeared in David Rockwood, "Op-ed: 'Democracy' Is the Umbrella Term for Our Government," *Salt Lake Tribune*, July 1, 2011; Ken Ivory, "Op-ed: Name of Government Matters," *Salt Lake Tribune*, July 8, 2011; and Adam Brown, "Do We Live in a 'Compound Constitutional Republic' or Something Else?," *Utah Data Points*, July 11, 2011, http://utahdatapoints.com/2011/07/do-we-live-in-a-compound-constitutional-republic-or-something-else/.

18. See Adam Brown, "The Tea Party's Declining Favorability," *Utah Data Points*, April 2, 2012, http://utahdatapoints.com/2012/04/the-tea-partys-declining-favorability/; Kyrene Gibb, "Brewing a Weaker Tea?," *Utah Data Points*, June 5, 2012, http://utahdatapoints.com/2012/06/brewing-a-weaker-tea/; Lee Davidson, "Patrick Henry Caucus Founders All Lose—but Claim Higher Victory," *Salt Lake Tribune*, April 30, 2012; Dennis Romboy, "Former Patrick Henry Caucus Pals Moving on without Each Other," *Deseret News* (Salt Lake City UT), April 30, 2012.

19. These figures are drawn from the 2010 Cooperative Congressional Election Study, a large-scale study coinciding with the November 2010 elections. Only neighboring Idaho (barely) exceeded Utah's support for the Tea Party—a state with the nation's second-highest LDS population.

20. When additional agencies—notably the U.S. Defense Department—are added to these four, federal management rises to 67 percent of Utah's territory (Gorte et al. 2012).

21. See Gorte et al. (2012).

22. For example, in a March 23, 2012, statement posted to his official blog, Governor Gary Herbert praised his fellow state leaders for "highlighting the interrelationship between public lands and education [funding]," claiming that "federal control of our public lands puts Utah at a distinct disadvantage with regard to . . . future fiscal needs" (see https://governorblog.utah.gov/2012/03/utahs-public -lands-a-new-paradigm/). On similar efforts in other states, see Hanson (2008) and Wilson (2014).

23. This historical overview of American public lands policy draws on Gorte et al. (2012), Muhn and Stuart (1988), Smith and Freemuth (2007), and especially Wilson (2014), as well as various government documents: the U.S. Constitution, the Northwest Ordinances, Utah's Enabling Act and Constitution, and legislative acts named in the text.

24. Claim based on author's examination of enabling acts archived on various state and federal government websites. Hawaii stands as an interesting exception. In its statehood act "the United States grants to the State of Hawaii, effective upon its admission into the Union, the United States' title to all the public lands and other public property" within Hawaii, with only a few exceptions.

25. Wilson (2014) provides a thorough summary of these ever-sweetening terms of sale.

26. See Muhn and Stuart (1988) and Wilson (2014) for additional information on these acts.

27. See Egan (2009), Rettie (1995), and Wilson (2014) on the origins of these agencies.

28. See Wilson (2014, 192).

29. Bernard DeVoto, "The West against Itself," *Harper's Magazine*, January 1947, 50. See Wilson (2014, 192) for further context.

30. Philip Bump, "That Time Ronald Reagan Joined a 'Rebellion'—but Still Couldn't Change Federal Land Laws," *Washington Post*, January 4, 2016.

31. See Rettie (1995, 4–5) and Wilson (2014).

32. Quoted in Lee Davidson, "Orton's Bill Would Erase Power to Declare Permanent Monument," *Deseret News* (Salt Lake City UT), September 27, 1996.

33. Sarah Kaplan and Carissa Wolf, "Cliven Bundy Arrested in Portland as Oregon Occupiers Say They Will Surrender," *Washington Post*, February 11, 2016.

34. Lee Davidson, "San Juan's Embattled Phil Lyman Gives up Commissioner of the Year Award," *Salt Lake Tribune*, October 22, 2015; Brian Maffly, "Utah Taxpayers Off the Hook, Gov. Gary Herbert First to Sign Up for Lyman's Legal Defense Fund," *Salt Lake Tribune*, June 24, 2015; Ben Winslow, "County Commissioner Phil Lyman Gets 10 Days Jail, 3 Years Probation for Recapture Canyon

Ride," *Fox 13 Now*, December 18, 2015, http://fox13now.com/2015/12/18/county
-commissioner-phil-lyman-gets-10-days-jail-3-years-probation-for-recapture
-canyon-ride/.

35. Julie Turkewitz and Kirk Johnson, "Ammon Bundy and 7 Oregon Protestors
Held; LaVoy Finicum Is Reported Dead," *New York Times*, January 27, 2016.

36. See Church of Jesus Christ of Latter-day Saints, "Church Responds to Inquiries
Regarding Oregon Armed Occupation," http://mormonnewsroom.org/article
/church-responds-to-inquiries-regarding-oregon-armed-occupation.

37. The bill exempted national parks, national historic sites and monuments (except
Grand Staircase-Escalante), and national wilderness areas created prior to January 1, 2012.

38. On the economic stakes of land transfer, see Utah Foundation (2013).

39. Michelle L. Price, "Utah Gears Up for Lands Fight as Deadline Passes," *Salt Lake
Tribune*, January 3, 3015.

40. HB148 directed the Constitutional Defense Council to prepare legislation to
create this public lands commission.

41. See Howard et al. (2015). See also Brian Maffly, "Republicans OK $14m Land-
Transfer Lawsuit, Say Utah Must Regain Sovereignty," *Salt Lake Tribune*, December 9, 2015.

42. Quoted in Michelle L. Price, "Western Attorneys General Cast Doubt on Utah's
Bid to Control Federal Lands," *Salt Lake Tribune*, September 30, 2016.

43. Proclamation 9558, issued December 28, 2016, has been archived at White House,
"Presidential Proclamation: Establishment of the Bears Ears National Monument," December 28, 2016, https://obamawhitehouse.archives.gov/the-press
-office/2016/12/28/proclamation-establishment-bears-ears-national-monument.

44. The December 4, 2017, White House proclamations may be found at White
House, "Presidential Proclamation Modifying the Bears Ears National Monument," December 4, 2017, https://www.whitehouse.gov/the-press-office/2017
/12/04/presidential-proclamation-modifying-bears-ears-national-monument;
White House, "Presidential Proclamation Modifying the Grand Staircase-
Escalante National Monument," December 4, 2017, https://www.whitehouse
.gov/the-press-office/2017/12/04/presidential-proclamation-modifying-grand
-staircase-escalante-national.

45. Trump's proclamation came as this book went to press, and the legal picture
remains a moving target. Within a day of Trump's proclamation, for example, a
coalition of five Native American tribes filed suit challenging his changes to Bears
Ears, and a separate coalition of environmental advocates filed suit challenging
changes to Grand Staircase-Escalante. See Courtney Tanner, "Five American

Indian Tribes, Furious over Trump Shrinking Bears Ears on His Trip to Utah, Sue the President," *Salt Lake Tribune*, December 4, 2017.

46. For opinion pieces from the bill's advocates, see Ivory, "Here Is Why Utah Should Acquire Its Federal Lands"; Robert G. Natelson, "Op-ed: There Is Legitimate Basis for States' Claims to Federal Lands," *Salt Lake Tribune*, July 31, 2015; David P. Hinkins, Keven J. Stratton, Wayne Niederhauser, and Greg Hughes, "Op-ed: Until Utah Controls Its Federal Lands, Utahns Will Be Second-Class Citizens," *Salt Lake Tribune*, April 2, 2016; see also Fretwell and Regan (2015). For critical opinions, see Arthur Caplan, "Op-ed: Land Transfer Study Based on Shakiest of Assumptions," *Salt Lake Tribune*, December 25, 2014; Ashley Korenblat, "Op-ed: Time to Let Ivory and His Empty Promises Go," *Salt Lake Tribune*, September 4, 2015; Veronica Egan, "Op-ed: Embattled Public Land Managers Need Our Support," *Salt Lake Tribune*, February 4, 2016; John D. Leshy, "Op-ed: Lands Transfer to States? It Would Take Another Dred Scott Decision," *Salt Lake Tribune*, January 30, 2016; Robert H. Nelson, "Op-ed: The Risks and Rewards of Federal Land Transfer? The Numbers Are Available," *Salt Lake Tribune*, March 17, 2016; Adam Cramer, John Sterling, and Amy Roberts, "Op-ed: Federal Lands Transfer Would Be a Blow to Utah's Recreation Economy," *Salt Lake Tribune*, January 6, 2016.

3. A PECULIARLY REPUBLICAN PEOPLE

1. For media characterizations of the "Mormon Moment," see Kristine Haglund, "What the 'Mormon Moment' Actually Accomplished," *Slate*, December 1, 2014, http://www.slate.com/articles/life/faithbased/2014/12/mormon_moment _is_over_but_it_changed_mormon_culture_for_good.html; Cadence Woodland, "The End of the 'Mormon Moment,'" *New York Times*, July 14, 2014; Matthew Crandall, "What the Mormon Moment Wrought," *Real Clear Religion*, May 13, 2015, http://www.realclearreligion.org/articles/2015/05/13/what_the_mormon _moment_wrought_106986.html.

2. For detailed historical comparisons, see Adam Brown, "Update: The 2015 Legislature Will Be Utah's 2nd Most Republican Since the Depression," *Utah Data Points*, November 20, 2014, http://utahdatapoints.com/2014/11/update-the-2015 -legislature-will-be-utahs-2nd-most-republican-since-the-depression/.

3. Data for 1897–2005 comes from Christensen et al. (2005); subsequent years compiled by author. Percentages omit the handful of seats held by independents and minor parties.

4. On these efforts to end religious-based partisan cleavages, see Alexander (2007, 201–3) and Fox (2006). See chapter 1 for further discussion of this theme.

5. Again see Alexander (2007, 201–3). Peterson and Cannon (2015) provide an especially detailed narrative of this period.

6. On following Church leaders' political cues, see Campbell and Monson (2007).

7. The lone exception arose in 1960. Kennedy won the close 1960 election by less than 0.2 percentage points nationally; Utah voted for Nixon by a similarly slim margin.

8. On this realigning dynamic generally, see Noel (2012).

9. See also Campbell et al. (2014, 86), Fox (2006), and Pew Forum on Religion and Public Life (2012) on Mormons' shift right in the 1970s, as well as on modern Mormons' voting habits.

10. Latter-day Saints call themselves "peculiar" in the sense of a people set apart from the world for a special purpose, evoking the ancient Abrahamic covenant. See, for example, Smith (1992).

11. Sells (2005) presents worthwhile perspectives from several prominent non-Mormon Utahns about their experience in the political minority.

12. Specifically I estimate an ordered probit model where the dependent variable is partisan self-identification (−1 for Democrats, 0 for independents, and +1 for Republicans, with leaners coded as partisans). I code education dichotomously based on whether the respondent had earned at least a four-year degree. Dichotomous racial indicators include black, Hispanic, and other nonwhite, with white as the omitted reference category. Age ranges from eighteen to ninety-five. A first (baseline) model includes only these variables. A second model includes dichotomous variables for Utahn, Mormon, and Mormon Utahn (an interaction of Utahn and Mormon); though these variables have unambiguous statistical significance, adding them does not appreciably change those coefficients that were included in the baseline model. Detailed statistical output available from author.

13. Conducting the same analysis using the 2012 CCES instead—the year of Romney's run—reveals marginally (but insignificantly) larger effects, with a Utah Mormon 40 percentage points more likely to be Republican than a typical American, and a Utah non-Mormon 7 points less likely.

14. I use 2014 data here owing to the unusual effects of Evan McMullin's independent 2016 candidacy.

15. To be clear, I compare a dichotomous Mormon-versus-other variable against a 3-point partisan identification scale (Democrat, independent, or Republican).

16. On polarization nationally, see McCarty et al. (2006), Jacobson (2007), and Levendusky (2009), but see also Fiorina et al. (2005).

17. Ideology is measured here along a 5-point scale from liberal to conservative.

18. Party balance rankings are based on Ranney indices from 2003 to 2006 as calculated by Gray and Hanson (2008, 84).

19. I define a "freshman" as somebody who has never previously served in either chamber of the legislature. Because many senators have previously served in the Utah House, this measure is less useful in analyzing turnover in the Utah Senate, which I omit from this discussion. I identify freshmen by examining each year's historical legislative roster, a copy of which can be found on the legislature's website as well as in archived legislative journals.

20. In 1922 the Utah House expanded from forty-seven to fifty-five seats; in 1932 it expanded again to sixty seats. These expansions naturally increased the percentage of freshmen in the following session.

21. For more on the link between imbalance and turnout in Utah, see an excellent report by the Utah Foundation (2012).

22. On the effect of competitiveness on turnout, see Downs (1957) and Riker and Ordeshook (1968).

23. The numerator is the number of votes cast for president. vap and vep are different denominators. vep subtracts from vap ineligible populations like felons, noncitizens, and institutionalized persons. On the superiority of vep over vap for multistate and multiyear comparisons, see McDonald and Popkin (2001). Data post-1980 courtesy of Michael McDonald (electproject.org). Data for earlier years compiled by the author from the Lieutenant Governor's Office (vote.utah.gov) and from the American Presidency Project at uc Santa Barbara (www.presidency.ucsb.edu/data/turnout.php).

24. See Rohde (1991), Aldrich (1995), and Aldrich and Rohde (2000a, 2000b), who include this dynamic in their concept of "conditional party government."

25. See Key's (1949) seminal dissection of one-party politics in the southern states for application of this insight outside Utah.

26. Even in 2010, at the height of the very conservative Tea Party movement, 39 percent of Republican respondents were "strongly conservative" compared to 49 percent "moderately conservative." Most remaining Republicans chose "middle of the road" (sometimes phrased in these polls as "moderate").

27. On the effects of mass intraparty division on elite intraparty division, see Ladewig (2005).

28. Although delegates are chosen only a few weeks before the convention, officeholders and candidates start wooing potential delegates far earlier. Since the same pool of people tend to serve repeatedly as delegates, wooing future delegates simply involves wooing past ones. In April and May 2012 byu's Center for the Study of Elections and Democracy cooperated with both state parties to survey Democratic and Republican delegates to the two state conventions. That year 58 percent of Democratic delegates and 47 percent of Republican delegates had served as a delegate in the past; 35 percent (Dem) and 24 percent

(Rep) had served more than once (J. Quin Monson, "Topline Results for Republican and Democratic Delegate Surveys," *Utah Data Points*, June 7, 2012, http://utahdatapoints.com/2012/06/topline-results-for-republican-and-democratic-delegate-surveys/).

29. Utah itself adopted a direct primary in 1937, reverting to a caucus-convention system in 1947. At that time the convention runner-up needed only 20 percent of delegates' support to force a primary; over the years the parties increased the cutoff, arriving at 40 percent in 1999 (Utah Foundation 2011).

30. Kelly Patterson, "Who Is a Better Filter, Caucus Attendees or Primary Voters?," *Utah Data Points*, February 24, 2014, http://utahdatapoints.com/2014/02/who-is-a-better-filter-caucus-attendees-or-primary-voters/.

31. Christopher Karpowitz and Jeremy Pope, "The Monkey Cage: The Problems with Caucuses and Conventions," *Washington Post*, February 10, 2014, https://www.washingtonpost.com/news/monkey-cage/wp/2014/02/10/the-problems-with-caucuses-and-conventions/?utm_term=.6efe60c47a5f.

32. Most 2016 Republican nomination contests ended at the state or county conventions. The 246,529 figure comes from the Republican gubernatorial primary.

33. Poll results reported by Bob Bernick, "Poll Shows Sen. Bob Bennett in Trouble with Utah GOP Delegates," *Deseret News* (Salt Lake City UT), April 25, 2010. To be sure, the poll showed that Bennett was in trouble; he pulled only 32 percent support among Republicans generally, followed by Lee at 12 percent. Giving this low support, it is not surprising that Bennett lost—only that he did not make it to the primary.

34. See Church of Jesus Christ of Latter-day Saints, "First Presidency Issues Letter on Utah Precinct Caucus Meetings," February 13, 2012, http://mormonnewsroom.org/article/first-presidency-issues-letter-utah-precinct-caucus-meetings.

35. Demographic statistics throughout this section draw on U.S. Census data unless stated otherwise.

36. These official LDS membership statistics were compiled by the Cumorah Project and are available at "Country Resources," http://www.cumorah.com/index.php?target=countries&cnt_res=2&wid=231&wid_state=306.

37. For 2009, see Pew Research Center, "A Portrait of Mormons in the U.S.," July 24, 2009, http://www.pewforum.org/2009/07/24/a-portrait-of-mormons-in-the-us/. For 2014, see Pew Research Center (2014).

38. Author's analysis of data from the 2014 Utah Colleges Exit Poll, with responses weighted by key demographic indicators. Data available at Brigham Young University, Utah Colleges Exit Poll, exitpolldata.byu.edu.

39. Income data from the U.S. Census. Fertility data from Centers for Disease Control, "Births: Final Data for 2010," *National Vital Statistics Reports* 61 (2011), https://

www.cdc.gov/nchs/data/nvsr/nvsr61/nvsr61_01.pdf, and Utah Department of Health, "Data List for General Fertility Rates, Utah vs. U.S., 2004–2014," at https://ibisdev.health.utah.gov/ibisph-view/indicator/view/FertRat.UT_US_Age.html.

4. LEGISLATING IN THE PEOPLE'S BRANCH

1. This view pervades pro-ratification writings. For example, Federalist 55 asserts that Congress has too much power for too few representatives to wield, while Federalist 70 exhibits no such fear about vesting all executive powers with a single president, whose veto would "check excesses in the majority" (Hamilton et al. [1787] 2003).

2. Seeing so much delegation, some conclude that Congress has abdicated its policymaking responsibilities altogether (Niskanen 1975; Lowi 1979; Healy 2010; Webb 2013). Others counter that Congress has simply found the most efficient way to govern a large, complex society, whose policy problems demand greater technical expertise than Congress could ever develop internally (McCubbins and Schwartz 1984; Kiewiet and McCubbins 1991). On the emergence of the American administrative state generally, see Skowronek (1982).

3. Recordings of past floor debates may be found at the Utah Legislature's website, le.utah.gov.

4. From Utah Governor, "Governor Acts on Remaining 52 Bills Today," press release, March 30, 2011, http://www.utah.gov/governor/news_media/article.html?article=4567.

5. At statehood there were forty-five seats in the house and eighteen in the senate. The legislature raised these numbers gradually until a 1972 amendment to the Utah Constitution capped the senate at twenty-nine seats, with a provision that the house would remain between two and three times this number—that is, between fifty-eight and eighty-seven seats. Without amending the constitution, the legislature can adjust the house's size within this range, though it has not done so since the 1970s.

6. Based on data in Council of State Governments (2015).

7. More precisely the numbers were 36,852 and 95,306 after the 2010 U.S. Census.

8. Calculations by author using chamber sizes from Council of State Governments (2015) and U.S. Census population estimates.

9. Forty state constitutions have some sort of germaneness provision; in the forty-first, Mississippi, germaneness is merely implied. The remaining nine states are Arkansas, Connecticut, Maine, Massachusetts, New Hampshire, North Carolina, Ohio, Rhode Island, and Vermont (National Conference of State Legislatures n.d.). Gilbert (2006) shows that state courts tend to enforce a narrow reading of single-subject rules. Brown (2012) addresses some implications of these provisions.

10. The following paragraphs summarize material from the Utah Legislature's rules, available in full via the legislature's website, le.utah.gov.

11. I estimate staffing numbers by counting employees listed in the public employee database at UtahsRight.com as earning $30,000 or more per year within these offices, a cutoff that leaves out interns and part-time employees.

12. On the effects of low legislator salary on candidate recruitment and electoral competitiveness, see Fiorina (1994, 1999), Rosenthal (1974), and Squire (1988, 1992, 2000, 2007).

13. Calculations from Hamm and Moncrief (2008, table 6-1) based on Squire's (2007) method.

14. Curiously the hours reported in the table add up to seventy-one per week during session and nineteen per week during the interim, exceeding the sixty-five and thirteen hours (respectively) that legislators reported when I asked simply for an estimate of total hours worked. Because legislators typically completed the survey quickly, perhaps it is unsurprising that their responses do not add up perfectly.

15. Current legislator compensation levels were enacted in 2013's HJR6. Legislators living far from the capitol can also receive reimbursements for travel and hotel stays.

16. In my survey the median legislator reports working 62.5 hours/week during session, 20.0 hours/week in the preceding month, and 12.5 hours/week the rest of the year. Even if I assume that legislators take two weeks totally away from politics each year, I calculate an estimate of 1,005 total hours per year. For context consider that a full-time employee with two weeks' vacation puts in 2,000 hours per year.

17. The Utah Code organizes the entire body of Utah's statutory law into titles, chapters, and sections. For example, Title 8, "Cemeteries," contains all Utah's statutes relevant to cemeteries; some chapters deal with donations to cemeteries, others with record keeping, and so on. Individual sections are cited as title-chapter-section; for example, Utah Code §8-5-1 (2016) states how unused or unkempt cemetery lots should be managed. A proposed bill may affect several parts of the Code. For example, a bill to ban cemeteries from advertising on billboards, with violations punishable as a misdemeanor, could reference Title 76 ("Utah Criminal Code"), which states punishments for misdemeanors; Title 32B ("Alcoholic Beverage Control Act"), which, for historical reasons, contains the legal definition of *billboard*; and, of course, Title 8, "Cemeteries."

18. Bills include the full text of any amended sections; if a bill changes a single word in a twenty-page section of Code, then the bill will nevertheless include the entire twenty-page section. The complete, searchable Utah Code is hosted on the legislature's website.

19. In addition committees may choose to return a bill to the Rules Committee without taking any action, at which point Rules can choose to send the bill to another committee.

20. Tabling is usually a "soft kill." For example, legislators might table a bill if they support its general aims but feel the bill needs further study over the interim before progressing. If the committee does not untable a bill by two-thirds vote at its next meeting, the bill returns to the Rules Committee. Rules then chooses whether to let the bill languish or send it to another committee.

21. If the committee does not vote to recommend, the bill is unlikely to pass that session. Passage is still technically possible, though; the bill's sponsor could persuade the committee chair to put the bill back on the agenda for another vote, or a floor motion could be made to lift the bill from committee and consider it on the house floor. These actions are rare.

22. I include votes that combine second and third readings under suspension in the latter group.

23. Statistics calculated from the author's Utah Legislative Voting Database. Margins calculated as the number of "aye" votes as a percentage of total votes cast (excluding those absent). For the 26 percent with changed margins, 13 percent gained support and 13 percent lost it. For further analysis of the second reading calendar, see Adam Brown, "Does It Matter That the Utah Senate Votes Twice on Each Bill?," *Utah Data Points*, February 11, 2014, http://utahdatapoints.com /2014/02/does-it-matter-that-the-utah-senate-votes-twice-on-each-bill/.

24. One need only type in a bill number or, failing that, a key word or sponsor's name into le.utah.gov to discover where in the legislative process a particular bill is.

25. Under JR4-4-105 each chamber devotes the third and fourth days of the week to bills originating in the other chamber.

26. HR4-3-101 and SR4-3-102 state that bills on the third reading calendar shall be heard in the order they appear unless directed otherwise by a majority vote; these rules govern floor debate through most of the session. However, HR3-1-101(2)(b) grants authority for the house floor to refer bills remaining on the third reading calendar back to House Rules Committee to "recommend to the House which legislation should be assigned [back] to the third reading calendar and the order in which it should be heard"; SR3-1-101 creates similar authority in the senate.

27. To the contrary, HR3-1-102 explicitly authorizes the House Rules Committee to hold legislation rather than send it back to the house floor with a recommendation; SR3-1-102 creates similar authority for the Senate Rules Committee.

28. SR3-2-302 requires senate standing committee chairs to "ensure that legislation referred to the committee is considered by the committee within a reasonable

time," an obligation repeated in SR3-2-403, but without defining *reasonable*. (House rules impose no such obligation on chairs.) However, senate rules also state unambiguously that "the chair shall set the agenda for a standing committee meeting" (SR3-2-302) and "[direct] the order of the agenda" (SR3-2-304). House rules grant similar authority to house standing committee chairs (in HR3-2-302 and HR3-2-304).

29. This section relies on logic from Cox and McCubbins (1993, 2005) and Cox et al. (2010).

30. On legislative leaders' greater procedural than substantive influence, see Cox and McCubbins (1993, 2005).

31. More precisely majority party legislators desire more active leaders when the majority party is more unified and when the ideological gap between parties is wider (Rohde 1991; Aldrich 1995; Aldrich and Rohde 2000a, 2000b). Because supermajority status tends to exacerbate intraparty differences (Key 1949), it follows that supermajority legislative leaders should feel less incentive to silence the minority party than bare-majority legislative leaders.

32. Quoted in Robert Gehrke, "Becky Lockhart, History-Making Utah Lawmaker, Dies at 46," *Salt Lake Tribune*, January 17, 2015.

33. The figure abbreviates the wording. In the survey the steps were described as follows: "Your chamber's Rules Committee"; "The standing committee that hears the bill"; "Discussions of the bill in party caucus meetings"; "Discussions of the bill in party leadership meetings"; "Floor debate about the bill in the House"; "Floor debate about the bill in the Senate."

34. See detailed bill statistics for each year at "Bills in the Utah Legislature, 2007–2017," adambrown.info/s/utleg/bills.

35. Author's calculations based on 2016 General Session weekly house schedules posted on the legislature's website, which allowed 7.0 floor time hours in the session's first week, 6.25 in the second, 13.75 in the third, 10.0 in the fourth, 22.0 in the fifth, 20.0 in the sixth, and 23.0 in the seventh, plus up to 18.0 evening floor time hours in the seventh, for a scheduled maximum of 120 hours.

36. JR4-2-101 prohibits opening a bill file after the General Session's eleventh day, except under special circumstances. However, LRGC drafting attorneys get so backlogged with bill requests in the weeks immediately prior to the session that requests submitted even a month prior to the session's start might not be ready for introduction until late in the session. The 2009–10 shift toward later introductions appears to coincide with a constitutional amendment that took effect in 2009 pushing the legislature's start date back from the third Monday to the fourth Monday in January. Prior to 2009 the General Session followed so quickly after Christmas that legislators hurried to submit bill requests prior to

the winter holidays; since then the delayed start date has apparently left legislators feeling free to submit their bill requests after the new year. For discussion
of other calendar decisions that may have reduced legislators' vetting time, see
Adam Brown, "The 2014 Legislature: Slow out of the Gate, Frantic in the Stretch,"
Utah Data Points, March 19, 2014, http://utahdatapoints.com/2014/03/the-2014
-legislature-slow-out-of-the-gate-frantic-in-the-stretch/.

37. Weekly schedules in 2016 reserved 12.0 hours to house standing committees in
the first week, 19.0 in the second, 11.67 in the third, 14.0 in the fourth, 16.0 in the
fifth, 20.0 in the sixth, and 10.0 in the seventh, a total of 102.67 scheduled hours
over the General Session. However, only one-third of the standing committees
are scheduled during any given time slot, implying an average of 34.22 scheduled
hours per committee. If bills were evenly distributed among the twelve major
house standing committees, and if each committee used its maximum scheduled
hours, then each committee would have heard 68.3 of the 819 bills introduced
that year; even if we set aside bills that failed, each committee would have heard
39.6 of the 475 bills that passed. With 34.22 scheduled hours, we calculate an
average of 30.0 committee minutes per introduced bill, or 52.0 minutes if only
enacted bills receive hearings.

38. Rebecca Lockhart, "Speaker's Opening Remarks 2013," *Vox Populi*, January 28,
2013, http://www.utahreps.net/representatives/speakers-opening-remarks-2013.

39. Averages for each year at "Voting Patterns in the Utah Legislature," adambrown
.info/s/utleg/floor_votes.

40. I apply the w-NOMINATE algorithm described in Poole and Rosenthal (1997).
Individual legislators' scores for both chambers and all years are available at
"Research about the Utah Legislature," adambrown.info/s/utleg.

5. REPRESENTING COMPETING VOICES

1. For a more far-reaching argument that legislators can present themselves as good
"representatives" without engaging in any lawmaking at all, see Mayhew (1974).

2. On Congress, see especially Fenno (1975). This chapter represents the first demon-
stration of this point within Utah specifically. Congressional research suggests
that candidates actively promote this dual thinking, running for Congress by
running "against" Congress; see, for example, Fenno (1978), Mayhew (1989),
and Jacobson (1996), but also Lipinski et al. (2003).

3. For the February 2016 poll results, see Lydia Saad, "Anti-incumbent Mood toward
Congress Still Going Strong," *Gallup*, February 12, 2016, http://www.gallup.com
/poll/189215/anti-incumbent-mood-toward-congress-going-strong.aspx.

4. Approval rose during the 1990s economic boom, followed by a brief patriotic
spike after the September 11, 2001, terrorist attacks, but approval in the 10 to

25 percent range has been common since 2006. Since 1970 only three elections (1976, 1992, and 2010) have seen fewer than 90 percent of house incumbents who sought reelection win.

5. All state polls discussed in this section are iterations of the Utah Voter Poll. A February 2012 poll found 48 percent approval, while an October poll found 58 percent.

6. I omit District 30 from this analysis, as redistricting pitted two incumbents (Fred Cox and Janice Fisher) against each other in the general election. Six incumbents lost renomination (Butterfield, Daw, Doughty, Hendrickson, Newbold, and Wright); only one lost in November (Watkins). Others left to run for Congress (Clark, Wimmer, Sandstrom, Herrod), statewide office (Sumsion, Dougall), or Utah Senate (Frank, Vickers, Painter, Harper). Three simply left politics, Litvack and Kiser after being drawn into new districts with fellow incumbents, and Morley for personal reasons. These voluntary departures led to the Utah House's highest turnover in twenty years; for details, see Adam Brown, "Lots of Freshmen in the Utah House?," *Utah Data Points*, November 7, 2012, http://utahdatapoints.com/2012/11/lots-of-freshmen-in-the-utah-house/.

7. Three representatives (Jim Bird, Jerry Anderson, and Dana Layton) lost to intraparty challengers; only one (Larry Wiley) lost in November. Richard Greenwood dropped out of the race fearing defeat in his party convention; treating Greenwood as a loss means five of sixty-five lost, a 92 percent reelection rate. The remaining ten representatives did not seek reelection.

8. Two representatives (Fred Cox, Earl Tanner) lost renomination; three lost in November (Mel Brown, Brad King, Sophia DiCaro). Kraig Powell dropped out fearing a convention loss; treating Powell as a loss means six of sixty-six lost, a 91 percent reelection rate. Of the remaining legislators, six retired from politics (Lifferth, Draxler, Oda, Anderson, Cunningham, McIff), two moved to the senate (Ipson, Anderegg), and one sought another office (Dee).

9. Fenno (1978) developed the "geographic," "reelection," and "primary" constituency labels employed here, though I have replaced his smallest group—the "personal" constituency—with the Utah-specific "delegate" constituency.

10. An important caveat is in order when reading this figure. Prior to the U.S. Supreme Court's 1964 ruling in *Reynolds v. Sims*, legislative districts in many states routinely had vastly unequal populations. As it happens, Utah's malapportioned districts were among those that motivated this case. Prior to the Court's ruling, Utah's least populous house district had only 165 residents, while the most populous had 32,380. Only since this ruling have Utah's districts consistently had near-equal population.

11. More precisely 12,311 votes were cast per Utah House district in the 2012 presi-

dential election, which is 33.4 percent of the average district's population in the 2010 census, 36,852.

12. In 2010, with gubernatorial and U.S. Senate races topping the ballot, 8,710 ballots were cast per Utah House district; in 2014, with no gubernatorial or U.S. Senate race topping the ballot, only 7,706 ballots were cast per district. Note that many voters participate only in top-of-the-ticket races—U.S. president, U.S. Senate, U.S. House, and Utah governor—leaving the rest of their ballots blank, behavior known as "roll-off." In 2010, 7.4 percent of voters skipped their local Utah House race, a rate that fell to 6.2 percent in 2012 and rose to 6.7 percent in 2014. Of course Utah's electronic voting machines allow voters to simply choose a party rather than take the time to select a candidate in every race. Generally around one-third of voters use the straight ticket option (32 percent in 2010, 37 percent in 2012, and 34 percent in 2014), which reduces roll-off by making it literally impossible for these voters to skip legislative races.

13. In 2014 winners of the seventy-five Utah House races averaged 5,359 votes each—75 percent of the 7,191 average votes actually cast in these races (a total that excludes roll-off ballots).

14. The Utah Republican Party estimated that 125,000 people attended the 2012 caucuses, an average of 1,667 per house district. GOP leadership characterized this attendance as easily setting a record; past years saw average caucus attendance around 533 per house district (roughly one in seventy-five constituents), though attendance remained high in 2014 at 800 to 900 per district. (Statistics from Lee Davidson, "Utah Caucus Attendance Down from 2012, but Higher than Average," *Salt Lake Tribune*, March 21, 2014.) Primaries attract more voters than caucuses; in 2016, 3,229 Republican primary ballots were cast per house district, roughly one for every twelve constituents.

15. Full wording for each group's or individual's description: "Your party's state chair"; "Your party's chamber leadership team"; "A constituent who is also a party delegate"; "A constituent who belongs to your party"; "A constituent who does not belong to your party"; "Your local newspaper's editorial board"; "A relevant interest group."

16. The survey used the following wording for each method: "Speaking with you on the telephone"; "Sending an email to your @le.utah.gov account"; "Communicating with you via Facebook or Twitter"; "Joining a group like the NRA, UEA, PCE, or SUWA"; "Attending your town hall meeting or other event"; "Speaking with you one-on-one"; "Sending you a letter by postal mail"; "Participating in a large rally outside the Capitol."

17. Though the data in this paragraph come from the Utah Legislature, this assertion applies elsewhere as well. In a study of Congress, for example, a congressional

staffer told researchers it was "goofy" to think members of Congress would check opinion polls prior to voting, explaining that U.S. representatives should lead, not follow, the public (Jacobs et al. 1998).

18. This question wording inspired by Rosenthal (2004), along with the next question reported here.

19. See Mayhew (1974) and Fenno (1978) for applications of this logic to the U.S. Congress.

20. The number of registered lobbyists has remained surprisingly stable over time. A 1987 analysis, for example, reported as few as 350 lobbyists in 1982 and as many as 775 in 1984 (Hrebenar et al. 1987, 116). The 2016 total of 503 falls easily within these bounds.

21. As of July 8, 2016. Utah maintains a public lobbyist registry at lobbyist.utah.gov.

22. On lobbying tactics generally, see Nownes (2006).

23. This survey involved only a few dozen respondents and therefore should be interpreted cautiously. See more results in Hrebenar et al. (1987, 118).

24. See HB311 and HB104, both passed in the 2010 General Session.

25. Julia Lyon, "Without Insurance for Autism, Utah Families Leave State," *Salt Lake Tribune*, June 18, 2012; Julia Lyon, "Utah Autism Solution Continues to Frustrate Parents," *Salt Lake Tribune*, July 30, 2012.

26. More senators voted against SB57 earlier in the process—it initially cleared the senate on an 18–7 vote (with 4 absent)—but when SB57 returned to the senate for concurrence after passing (with amendments) the house, many senators dropped their opposition.

27. Quoted in Lee Davidson, "Autism Bill Passes Both Utah Houses," *Salt Lake Tribune*, March 13, 2014.

28. This claim, and the following hypothetical example, come from Olson (1965).

29. In LDS parlance, "home teachers" are fellow congregants assigned to visit families at home once a month to check on the family's well-being and deliver a brief religious message. All active LDS men are expected to serve as home teachers (in pairs), so that each pair visits a short list of two to four assigned households each month. On this usage among legislators, see Lee Davidson and Matt Canham, "Mormon Church Lobbying in Utah's Capitol—Hardball or Light Touch," *Salt Lake Tribune*, March 29, 2015, which also serves as the source for all legislator quotes in this paragraph and the next from legislators other than Wimmer.

30. All quotes from Wimmer from his blog post, "The Role of the LDS Church in Utah's Politics," posted at *An American Dream Revealed* in March 2015, now defunct.

31. On alcopops, see Davidson and Canham, "Mormon Church Lobbying in Utah's Capitol."

32. Jesse McKinley and Kirk Johnson, "Mormons Tipped Scale in Ban on Gay Marriage," *New York Times*, November 14, 2008.

33. The LDS Church weighed in once more against alcohol liberalization in 2014. See Robert Gehrke, "LDS Church: Don't Change Utah's Liquor Laws," *Salt Lake Tribune*, January 23, 2014.

34. See, for example, the LDS newsroom's "Immigration Response," praising HB116 as a "responsible attempt to address the principles outlined" in previous Church statements, available at http://mormonnewsroom.org/article/immigration -response.

35. J. Quin Monson, "Did the Utah Compact Actually Change Attitudes about Immigration?," *Utah Data Points*, April 20, 2011, http://utahdatapoints.com/2011/04 /did-the-utah-compact-actually-change-attitudes-about-immigration/.

36. The Utah Legislature does not publicize legislators' religion. This estimate is based on the author's own inquiries during recent sessions, though some legislators decline to answer and others wish to remain off the record. Not all Mormon legislators are strictly observant, of course, as revealed by occasional scandals. In 2010, for example, a professed Mormon (and Republican) senator resigned in disgrace after being arrested and charged with driving under the influence; his passenger, a lobbyist, was also intoxicated. LDS tenets forbid consumption of alcohol.

37. At the local level all LDS congregations are led by unpaid local members. To spread the leadership burden, each congregation has numerous positions of responsibility (referred to as "callings"). Active members, especially those (like legislators) with organizational or professional skills, can expect to rotate through many responsible callings throughout their adult lives.

38. From Wimmer's blog post, "The Role of the LDS Church in Utah's Politics."

39. The candidate was Jonathan Johnson, who waged an intraparty challenge against incumbent governor Gary Herbert for the Republican nomination in 2016. Data drawn from Utah's campaign finance disclosures at "State of Utah Financial Disclosures," disclosures.utah.gov. On Johnson's relationship to this donor, Patrick Byrne, see Robert Gehrke, "Johnson Gets Another Fat Check; Herbert Campaign Asks, Is He Beholden to His Sugar Daddy," *Salt Lake Tribune*, May 21, 2016.

40. Official campaign finance disclosures are at disclosures.utah.gov, but the National Institute on Money in State Politics presents the data in a more accessible form (along with data from the other forty-nine states) at its website, followthemoney .org. I rely on NIMSP's data in the remainder of this section.

41. I have omitted from this discussion a small handful of legislative candidates in highly competitive races who aggressively raised funds. What makes these legislative leaders (and leadership candidates) different is that they received

more funds than nearly all of their chamber colleagues despite facing little or no electoral competition and engaging in little or no serious fundraising—the money simply found its way to them anyway.

42. I mention by name any Utah representative who gave to ten or more house candidates and any Utah senator who gave to four.

43. Democratic senator Karen Morgan also contributed to four senate candidates, though three of them lost their races.

44. Though there were not open leadership races on the house Republican side in 2012, Representative Ipson gave to twenty-four peers.

6. LEGISLATING AT THE BALLOT BOX

1. Initially the act would provide vouchers only to children then enrolled in public schools and also to low-income children already enrolled in private schools, but over several years the bill would eventually allow all Utah children to receive school vouchers. The cash value would vary depending on family income. Funding for each voucher would come out of the budget of whichever public school the voucher's recipient would have otherwise attended, though the bill provided some funding guarantees to public schools in the first five years after a student transferred out. In addition to the bill's text, see an analysis in Julia Lyon and Nicole Stricker, "Tuition Still Unaffordable for Poorest," *Salt Lake Tribune*, February 25, 2007.

2. Dan Lips and Evan Feinberg, "Utah's Revolutionary New School Voucher Program," *Heritage Foundation WebMemo* 1362, February 2007, http://www.heritage.org/research/reports/2007/02/utahs-revolutionary-new-school-voucher-program.

3. Quotes from "Utah Creates Nation's First Universal School Voucher Program," *Heartland Institute*, https://www.heartland.org/news-opinion/news/utah-creates-nations-first-universal-school-voucher-program.

4. That is, signatures exceeding 10 percent of the 927,801 votes cast in Utah for all candidates for president in the 2004 election.

5. This statistic and the subsequent reaction quote from PCE's director from Tiffany Erickson, "Voucher Foes Win a Round: Number of Signatures on Petition Sets a Record," *Deseret News* (Salt Lake City UT), May 1, 2007.

6. Glen Warchol and Robert Gehrke, "Utah School Vouchers Bill Is Battleground for Out-of-State Donors," *Salt Lake Tribune*, September 18, 2007.

7. Quoted in Glen Warchol, "Vouchers Go Down in Crushing Defeat," *Salt Lake Tribune*, November 7, 2007.

8. Voters supported vouchers in only two legislative districts: Senator Curt Bramble's

(the Senate sponsor of HB148) and Representative Stephen Sandstrom's, both centered around Provo-Orem.

9. Quoted in Robert Gehrke, "Voucher Defeat May Cost Utah Republicans in '08 Polls," *Salt Lake Tribune*, November 14, 2007.

10. In Curtis's case accusations of ethical impropriety also contributed to his loss; see Brandon Loomis, "Did Lawmaker-Turned Lobbyist Curtis Derail Indian Site Protection," *Salt Lake Tribune*, March 4, 2009.

11. Erickson, "Voucher Foes Win a Round."

12. Should the legislature reject the indirect initiative, the petitioner can resume gathering signatures in hopes of meeting the higher threshold required of direct initiatives. See Utah Code §20A-7-208 (2016).

13. See generally Utah Code §20A-7-101 (2016) and following for details.

14. Oregon requires a 6 percent threshold for direct initiatives, and California requires 5 percent, but both states denominate these percentages in terms of turnout in the most recent gubernatorial election, unlike Utah, which uses the most recent presidential election.

15. Some studies find no initiative effect on policy responsiveness, including Monogan et al. (2009) and Lascher et al. (1996). One comprehensive study accounting for many diverse variables likewise finds no effect, though its authors note that their term-limits variable might be absorbing the initiative's effects, since term limits are most common in states with workable initiative processes (Lax and Phillips 2012).

16. Meanwhile the legislature also took other steps to complicate future initiative drives, including prohibiting electronic signatures, allowing voters to "unsign" a petition up to thirty days after the signature-gathering deadline had passed, increasing the signature threshold, and more.

17. UEG continued gathering signatures through August and exceeded the requirement, but the Utah Supreme Court ruled that signatures collected after April 15 were invalid.

18. I thank Dixie Huefner, UEG communications chair, for providing information in this paragraph.

19. Numbers from Robert Gehrke, "Bill Could Make Count My Vote Initiative Moot," *Salt Lake Tribune*, February 4, 2014.

7. THE MOST POWERFUL GOVERNOR

1. Had Lee's successor, George D. Clyde, sought a third term in 1964, he too might have lost. Clyde's contentious second term alienated many voter blocs; recognizing the risk, he wisely chose to retire after two terms.

2. Bob Bernick, "No 3rd Term for Bangerter," *Deseret News* (Salt Lake City UT), November 29, 1990.

3. On Walker's brief gubernatorial career, see Dan Harrie, "Sweet, 'Tough' Olene Walker Was a Pioneer and an Advocate for Bettering Lives in Utah," *Salt Lake Tribune*, November 28, 2015.

4. Polling from SurveyUSA, poll 11166, reported November 2006.

5. Approval rating from Bob Bernick, "90% of Utahns Like How Huntsman Does Job," *Deseret News* (Salt Lake City UT), January 26, 2009. Nationwide, voters generally view their governor through a partisan lens, making this bipartisan appeal even more remarkable; see Brown (2010).

6. Huntsman accepted the call even though the national press speculated that Obama was sending Huntsman abroad to defuse a potential 2012 challenge from the popular, moderate Republican governor; see, for example, "Obama Names Moderate Republican as Envoy to China," CNN, May 16, 2009, http://www.cnn .com/2009/POLITICS/05/16/huntsman.china/index.html.

7. I rely on an updated version of the dataset described in Brown (2013a).

8. There were 193 total elections during this period, of which 106 featured an incumbent seeking reelection and 87 were open races. Across all 193 races, seven featured two (current or recent) plural executives running against each other in the general election, for a total of seventy-six plural executive candidates during this period; included were twenty-seven lieutenant governors, twenty-six attorneys general, nine treasurers, eight secretaries of state, and a few others. On the importance of challenger experience and candidate quality generally in gubernatorial elections, see Brown and Jacobson (2008) and Brown (2013a).

9. According to the Council of State Governments (2015, table 4.4), eleven governors have item veto authority in all bills (those in Alabama, Connecticut, Delaware, Idaho, Illinois, Kentucky, Maryland, Massachusetts, New York, Washington, and Wyoming), six governors lack any item veto authority at all (in Indiana, Nevada, New Hampshire, North Carolina, Rhode Island, and Vermont), and the remaining thirty-three (including Utah's) have item veto authority only on certain bills—typically appropriations bills.

10. Polling data on HB363 was reported by Chris Karpowitz, "Poll: Should Utah Schools Teach about Contraception?," *Utah Data Points*, March 12, 2012, http://utahdatapoints.com/2012/03/poll-should-utah-schools-teach-about -contraception/; see also Robert Gehrke and Lisa Schencker, "Herbert Vetoes Sex-Ed Bill, Says It Constricts Parent Choice," *Salt Lake Tribune*, March 18, 2012.

11. Though he has not fully tested it at the gubernatorial level, Benedictis-Kessner (2018) uses an analysis of ten thousand mayoral races over the past sixty years to show that the incumbency advantage grows in off-cycle elections.

12. Analysis by author, based on turnout data from all fifty states from 1980 through 2016; data for Louisiana 1982 are missing, hence N=949, with nineteen observations per state (but eighteen for Louisiana). Because several states changed the timing of their gubernatorial elections during this period, and others had special elections to fill midterm vacancies (such as Utah's 2010 gubernatorial special election), the data provide abundant within and between variance. Data courtesy of Michael McDonald (electproject.org). I analyze the data using a random effects generalized least squares regression with several dichotomous regressors: presidential year, presidential year with gubernatorial race, presidential year with U.S. Senate race, presidential year with both gubernatorial and U.S. Senate race, midterm year with gubernatorial race, midterm year with U.S. Senate race, and midterm year with both gubernatorial and U.S. Senate race. (Midterm year without gubernatorial or U.S. Senate race is the omitted category.) Base turnout in a midterm year is estimated at 35.6 percent. Adding a U.S. Senate race boosts this expectation by 5.2 percentage points; adding a gubernatorial race boosts it by 6.6 points; adding both boosts it by 8.3 points; all these effects are statistically significant ($p<0.05$). In a presidential year, base turnout is estimated at 58.3 percent. Adding a gubernatorial race, U.S. Senate race, or both does not have a statistically significant effect on expected turnout (and the coefficients themselves are trivial). Findings are driven heavily by a "within" effect (over time within each state) rather than a "between" effect, supporting the interpretation given here. I measure turnout as the number of ballots cast in the state's highest race, divided by the voting eligible population.

13. Claim based on data from Council of State Governments (2015).

14. Kousser and Phillips (2012) found this pattern so consistently that they subtitled their book, *The Power of American Governors*, as *Winning on Budgets and Losing on Policy*.

15. Governors began expanding their staff capabilities in the 1960s and 1970s under the Clyde and Rampton administrations.

16. See Squire (1992, 2007) for the canonical definitions of legislative professionalism.

17. A complete list is available at "Boards & Commissions," boards.utah.gov.

18. See table 7-5 in Beyle and Ferguson (2008). Utah ranks behind only Massachusetts, West Virginia, New York, New Jersey, Maryland, and Alaska.

19. Hamm and Moncrief (2008, table 6-1) identify only South Dakota, Wyoming, North Dakota, and New Hampshire as having fewer legislative resources (staff, session days, and legislator salary) than Utah.

8. JUDGES AND COURTS

1. Claims based on Pew Research Center, "What the Public Knows—In Words and Pictures," 2011 edition, http://www.people-press.org/2011/11/07/what-the-public

-knows-in-words-and-pictures/, 2013 edition, http://www.people-press.org/2013
/09/05/what-the-public-knows-in-words-pictures-maps-and-graphs/, and 2015
edition, http://www.people-press.org/2015/04/28/what-the-public-knows-in
-pictures-words-maps-and-graphs/.

2. Chapter 4 provides support for this claim.

3. In 2006, for example, federal courts heard a total of 88,094 cases, while America's
fifty state court systems heard a total of 9,312,716 cases (Donovan et al. 2013, 326).

4. Readers should not confuse these state district courts with the federal court for
the District of Utah, headquartered in Salt Lake City, which is the entry-level
federal court for cases originating in Utah.

5. Caseload statistics compiled from Utah Courts, "Utah Courts Caseload," utcourts
.gov/stats/.

6. For profiles of the teen court system, see Lori Prichard, "Youth Court: An Inter-
vention Where Peers Decide Appropriate Punishment," *Deseret News* (Salt Lake
City UT), April 12, 2012; Janelle Stecklein, "Utah Teens Find Justice in Peer
Courts," *Salt Lake Tribune*, February 3, 2013.

7. For profiles of Utah's drug courts, see Jennifer Stagg and Amy Joi O'Donoghue,
"Drug Court Program Offering Hope and a Brighter Future for Many Addicts,"
Deseret News (Salt Lake City UT), November 18, 2010; Greg Skordas, "Op-ed:
Utah Celebrates 20 Years of Saving Lives through Drug Court," *Salt Lake Tribune*,
September 26, 2015.

8. For a profile of these courts, see Carlos Mayorga, "Graduates of Mental-Health
Court Stay Out of Jail Longer," *Salt Lake Tribune*, September 22, 2008.

9. Federal caseload statistics are available online at http://www.uscourts.gov/statistics
-reports/analysis-reports/federal-judicial-caseload-statistics and Utah caseload
statistics at Utah Courts, "Utah Courts Caseload," http://utcourts.gov/stats/.

10. I compare fiscal year totals for district courts (from Utah Courts, "Utah Courts
Caseload," utcourts.gov/stats/) to calendar year totals for appellate courts (by
tallying rulings published at Utah Courts, "Appellate Court Opinions," utcourts
.gov/opinions/).

11. Article VIII, Section 3, of Utah's constitution specifies the rare circumstances
when Utah's supreme court holds original rather than appellate jurisdiction.

12. Author's analysis based on data from Spaeth et al. (2016).

13. These claims are based on author's analysis of the extraordinarily detailed State
Supreme Court Data Project (Brace and Hall 1999; Hall 2014), which unfortu-
nately spans only four years, 1995–98. See also Brown (2016). On judicial review
in state supreme courts generally, see Langer (2002).

14. See Huber and Shipan (2002), Tsebelis and Nardi (2016), and Brown (2016) on
the connection between length and specificity.

15. Additionally Langer (2002) argues that easily amended constitutions deter state judges from striking down state actions, since they fear retaliatory constitutional amendments.

16. See Brown (2016) for a thorough development of these three arguments, along with empirical tests based on analysis of the fifty states.

17. On measuring ideological behavior in the U.S. Supreme Court, see Segal and Spaeth (1993); Epstein and Knight (1998); Grofman and Brazill (2002); Martin and Quinn (2002).

18. These arguments were especially common in 2016 among Republicans concerned about Donald Trump. For examples, see Makan Delrahim, "To Save the Supreme Court, Vote Trump over Clinton," *New York Post*, March 9, 2016; Ken Klukowski, "Trump's SCOTUS List Gives America Clear Choice," *Brietbart*, May 19, 2016; Curt Levey, "What Trump's Supreme Court List (and Hillary Clinton's Reaction to It) Tells Us," *Fox News*, May 19, 2016, http://www.foxnews.com/opinion/2016/05/19/what-trumps-supreme-court-list-and-hillary-clintons-reaction-to-it-tells-us.html; and Jay Nordlinger, "Spooked by SCOTUS," *National Review*, June 17, 2016.

19. In 1984 the legislature proposed this amendment to Article VIII of Utah's constitution in SJR1; voters ratified the amendment later that year.

20. These procedures are specific to filling vacancies in the state's two appellate courts, although vacancies in the various district courts are filled using a broadly similar process. For details, see Utah Code §78A-10 (2016) and Article VIII, Section 8, of the Utah Constitution.

21. To be clear, I define a decision as unanimous if all judges joined either the majority opinion or a concurring opinion. If any judges signed a dissenting opinion, the decision was not unanimous. Statistics in figure 26 calculated using the author's Utah Supreme Court Rulings Database.

22. Percentages here include any opinion authored by each justice, including majority, concurring, and dissenting opinions. For data on other judges, see Adam Brown, "Utah's Supreme Court, Where Unanimity Is the Rule," *Utah Data Points*, June 10, 2013, http://utahdatapoints.com/2013/06/utahs-supreme-court-where-unanimity-is-the-rule/.

23. Based on author's analysis of the 1995–98 State Supreme Court Data Project referenced in an earlier note (Brace and Hall 1999; Hall 2014). A handful of states lack an intermediate court of appeals, so that all appeals go to the state supreme court (Council of Chief Judges of State Courts of Appeal 2012). Because the Utah Court of Appeals reduces the Utah Supreme Court's caseload, only the most difficult cases proceed to the higher court. That the Utah Supreme Court nevertheless stands out for its consensus thus seems all the more remarkable.

9. LOCAL GOVERNMENTS

1. Quoted in Brian Carlson, "Salt Lake City Okays Fast Food Drive Thru Service for Bicycle Riders," KTVX *Good4Utah*, September 30, 2014.

2. Quoted in Annie Knox, "Bikes at the Drive-Thru? City, Legislature at Odds," *Salt Lake Tribune*, February 9, 2015.

3. On Salt Lake's 1993 actions, see Marianne Funk and Jay Evensen, "Gun Supporters File Suit to Block SL's New Law," *Deseret News* (Salt Lake City UT), October 29, 1993. Separately the legislature updated the uniform firearm law (with SB48 in the 2004 General Session) after the Utah Supreme Court ruled that the University of Utah's campus firearm ban did not violate the act, since the university is a state agency rather than a local government. Utah Code now declares that neither "a local authority" nor a "state entity" may restrict firearms "except as specifically provided by state law"; see Utah Code §53-5A-102 (2016).

4. Derek P. Jensen, "Bill Would Ice Yalecrest Historic District for a Year," *Salt Lake Tribune*, February 15, 2011.

5. "Crazy Quilt Gay Agenda in SLC," *Daily Herald*, August 9, 2009.

6. Church of Jesus Christ of Latter-day Saints, "Church Supports Salt Lake City Non-discrimination Ordinance," November 10, 2009, http://www.mormonnewsroom .org/ldsnewsroom/eng/news-releases-stories/church-supports-nondiscrimination -ordinances. By 2015 Salt Lake City's ordinance had been copied by Salt Lake County, West Valley City, Ogden, Taylorsville, Logan, Murray, Summit County, Midvale, Grand County, Park City, and Moab.

7. For an overview of 2015's successful SB296, see Jennifer Dobner, "LGBT Anti-Discrimination Bill Clears Legislature, on Its Way to Utah Governor," *Salt Lake Tribune*, March 11, 2015.

8. All quotations in paragraph from Heidi Toth, "Bill over Zoning Law Divides Provo Politicians," *Daily Herald*, March 21, 2010.

9. Quoted from *Clinton v. Cedar Rapids and the Missouri River Railroad*, 24 Iowa 455 (1868).

10. In doing so these state courts draw on a later opinion written by Dillon expanding his earlier view, sometimes (confusingly) also called "Dillon's rule" (in *Merriam v. Moody's Executors*, 25 Iowa 163 [1868]). Because local governments have no authority beyond what the state expressly delegates to them, he reasoned in this latter case, they may exercise only those powers "granted in express words" or necessarily implied.

11. In *State v. Hutchinson*, 624 P.2d 116 (1980). The legislature later codified this principle. For counties, see Utah Code §17-50-302 (2016): a county may "provide a service, exercise a power, or perform a function that is reasonably related to the safety, health, morals, and welfare of county inhabitants, except as limited

or prohibited by statute." For cities, see Utah Code §10-8-1 (2016): "The municipal legislative body may pass all ordinances . . . as are necessary and proper
to provide for the safety and preserve the health, and promote the prosperity,
improve the morals, peace and good order, comfort, and convenience of the city
and its inhabitants, and for the protection of property in the city." As Anderson
(2013, 18) points out, however, *Hutchinson* applies only to police (i.e., regulatory)
powers, not to revenue powers: local governments may not impose taxes or fees
not authorized by state statute. Hutchinson's rule applies only to Utah's general-
purpose governments (cities and counties), not to single-purpose governments
(special districts and school districts).

12. Fewer than 1 percent nationwide use commissions, while the rest use other
forms, such as town meetings and representative town meetings. See National
League of Cities (1989) for these statistics, as well as for more detailed overviews
of common municipal government systems.

13. The Utah Association of Counties maintains a directory of county officials that
can be used to infer each county's form of government, depending on whether
that county has commissioners or councilors.

14. Permissible forms of county government are described in Utah Code §17-52-5
(2016).

15. These officers are described in Utah Code Title 17 (2016). On consolidation, see
Utah Code §17-16-3 (2016).

16. Utah League of Cities and Towns, "City Facts and Statistics," http://www.ulct
.org/about/city-facts-and-statistics/.

17. See Utah Code §10-3b-1 (2016), as well as a summary at Utah League of Cities
and Towns, "Municipal Forms of Government in Utah," http://www.ulct.org/wp
-content/uploads/sites/4/2013/02/forms-of-municipal-government.pdf.

18. Moving executive powers from the mayor to a city councilor or to a manager
(or back) requires either a majority council vote with the mayor's consent or a
unanimous vote over the mayor's dissent.

19. Tooele was founded in 1853 but did not adopt its current charter until 1965.
Details about its charter may be found at the city website, tooelecity.org.

20. District-based cities in Utah may also include at-large council members.
Although elected citywide, they are equal in authority to the district-based
councilors.

21. This book omits similar concepts for brevity, such as conservation districts
and local building authorities. Utah Code §17C (2016) addresses special service
districts, while Utah Code §17B (2016) addresses local districts.

22. The Utah Association of Special Districts maintains a list of districts at uasd.org
/district-listing.php.

23. On these general patterns, see Lawless and Fox (2010) and Wayne (2007, tables 3.1 and 3.3).

24. Respondents included mayors, city councilors, county commissioners and councilors, state legislators, and planning commission members, though local officials, particularly city councilors, dominate the sample. The survey was fielded online from August 10 to September 13, 2010, garnering 898 responses, a 46.8 percent response rate. See Hall et al. (2010) for additional details.

25. Statistics on Utah voters drawn from the 2010 Utah Colleges Exit Poll, exitpoll .byu.edu. For Utahns generally, statistics on education, age, gender, and race drawn from the 2010 U.S. Census; religion drawn from Pew Research Center (2014); party affiliations from the publicly available database of all registered voters, as of 2010.

26. The question asked respondents to rate their government's in-house capacity in each area on a scale from 0 (no capacity) to 5 (very high capacity). I report as "high capacity" those choosing 4 or 5 on these scales, and as "inadequate capacity" those choosing 0 or 1.

10. A MULTIBILLION-DOLLAR BUDGET

1. Quotes from Herbert and Hughes found in Robert Gehrke, "Herbert Proposes $14.8 Billion Budget with Emphasis on Education," *Salt Lake Tribune*, December 9, 2015.

2. Quotes from Morgan Jacobsen, "Utah Schools Get $445M Funding Boost, New Direction for Leadership Elections," *Deseret News* (Salt Lake City UT), March 10, 2016.

3. Per pupil spending statistics from U.S. Census Bureau release CB15–98, "Per Pupil Spending Varies Heavily across the United States," based on FY2013 data, June 2, 2015. See also "Education Spending per Student by State," *Governing Magazine*, n.d., http://www.governing.com/gov-data/education-data/state-education -spending-per-pupil-data.html.

4. Quoted in Utah Taxpayers Association, "My Corner: Why Utah's Rank on Per Student Spending Is Just One Data Point—Not a Vice," June 13, 2015, http://www .utahtaxpayers.org/?p=7160.

5. Quoted in Gehrke, "Herbert Proposes $14.8 Billion Budget."

6. I divide total expenditures per fiscal year by current year GDP as reported by the U.S. Bureau of Economic Analysis.

7. Statistics in this paragraph draw on tables 5 and 6 in Stevenson et al. (2017).

8. In FY2018 the General Fund (excluding the General Fund Restricted, which holds earmarked sales taxes) totaled $2.5 billion, and the Education Fund (including the Uniform School Fund and Education Special Revenue) totaled $4.4 billion,

adding to $6.8 billion of the state's $16.2 billion authorized spending, of which federal transfers provided $4.3 billion. See table 1 in Stevenson et al. (2017).

9. These staff are housed in the Office of the Legislative Fiscal Analyst and in the Governor's Office of Management and Budget.

10. Chapter 4 reviewed the structure of these appropriations subcommittees.

11. There were six additional funding gaps between 1976 and 1979, but they did not result in shutdown. There were no funding gaps prior to 1976.

11. DIFFERENT PEOPLE, SIMILAR PROCESSES

1. Quoted in Rob Story, "Robert Redford: The Sundance Kid Rides Again," *Men's Journal*, August 8, 2013.

2. Trump still won Utah, even with only 47 percent of the vote, since Democratic nominee Hillary Clinton and Utah-born protest candidate Evan McMullin split the other 53 percent.

3. Most of the rest of this group—26 percent—supported protest candidate Evan McMullin.

4. These are not misprints; 100 percent is rounded off from 99.8 percent in 2012 and 99.6 percent in 2004.

5. The full statement can be found at an official LDS website, "Church Points to Joseph Smith's Statements on Religious Freedom, Pluralism," December 8, 2015, http://mormonnewsroom.org/article/church-statement-religious-freedom-pluralism.

6. Utahns cast their preference at precinct caucuses, not in a primary; this 14 percent figure comes from mass caucus attendees, not convention delegates. I omit territories such as Puerto Rico and Washington DC from this comparison. I also omit states that hold only a convention, with neither a caucus nor a primary.

7. Quoted in Tom Hamburger and Sean Sullivan, "Trump Makes Play for Evangelicals by Noting His Problems in Mormon-Rich Utah," *Washington Post*, August 11, 2016.

8. To be clear, Salt Lake City served as the home of mining financiers and executives, not of actual mines.

9. Though no longer available at *The Advocate*'s website, the ranking was reported widely. For example, see "Salt Lake City as 'Gayest City' in America," *Huffington Post*, January 11, 2012, https://www.huffingtonpost.com/2012/01/11/salt-lake-city-as-gayest-_n_1199918.html.

APPENDIX 1

1. Lynn Arave, "The Day the Sky Fell," *Deseret News* (Salt Lake City UT), April 2, 1995. Additional information about these events may be found at the Utah capitol's website, utahstatecapitol.utah.gov.

BIBLIOGRAPHY

Aird, Polly. 2011. "Not Just Buchanan's Blunder." *Dialogue: A Journal of Mormon Thought* 44 (Summer): 180–90.

Aldrich, John H. 1995. *Why Parties? The Origin and Transformation of Political Parties.* Chicago: University of Chicago Press.

Aldrich, John H., and David W. Rohde. 2000a. "The Consequences of Party Organization in the House: The Role of the Majority and Minority Parties in Conditional Party Government." In *Polarized Politics: Congress and the President in a Partisan Era*, ed. Jon R. Bond and Richard Fleisher. Washington DC: CQ Press.

———. 2000b. "The Republican Revolution and the House Appropriation Committee." *Journal of Politics* 62(1): 1–33.

Alexander, Thomas G. 2007. *Utah: The Right Place.* Revised and updated edition. Layton UT: Gibbs Smith.

Anderson, Gavin. 2013. *County Government in Utah: The Official County Government Resource Guide of the Utah Association of Counties.* Murray UT: Utah Association of Counties.

Arceneaux, Kevin. 2002. "Direct Democracy and the Link between Public Opinion and State Abortion Policy." *State Politics and Policy Quarterly* 2(4): 372–87.

Arceneaux, Kevin, Chris W. Bonneau, and Paul Brace. 2007. "On Consensus in State Supreme Courts." Paper presented at the annual meeting of the Midwest Political Science Association, Chicago, April 12–15.

Bailey, Paul. 1978. *Holy Smoke: A Dissertation on the Utah War.* Los Angeles: Westernlore Books.

Beck, Paul Allen. 1974. "A Socialization Theory of Partisan Realignment." In *The Politics of Future Citizens*, ed. Richard G. Niemi. San Francisco: Jossey-Bass.

Benedictis-Kessner, Justin de. 2018. "Off-Cycle and Out of Office: Election Timing and the Incumbency Advantage." *Journal of Politics* 80(1): 119–32.

Berkman, Michael B. 2001. "Legislative Professionalism and the Demand for Groups: The Institutional Context of Interest Population Density." *Legislative Studies Quarterly* 26 (November): 661–79.

Beyle, Thad L., and Margaret Ferguson. 2008. "Governors and the Executive Branch."

In *Politics in the American States*, ed. Virginia Gray and Russell L. Hanson. 9th edition. Washington DC: CQ Press.

Black, Susan Easton. 1995. "How Large Was the Population of Nauvoo?" *BYU Studies Quarterly* 35(2): 91–94.

Bonneau, Chris W., and Melinda Gann Hall. 2009. *In Defense of Judicial Elections.* New York: Routledge.

——, eds. 2017. *Judicial Elections in the 21st century.* New York: Routledge.

Bowler, Shaun, and Todd Donovan. 2004. "Measuring the Effect of Direct Democracy on State Policy: Not All Initiatives Are Created Equal." *State Politics and Policy Quarterly* 4 (December): 345–63.

Brace, Paul, and Brent D. Boyea. 2008. "State Public Opinion, the Death Penalty, and the Practice of Electing Judges." *American Journal of Political Science* 52 (April): 360–72.

Brace, Paul, and Melinda Gann Hall. 1997. "The Interplay of Preferences, Case Facts, Context, and Structure in the Politics of Judicial Choice." *Journal of Politics* 59 (November): 1206–31.

——. 1999. "The State Supreme Court Data Project." *Law and Courts* 9 (Spring): 21–21.

——. 2001. "'Haves' versus 'Have Nots' in State Supreme Courts: Allocating Docket Space and Wins in Power Asymmetric Cases." *Law and Society Review* 35(2): 393–417.

Brown, Adam R. 2010. "Are Governors Responsible for the State Economy? Partisanship, Blame, and Divided Federalism." *Journal of Politics* 72 (July): 605–15.

——. 2011. "Losing to Nobody? Nevada's 'None of These Candidates' Ballot Reform." *Social Science Journal* 48 (June): 364–70.

——. 2012. "The Item Veto's Sting." *State Politics and Policy Quarterly* 12(2): 183–203.

——. 2013a. "Does Money Buy Votes? The Case of Self-Financed Gubernatorial Candidates, 1998–2008." *Political Behavior* 35 (March): 21–41.

——. 2013b. "Utah: Pizza Slices, Doughnut Holes, and One-Party Dominance." In *The Political Battle over Congressional Redistricting*, ed. William J. Miller and Jeremy D. Walling. Lanham MD: Lexington Books.

——. 2015. "When Do States Amend Their Constitutions?" Paper presented at the annual meeting of the American Political Science Association, San Francisco, September 3–6.

——. Forthcoming. "The Role of Constitutional Features in Judicial Review." *State Politics and Policy Quarterly.*

Brown, Adam R., and Jay Goodliffe. 2017. "Why Do Legislators Skip Votes? Position Taking versus Policy Influence." *Political Behavior* 39(2): 425–55.

Brown, Adam R., and Gary C. Jacobson. 2008. "Party, Performance, and Strategic Politicians: The Dynamics of Elections for Senator and Governor in 2006." *State Politics and Policy Quarterly* 8 (Winter): 384–409.

Cameron, Charles M. 2000. *Veto Bargaining: Presidents and the Politics of Negative Power*. Cambridge, UK: Cambridge University Press.

Campbell, David E., John C. Green, and J. Quin Monson. 2014. *Seeking the Promised Land: Mormons and American Politics*. New York: Cambridge University Press.

Campbell, David E., and J. Quin Monson. 2007. "Dry Kindling: A Political Profile of American Mormons." In *From Pews to Polling Places: Faith and Politics in the American Religious Mosaic*, ed. J. Matthew Wilson. Washington DC: Georgetown University Press.

Cann, Damon M. 2007. "Justice for Sale? Campaign Contributions and Judicial Decisionmaking." *State Politics and Policy Quarterly* 7 (Fall): 281–97.

——. 2008. *Sharing the Wealth: Member Contributions and the Exchange Theory of Party Influence in the U.S. House of Representatives*. Albany: State University of New York Press.

Cann, Damon M., and Jeff Yates. 2016. *These Estimable Courts: Understanding Public Perceptions of State Judicial Institutions and Legal Policy-Making*. New York: Oxford University Press.

Carsey, Thomas M. 2000. *Campaign Dynamics: The Race for Governor*. Ann Arbor: University of Michigan Press.

Carter, D. Robert. 2002. *Utah Lake: Legacy*. Provo UT: June Sucker Recovery Implementation Program.

——. 2003. *Founding Fort Utah: Provo's Native Inhabitants, Early Explorers, and First Year of Settlement*. Provo UT: Provo City Corporation.

Carter, John R., and David Schap. 1990. "Line-Item Veto, Where Is Thy Sting?" *Journal of Economic Perspectives* 4 (Spring): 103–18.

Choi, Stephen J., G. Mitu Gulati, and Eric A. Posner. 2007. "Professionals or Politicians: The Uncertain Empirical Case for an Elected Rather Than Appointed Judiciary." John M. Olin Law & Economics Working Paper No. 357, Stanford Law School.

Christensen, Michael E., Mary Catherine Perry, M. Gay Taylor, John Q. Cannon, and Cassandra N. Bauman, eds. 2005. *A Citizen's Guide to Utah State Government*. Salt Lake City UT: Legislative Printing.

Council of Chief Judges of the State Courts of Appeal. 2012. *The Role of Intermediate Appellate Courts: Principles for Adapting to Change*. White paper. http://www.sji .gov/wp/wp-content/uploads/Report_5_CCJSCA_Report.pdf.

Council of State Governments. 2015. *The Book of the States*. Lexington KY: Council of State Governments.

Cox, Gary W., and Mathew D. McCubbins. 1993. *Legislative Leviathan: Party Government in the House*. Berkeley: University of California Press.

——. 2005. *Setting the Agenda: Responsible Party Government in the US House of Representatives*. New York: Cambridge University Press.

Cox, Gary W., Thad Kousser, and Mathew D. McCubbins. 2010. "Party, Power, or Preferences? Quasi-experimental Evidence from American State Legislatures." *Journal of Politics* 72 (July): 799–811.

Curry, James M. 2015. *Legislating in the Dark: Information and Power in the House of Representatives*. Chicago: University of Chicago Press.

Davis, Richard. 2005. *Electing Justice: Fixing the Supreme Court Nomination Process*. New York: Oxford University Press.

Donovan, Todd, Christopher Z. Mooney, and Daniel A. Smith. 2013. *State and Local Politics: Institutions and Reform*. 3rd edition. Boston: Wadsworth.

Downs, Anthony. 1957. *An Economic Theory of Democracy*. New York: Harper and Row.

Egan, Timothy. 2009. *The Big Burn: Teddy Roosevelt and the Fire That Saved America*. Boston: Mariner Books.

Elazar, Daniel J. 1966. *American Federalism: A View from the States*. New York: Thomas Y. Crowell.

Ellis, Richard E. 2007. *Aggressive Nationalism: McCulloch vs Maryland and the Foundation of Federal Authority in the Young Republic*. New York: Oxford University Press.

Epstein, Lee, and Jack Knight. 1998. *The Choices Justices Make*. Washington DC: Congressional Quarterly Press.

Farmer, Jared. 2008. *On Zion's Mount: Mormons, Indians, and the American Landscape*. Cambridge MA: Harvard University Press.

Fenno, Richard F. 1975. "If, as Ralph Nader says, Congress Is 'the Broken Branch,' How Come We Love Our Congressmen so Much?" In *Congress in Change: Evolution and Reform*, ed. Norman Ornstein. New York: Praeger.

————. 1978. *Home Style: House Members in Their Districts*. Boston: Little, Brown.

Fiorina, Morris P. 1994. "Divided Government in the American States: A Byproduct of Legislative Professionalism?" *American Political Science Review* 88: 304–16.

————. 1999. "Further Evidence of the Partisan Consequences of Legislative Professionalism." *American Journal of Political Science* 43: 974–77.

Fiorina, Morris, Samuel J. Abrams, and Jeremy C. Pope. 2005. *Culture War? The Myth of a Polarized America*. New York: Longman Press.

Flanders, Robert Bruce. 1965. *Nauvoo: Kingdom on the Mississippi*. Urbana: University of Illinois Press.

Fox, Jeffrey Carl. 2006. *Latter-Day Political Views*. Lanham MD: Lexington Books.

Francia, Peter L., John C. Green, Paul S. Herrnson, Lynda W. Powell, and Clyde Wilcox. 2003. *The Financiers of Congressional Elections: Investors, Ideologues, and Intimates*. New York: Columbia University Press.

Fretwell, Holly, and Shawn Regan. 2015. *Divided Lands: State vs Federal Management in the West*. Bozeman MT: Property and Environment Research Center.

Gerber, Elisabeth R. 1996. "Legislative Response to the Threat of Popular Initiatives." *American Journal of Political Science* 40 (February): 99–128.

———. 1999. *The Populist Paradox: Interest Group Influence and the Promise of Direct Legislation*. Princeton NJ: Princeton University Press.

Gilbert, Michael D. 2006. "Single Subject Rules and the Legislative Process." *University of Pittsburgh Law Review* 67(4): 803–70.

Goelzhauser, Greg, and Damon M. Cann. 2014. "Judicial Independence and Opinion Clarity on State Supreme Courts." *State Politics and Policy Quarterly* 14(2): 123–41.

Gordon, Sanford C., and Gregory A. Huber. 2007. "The Effect of Electoral Competitiveness on Incumbent Behavior." *Quarterly Journal of Political Science* 2(2): 107–38.

Gorte, Ross W., Carol Hardy Vincent, Laura A. Hanson, and Marc R. Rosenblum. 2012. *Federal Land Ownership: Overview and Data*. Washington DC: Congressional Research Service.

Gray, Virginia, John Cluverius, Jeffrey J. Harden, Boris Shor, and David Lowery. 2015. "Party Competition, Party Polarization, and the Changing Demand for Lobbying in the American States." *American Politics Research* 43 (March): 175–204.

Gray, Virginia, and Russell L. Hanson, eds. 2008. *Politics in the American States: A Comparative Analysis*. 9th edition. Washington DC: CQ Press.

Greene, John P. 1839. *Facts Relative to the Expulsion of the Mormons or Latter Day Saints, from the State of Missouri, under the "Exterminating Order."* Cincinnati OH: R. P. Brooks.

Grimshaw, Scott D., Howard B. Christensen, David B. Magleby, and Kelly D. Patterson. 2004. "Twenty Years of the Utah Colleges Exit Poll: Learning by Doing." *Chance* 17(2): 32–38.

Grodzins, Morton. 1966. *The American Political System*. Chicago: Rand-McNally.

Grofman, Bernard, and Timothy J. Brazill. 2002. "Identifying the Median Justice on the Supreme Court through Multidimensional Scaling: Analysis of 'Natural Courts' 1953–1991." *Public Choice* 112: 55–79.

Grossman, Matt, and David A. Hopkins. 2016. *Asymmetric Politics: Ideological Republicans and Group Interest Democrats*. New York: Oxford University Press.

Hall, Melinda Gann. 2014. "Representation in State Supreme Courts: Evidence from the Terminal Term." *Political Research Quarterly* 67(2): 335–46.

Hall, Thad, Chris F. Karpowitz, and J. Quin Monson. 2010. *Utah Elected Officials Survey*. Provo UT: Center for the Study of Elections and Democracy, Brigham Young University.

Hamilton, Alexander, James Madison, and John Jay. (1787) 2003. *The Federalist Papers*. Ed. Clinton Rossiter. New York: Signet Classic.

Hamm, Keith E., and Gary F. Moncrief. 2008. "Legislative Politics in the States." In

Politics in the American States, ed. Virginia Gray and Russell L. Hanson. 9th edition. Washington DC: CQ Press.

Hanson, Russell L. 2008. "Intergovernmental Relations." In *Politics in the American States: A Comparative Analysis*, ed. Virginia Gray and Russell L. Hanson. 9th edition. Washington DC: CQ Press.

Healy, Gene. 2010. "Congressional Abdication and the Cult of the Presidency." *White House Studies* 10(2): 85–103.

Herbert, Gary R. 2016. *Investing in the Future of Utah: Budget Recommendations, Fiscal Year 2017—Fiscal Year 2016 Supplementals*. Salt Lake City UT: Governor's Office of Management and Budget.

Hicks, William D. 2013. "Initiatives within Representative Government: Political Competition and Initiative Use in the American States." *State Politics and Policy Quarterly* 13(4): 471–94.

Howard, John W., James S. Jardine, Ronald D. Rotunda, Richard Seamon, and George R. Wentz Jr. 2015. *Legal Analysis of the Legal Consulting Services Team Prepared for the Utah Commission for the Stewardship of Public Lands Pursuant to the Legal Consulting Services and Relations Services Agreement (2015-01) with the Davillier Law Group, LLC*. New Orleans LA: Davillier Law Group.

Hoyt, Homer. 1933. *One Hundred Years of Land Values in Chicago*. Chicago: University of Chicago Press.

Hrebenar, Ronald J., Melanee Cherry, and Kathanne Greene. 1987. "Utah: Church and Corporate Power in the Nation's Most Conservative State." In *Interest Group Politics in the American West*, ed. Ronald J. Hrebenar and Clive S. Thomas. Salt Lake City: University of Utah Press.

Huber, Gregory A., and Sanford C. Gordon. 2004. "Accountability and Coercion: Is Justice Blind When It Runs for Office?" *American Journal of Political Science* 48(2): 247–63.

Huber, John D., and Charles R. Shipan. 2002. *Deliberate Discretion? The Institutional Foundations of Bureaucratic Autonomy*. Cambridge, UK: Cambridge University Press.

Ivory, Ken. 2011. *Where's the Line? How States Protect the Constitution*. 2nd edition. West Jordan UT: Where's the Line America Foundation.

Jacobs, Lawrence R., Eric D. Lawrence, Robert Y. Shapiro, and Steven S. Smith. 1998. "Congressional Leadership of Public Opinion." *Political Science Quarterly* 113 (Spring): 21–41.

Jacobson, Gary C. 1996. "The 1994 House Elections in Perspective." *Political Science Quarterly* 111 (Summer): 203–23.

———. 2007. *A Divider Not a Uniter: George W. Bush and the American People*. Boston: Routledge.

——— . 2013. *The Politics of Congressional Elections*. 8th edition. Boston: Pearson.

James, Scott. 2005. "The Evolution of the Presidency: Between the Promise and the Fear." In *Institutions of American Democracy: The Executive Branch*, ed. Joel D. Aberbach and Mark A. Peterson. Oxford: Oxford University Press.

Jonas, Frank. 1969. *Politics in the American West*. Salt Lake City: University of Utah Press.

Kernell, Samuel. 2007. *Going Public: New Strategies of Presidential Leadership*. 4th edition. Washington DC: CQ Press.

Key, V. O. 1949. *Southern Politics in State and Nation*. Knoxville: University of Tennessee Press.

Kiewiet, D. Roderick, and Mathew D. McCubbins. 1985. "Appropriations Decisions as a Bilateral Bargaining Game between President and Congress." *Legislative Studies Quarterly* 10 (May): 181–201.

——— . 1991. *The Logic of Delegation: Congressional Parties and the Appropriations Process*. Chicago: University of Chicago Press.

Kousser, Thad, and Justin H. Phillips. 2012. *The Power of American Governors: Winning on Budgets and Losing on Policy*. New York: Cambridge University Press.

Ladewig, Jeffrey W. 2005. "Conditional Party Government and the Homogeneity of Constituent Interests." *Journal of Politics* 67 (November): 1006–29.

Langer, Laura. 2002. *Judicial Review in State Supreme Courts: A Comparative Study*. Albany: State University of New York Press.

Lascher, Edward L., Michael G. Hagen, and Steven A. Rochlin. 1996. "Gun behind the Door? Ballot Initiatives, State Policies, and Public Opinion." *Journal of Politics* 58 (August): 760–75.

Lawless, Jennifer L., and Richard L. Fox. 2010. *It Still Takes a Candidate: Why Women Don't Run for Office*. New York: Cambridge University Press.

Lax, Jeffrey R., and Justin H. Phillips. 2012. "The Democratic Deficit in the States." *American Journal of Political Science* 56 (January): 148–66.

Leonard, Glen M. 1992. "Nauvoo." In *Encyclopedia of Mormonism*, ed. Daniel H. Ludlow. New York: Macmillan.

Leonard, Meghan E., and Joseph V. Ross. 2016. "Understanding the Length of State Supreme Court Opinions." *American Politics Research* 44: 710–33.

Levendusky, Matthew. 2009. *The Partisan Sort: How Liberals Became Democrats and Conservatives Became Republicans*. Chicago: University of Chicago Press.

Lieske, Joel. 1993. "Regional Subcultures of the United States." *Journal of Politics* 55 (November): 888–913.

——— . 2012. "American State Cultures: Testing a New Measure and Theory." *Publius* 42 (Winter): 108–33.

Lipinski, Daniel, William T. Bianco, and Ryan Work. 2003. "What Happens When

House Members 'Run with Congress'? The Electoral Consequences of Institutional Loyalty." *Legislative Studies Quarterly* 28 (August): 413–29.

Lowi, Theodore J. 1979. *The End of Liberalism*. New York: Norton.

Lyman, Edward Leo. 1986. *Political Deliverance: The Mormon Quest for Utah Statehood*. Urbana: University of Illinois Press.

Lyons, Jeffrey, William P. Jaeger, and Jennifer Wolak. 2013. "The Roots of Citizens' Knowledge of State Politics." *State Politics and Policy Quarterly* 13(2): 183–202.

Madison, James. 1920. *The Debates in the Federal Convention of 1787*. Ed. Gaillard Hunt and James Brown Scott. Oxford: Oxford University Press.

Magleby, David B. 1984. *Direct Legislation: Voting on Ballot Propositions in the United States*. Baltimore MD: Johns Hopkins University Press.

———. 1992. "Contemporary American Politics." In *Encyclopedia of Mormonism*, ed. Daniel H. Ludlow. New York: Macmillan.

———. 2006. "Religious Interest Group Activity in Utah State Government." In *Representing God at the Statehouse*, ed. Edward L. Cleary and Allen D. Hertzke. Lanham MD: Rowman and Littlefield.

Marchant-Shapiro, Theresa, and Kelly D. Patterson. 1995. "Partisan Change in the Mountain West." *Political Behavior* 17(4): 359–78.

Martin, Andrew D., and Kevin M. Quinn. 2002. "Dynamic Ideal Point Estimation via Markov Chain Monte Carlo for the US Supreme Court, 1953–1999." *Political Analysis* 10: 134–53.

Matsusaka, John G. 2010. "Popular Control of Public Policy: A Quantitative Approach." *Quarterly Journal of Political Science* 5(2): 133–67.

Matthews, Steven A. 1989. "Veto Threats: Rhetoric in a Bargaining Game." *Quarterly Journal of Economics* 104(2): 347–69.

Mauss, Armand L. 1966. "Mormonism and Secular Attitudes toward Negroes." *Pacific Sociological Review* 9 (Autumn): 91–99.

———. 1994. *The Angel and the Beehive: The Mormon Struggle with Assimilation*. Urbana: University of Illinois Press.

May, Dean L. 1987. *Utah: A People's History*. Salt Lake City: University of Utah Press.

Mayhew, David R. 1974. *Congress: The Electoral Connection*. New Haven CT: Yale University Press.

———. 1989. *Congress: Keystone of the Washington Establishment*. New Haven CT: Yale University Press.

McCarty, Nolan, Keith T. Poole, and Howard Rosenthal. 2006. *Polarized America: The Dance of Ideology and Unequal Riches*. Cambridge MA: MIT Press.

McCubbins, Mathew D., and Thomas Schwartz. 1984. "Congressional Oversight Overlooked: Policy Patrols versus Fire Alarms." *American Journal of Political Science* 28 (February): 165–79.

McDonald, Michael P., and Samuel L. Popkin. 2001. "The Myth of the Vanishing Voter." *American Political Science Review* 95 (December): 963–74.

Miller, David Y., David C. Barker, and Christopher J. Carman. 2006. "Mapping the Genome of American Political Subcultures: A Proposed Methodology and Pilot Study." *Publius* 36(2): 303–15.

Monogan, James, Virginia Gray, and David Lowery. 2009. "Public Opinion, Organized Interests, and Policy Congruence in Initiative and Noninitiative States." *State Politics and Policy Quarterly* 9(3): 304–24.

Monson, J. Quin, Brian Reed, and Zach Smith. 2013. "Religion and Secular Realignment: Explaining Why Mormons Are So Republican." Paper presented at the annual conference of the American Political Science Association, Chicago, August 29–September 1.

Muhn, James, and Hanson R. Stuart. 1988. *Opportunity and Challenge: The Story of BLM*. Washington DC: U.S. Government Printing Office.

Nardulli, Peter F. 1990. "Political Subcultures in the American States: An Empirical Examination of Elazar's Formulation." *American Politics Quarterly* 18 (July): 287–315.

National Center for State Courts. 2009. *Separate Branches, Shared Responsibilities: A National Survey of Public Expectations on Solving Justice Issues*. http://www.ncsc .org/Services-and-Experts/Court-leadership/Poll--Separate-Branches-and-Shared -Responsibilities.aspx.

National Conference of State Legislatures. N.d. "Germaneness Requirements." Accessed June 2014. http://www.ncsl.org/research/about-state-legislatures/germaneness -requirements.aspx.

National League of Cities. 1989. *Choices of the Citizenry: Forms of Municipal Government*. Washington DC: National League of Cities. http://www.nlc.org/forms-of -municipal-government.

Neustadt, Richard E. 1991. *Presidential Power and the Modern Presidents: The Politics of Leadership from Roosevelt to Reagan*. New York: Free Press.

Niskanen, William A. 1975. "Bureaucrats and Politicians." *Journal of Law and Economics* 18 (December): 617–43.

Noel, Hans. 2012. "The Coalition Merchants: The Ideological Roots of the Civil Rights Realignment." *Journal of Politics* 74(1): 156–73.

Nownes, Anthony J. 2006. *Total Lobbying: What Lobbyists Want (and How They Try to Get It)*. New York: Cambridge University Press.

Olson, Mancur. 1965. *The Logic of Collective Action: Public Goods and the Theory of Groups*. Cambridge MA: Harvard University Press.

Ornstein, Norman J., Thomas E. Mann, and Michael J. Malbin. 2012. *Vital Statistics on Congress*. Washington DC: Brookings Institution Press.

Owens, Ryan J., Alexander Tahk, Patrick C. Wohlfarth, and Amanda C. Bryan. 2015.

"Nominating Commissions, Judicial Retention, and Forward-Looking Behavior on State Supreme Courts: An Empirical Examination of Selection and Retention Methods." *State Politics and Policy Quarterly* 15(2): 211–38.

Peterson, Charles S., and Brian Q. Cannon. 2015. *The Awkward State of Utah: Coming of Age in the Nation, 1896–1945*. Salt Lake City: University of Utah Press.

Pew Forum on Religion and Public Life. 2012. *Mormons in America: Certain of Their Beliefs, Uncertain of Their Place in Society*. Washington DC: Pew Research Center.

Pew Research Center. 2014. *US Religious Landscape Study*. Washington DC: Pew Research Center.

Phillips, Justin H. 2008. "Does the Citizen Initiative Weaken Party Government in the U.S. States?" *State Politics and Policy Quarterly* 8(2): 127–49.

Piacenza, Joanna. 2015. "The Three Religious Traditions That Dominate the US." Public Religion Research Institute. http://www.prri.org/spotlight/top-three-religions-in -each-state/.

Poll, Richard D., Thomas G. Alexander, Eugene E. Campbell, and David E. Miller. 1989. *Utah's History*. Logan: Utah State University Press.

Poll, Richard D., and Ralph W. Hansen. 1961. "'Buchanan's Blunder': The Utah War, 1857–1858." *Military Affairs* 25 (Autumn): 121–31.

Poole, Keith T., and Howard Rosenthal. 1997. *Congress: A Political-Economic History of Roll Call Voting*. Oxford: Oxford University Press.

Powell, Allan Kent, ed. 1994. *Utah History Encyclopedia*. Salt Lake City: University of Utah Press. http://www.uen.org/utah_history_encyclopedia/.

Prince, Gregory A., and Wm. Robert Wright. 2005. *David O. McKay and the Rise of Modern Mormonism*. Salt Lake City: University of Utah Press.

Quinn, D. Michael. 1994. *The Mormon Hierarchy: Origins of Power*. Salt Lake City UT: Signature Books.

——. 1997. *The Mormon Hierarchy: Extensions of Power*. Salt Lake City UT: Signature Books.

Rettie, Dwight F. 1995. *Our National Park System: Caring for America's Greatest Natural and Historic Treasures*. Urbana: University of Illinois Press.

Rice, Tom W., and Alexander Sumberg. 1997. "Civic Culture and Government Performance in the American States." *Publius* 27 (Winter): 99–114.

Riker, William H. 1975. "Federalism." In *The Handbook of Political Science*, vol. 5, ed. Frank Greenstein and Nelson Polsby. Reading MA: Addison-Wesley.

Riker, William H., and Peter C. Ordeshook. 1968. "A Theory of the Calculus of Voting." *American Political Science Review* 62 (March): 25–42.

Rohde, David W. 1991. *Parties and Leaders in the Postreform House*. Chicago: University of Chicago Press.

Roosevelt, Theodore. 1913. *Theodore Roosevelt: An Autobiography*. New York: Charles Scribner's Sons.

Rosenthal, Alan. 1974. "Turnover in State Legislatures." *American Journal of Political Science* 18: 609–16.

———. 2004. *Heavy Lifting: The Job of the American Legislature*. Washington DC: CQ Press.

———. 2013. *The Best Job in Politics: Exploring How Governors Succeed as Policy Leaders*. Washington DC: CQ Press.

Segal, Jeffrey A., and Harold J. Spaeth. 1993. *The Supreme Court and the Attitudinal Model*. Cambridge, UK: Cambridge University Press.

Sells, Jeffery E, ed. 2005. *God and Country: Politics in Utah*. Salt Lake City UT: Signature Books.

Skowronek, Stephen. 1982. *Building a New American State: The Expansion of National Administrative Capacities, 1877–1920*. New York: Cambridge University Press.

Smith, Wilford E. 1992. "'Peculiar' People." In *Encyclopedia of Mormonism*, ed. Daniel H. Ludlow. New York: Macmillan.

Smith, Zachary A., and John C. Freemuth, eds. 2007. *Environmental Politics and Policy in the West*. Revised edition. Boulder: University Press of Colorado.

Spaeth, Harold J., Lee Epstein, Andrew D. Martin, Jeffrey A. Segal, Theodore J. Ruger, and Sara C. Benesh. 2016. *Supreme Court Database*. Version 2015, release 03. Washington University Law. http://supremecourtdatabase.org.

Squire, Peverill. 1988. "Career Opportunities and Membership Stability in Legislatures." *Legislative Studies Quarterly* 13: 65–82.

———. 1992. "Legislative Professionalization and Membership Diversity in State Legislatures." *Legislative Studies Quarterly* 17: 69–79.

———. 2000. "Uncontested Seats in State Legislative Elections." *Legislative Studies Quarterly* 25: 131–46.

———. 2007. "Measuring State Legislative Professionalism: The Squire Index Revisited." *State Politics and Policy Quarterly* 7 (June): 211–27.

Stanlis, Peter J. 1963. *Edmund Burke: Selected Writings and Speeches*. London: Transaction.

Stenhouse, T. B. H. 1873. *The Rocky Mountain Saints: A Full and Complete History of the Mormons*. New York: D. Appleton.

Stevenson, Jerry, W. Dean Sanpei, and Jonathan C. Ball. 2017. *2017–2018 Budget of the State of Utah and Related Appropriations: A Report on the Actions of the Utah State Legislature*. Salt Lake City UT: Office of the Legislative Fiscal Analyst. https://le.utah.gov/interim/2017/pdf/00002431.pdf.

Tausanovitch, Chris, and Christopher Warshaw. 2014. "Representation in Municipal Government." *American Political Science Review* 108(3): 605–41.

Tiebout, Charles M. 1956. "A Pure Theory of Local Expenditures." *Journal of Political Economy* 64 (October): 416–24.

Tocqueville, Alexis de. (1831) 1969. *Democracy in America*. Ed. J. P. Mayer. Trans. George Lawrence. Garden City NY: Doubleday, Anchor Books.

Trounstine, Jessica. 2010. "Representation and Accountability in Cities." *Annual Review of Political Science* 13 (June): 407–23.

Tsebelis, George, and Dominic J. Nardi. 2016. "A Long Constitution Is a (Positively) Bad Constitution: Evidence from OECD Countries." *British Journal of Political Science* 46: 457–78.

Turner, John G. 2016. *Out of Obscurity: Mormonism since 1945*. New York: Oxford University Press.

Utah Foundation. 2011. *Nominating Candidates: The Politics and Process of Utah's Unique Convention and Primary System*. Research Report No. 704. November. http://www.utahfoundation.org/uploads/rr704.pdf.

———. 2012. *Partisan Politics, Polarization, and Participation*. Research Report No. 710. June. http://www.utahfoundation.org/uploads/rr710.pdf.

———. 2013. *Sagebrush Rebellion Part II: Analysis of the Public Lands Debate in Utah*. Research Report No. 714. June. http://www.utahfoundation.org/uploads/rr714.pdf.

Utah State Historical Society. N.d. *Utah History to Go*. Accessed December 4, 2017. http://historytogo.utah.gov/.

Verdoia, Ken, and Richard Firmage. 1996. *Utah: The Struggle for Statehood*. Salt Lake City: University of Utah Press.

Walker, Ronald W., Richard E. Turley, and Glen M. Leonard. 2011. *Massacre at Mountain Meadows*. Oxford: Oxford University Press.

Wayne, Stephen J. 2007. *Is This Any Way to Run a Democratic Election?* 3rd edition. Washington DC: CQ Press.

Webb, Jim. 2013. "Congressional Abdication." *National Interest* (March–April). http://nationalinterest.org/article/congressional-abdication-8138.

White, Jean Bickmore. 2011. *The Utah State Constitution*. Oxford: Oxford University Press.

Whitley, Colleen. 2006. *From the Ground Up: The History of Mining in Utah*. Logan: Utah State University Press.

Wills, John A. 1890. "The Twin Relics of Barbarism." *Historical Society of Southern California, Los Angeles* 1(5): 40–44.

Wilson, Randall K. 2014. *America's Public Lands: From Yellowstone to Smokey Bear and Beyond*. Lanham MD: Rowan and Littlefield.

Winder, Michael K. 2007. *Presidents and Prophets: The Story of America's Presidents and the LDS Church*. American Fork UT: Covenant Communications.

Alabama Government and Politics
By James D. Thomas and
William H. Stewart

Alaska Politics and Government
By Gerald A. McBeath and
Thomas A. Morehouse

Arizona Politics and Government:
The Quest for Autonomy,
Democracy, and Development
By David R. Berman

Arkansas Politics and Government,
second edition
By Diane D. Blair and Jay Barth

Colorado Politics and Government:
Governing the Centennial State
By Thomas E. Cronin and
Robert D. Loevy

Colorado Politics and Policy:
Governing a Purple State
By Thomas E. Cronin and
Robert D. Loevy

Delaware Politics and Government
By William W. Boyer and
Edward C. Ratledge

Hawai'i Politics and Government:
An American State in a Pacific World
By Richard C. Pratt with Zachary Smith

Illinois Politics and Government:
The Expanding Metropolitan Frontier
By Samuel K. Gove and
James D. Nowlan

Kansas Politics and Government:
The Clash of Political Cultures
By H. Edward Flentje and
Joseph A. Aistrup

Kentucky Politics and Government:
Do We Stand United?
By Penny M. Miller

Maine Politics and Government,
second edition
By Kenneth T. Palmer, G. Thomas
Taylor, Marcus A. LiBrizzi,
and Jean E. Lavigne

Maryland Politics and Government:
Democratic Dominance
By Herbert C. Smith and John T. Willis

Michigan Politics and Government:
Facing Change in a Complex State
By William P. Browne and
Kenneth VerBurg

Minnesota Politics and Government
By Daniel J. Elazar, Virginia Gray,
and Wyman Spano

Mississippi Government and Politics:
Modernizers versus Traditionalists
By Dale Krane and Stephen D. Shaffer

Nebraska Government and Politics
Edited by Robert D. Miewald

Nevada Politics and Government:
Conservatism in an Open Society
By Don W. Driggs and
Leonard E. Goodall

New Jersey Politics and Government:
Suburban Politics Comes of Age,
second edition
By Barbara G. Salmore and
Stephen A. Salmore

New York Politics and Government:
Competition and Compassion
By Sarah F. Liebschutz, with Robert W.
Bailey, Jeffrey M. Stonecash,
Jane Shapiro Zacek, and Joseph F.
Zimmerman

North Carolina Government and Politics
By Jack D. Fleer

Oklahoma Politics and Policies:
Governing the Sooner State
By David R. Morgan, Robert E.
England, and George G. Humphreys

Oregon Politics and Government:
Progressives versus Conservative
Populists
By Richard A. Clucas, Mark Henkels,
and Brent S. Steel

Rhode Island Politics and Government
By Maureen Moakley and
Elmer Cornwell

South Carolina Politics and Government
By Cole Blease Graham Jr. and
William V. Moore

Utah Politics and Government:
American Democracy among a
Unique Electorate
By Adam R. Brown

West Virginia Politics and Government
By Richard A. Brisbin Jr., Robert
Jay Dilger, Allan S. Hammock,
and Christopher Z. Mooney

West Virginia Politics and Government,
second edition
By Richard A. Brisbin Jr., Robert
Jay Dilger, Allan S. Hammock,
and L. Christopher Plein

Wisconsin Politics and Government:
America's Laboratory of Democracy
By James K. Conant

To order or obtain more information on these or other University of Nebraska Press
titles, visit nebraskapress.unl.edu.

CPSIA information can be obtained
at www.ICGtesting.com
Printed in the USA
LVHW02s0744140818
586839LV00005B/483/P